King Arthur and the Battle for Britannia

King Arthur and the Battle for Britannia

Dux Bellorum and the Kings of the Britons

Tony Sullivan

First published in Great Britain in 2024 by
Pen & Sword History
An imprint of Pen & Sword Books Limited
Yorkshire – Philadelphia

Copyright © Tony Sullivan 2024

ISBN 978 1 39904 868 2

The right of Tony Sullivan to be identified as
Author of this Work has been asserted by him in accordance
with the Copyright, Designs and Patents Act 1988.

A CIP catalogue record for this book is
available from the British Library

All rights reserved. No part of this book may be reproduced or transmitted in any form or by any means, electronic or mechanical including photocopying, recording or by any information storage and retrieval system, without permission from the Publisher in writing.

Typeset by Mac Style
Printed in the UK by CPI Group (UK) Ltd, Croydon, CR0 4YY.

Pen & Sword Books Limited incorporates the imprints of After the Battle, Atlas, Archaeology, Aviation, Discovery, Family History, Fiction, History, Maritime, Military, Military Classics, Politics, Select, Transport, True Crime, Air World, Frontline Publishing, Leo Cooper, Remember When, Seaforth Publishing, The Praetorian Press, Wharncliffe Local History, Wharncliffe Transport, Wharncliffe True Crime and White Owl.

For a complete list of Pen & Sword titles please contact

PEN & SWORD BOOKS LIMITED
47 Church Street, Barnsley, South Yorkshire, S70 2AS, England
E-mail: enquiries@pen-and-sword.co.uk
Website: www.pen-and-sword.co.uk
or
PEN AND SWORD BOOKS
1950 Lawrence Rd, Havertown, PA 19083, USA
E-mail: uspen-and-sword@casematepublishers.com
Website: www.penandswordbooks.com

Many thanks to Charles Evans-Gunther for his help and advice and reading through the first draft and correcting my many mistakes. Also for use of his drawing of the stone inscription of Lucius Artorius Castus. Also thanks to Stephen Holden for his help and advice especially with northern locations and battles, in particular Hexham, once called Hagustealde meaning 'young warriors' enclosure'.

Contents

Tables	viii
Figures	ix
Abbreviations	x
Introduction	xi
Chapter 1 Overview	1
Chapter 2 The Historical Background	14
Chapter 3 The First Whispers of Arthur	57
Chapter 4 Arthur, the Earliest Traditions	83
Chapter 5 Saints' Lives	107
Chapter 6 Geoffrey of Monmouth	119
Chapter 7 The French Connection	133
Chapter 8 *Le Morte D'Arthur* by Thomas Malory	150
Chapter 9 Genealogies	155
Chapter 10 Alleged Forgeries, Burials, Crosses and Stones	175
Chapter 11 Theories	184
Chapter 12 Conclusions	206
Notes	219
References and Bibliography	231
Index	238

Tables

Table 1	Genealogies of Welsh kings and saints	8
Table 2	Earliest Anglo-Saxon kings	25
Table 3	The Annales Cambriae	78
Table 4	Earliest Welsh sources	84
Table 5	Triads of the island of Britain referencing Arthur	101
Table 6	Saints' Lives connected to Arthur	108
Table 7	Roman Emperors of Britain invading Gaul	134
Table 8	The Vulgate and Post-Vulgate Cycles	143
Table 9	Genealogies of Welsh kings and saints	158
Table 10	Manuscript dates	159
Table 11	List of potential candidates for King Arthur	185

Figures

Figure 1	One version of Arthur's family tree	10
Figure 2	The potential evolution of the legend	11
Figure 3	The five provinces of the Diocese of Britain c.400	15
Figure 4	Map of late Roman Britain	16
Figure 5	Map of Roman villas in Britain	17
Figure 6	The Organisation of the late-Roman Western Empire	20
Figure 7	Map of early kingdoms c.600	26
Figure 8	Map of Roman Gaul c.460s	30
Figure 9	Possible routes for army of Riothamus	31
Figure 10	Map of fifth-century Germanic burials	35
Figure 11	Map of Angle, Saxon and Jute settlement in fifth-century Britain according to Bede	37
Figure 12	Map of early battle sites in the Anglo-Saxon Chronicles	54
Figure 13	Northern kingdoms and battles of the late sixth century	60
Figure 14	Map of Arthurian landmarks	63
Figure 15	Map showing most likely locations of Arthur's battles	77
Figure 16	Arthur's family tree from Cuhlwch and Olwen	92
Figure 17	Arthur in the Saints' Lives and Culhwch and Olwen	114
Figure 18	Arthur's family tree from HRB	126
Figure 19	Arthur's war against the Romans in Gaul in HRB	134
Figure 20	Genealogies showing Arthur's paternal family tree	161
Figure 21	Arthur's paternal Dumnonian family tree	161
Figure 22	Arthur's maternal family tree	162
Figure 23	The descendants of Cunedda	164
Figure 24	The descendants of Coel Hen	165
Figure 25	Genealogies of the Anglo-Saxons	170
Figure 26	The Glastonbury Cross inscription	179
Figure 27	Drawing of stone inscription by Charles Evans-Gunther	187
Figure 28	Timeline 400–600	207
Figure 29	Evolution of Arthurian tradition up to c.1485	208
Figure 30	Insular and continental sources	209
Figure 31	Arthur's Britain	214
Figure 32	A revised family tree	216

Abbreviations

AC   *Annales Cambriae* 'Annales Cambriae, mid-tenth century
ASC   Anglo-Saxon Chronicles, late ninth century
DEB   *De Excidio et Conquestu Britanniae*, 'On the Ruin and Conquest of Britain', Gildas c.479–550
GC   *Gallica Chronica*, Gallic Chronicle, 452 and 511
HB   *Historia Brittonum*, c.830
HE   *Historia ecclesiastica gentis Anglorum*, History of the English, Bede 731
HRB   *Historia regum Britanniae* 'History of the Kings of Britain', Geoffrey of Monmouth c.1136

Introduction

One of the aims of this book is to save the reader time, effort and money. It may not have escaped the reader's notice there are a huge plethora of books claiming to reveal the identity of King Arthur. They place our hero in every corner of the islands of Britain, from Cornwall to Southern Scotland. Even Ireland and Brittany have their proponents. Not forgetting of course Wales which, perhaps uniquely, retained a strong memory of an oral tradition relating to Arthur into the late middle ages. Theorists also disagree as to his floruit. Some place him soon after the Romans left in c.410, others as late as the end of the sixth century when the first attested kings of various petty kingdoms are named by the sources. Most place him sometime within these two dates, c.400 to 600, although as we shall see, we can narrow this down much further. A small number have tried to date him outside this timeframe, with one notable example placing the origin of the legend in the second century. This will be addressed later.

It should be obvious when looking at these theories that they cannot all be correct. Most are mutually exclusive. Yet they tug at something within us: a mystery to be solved; a yearning for a nobler age; or simple human curiosity. They tease us down the various rabbit holes only to come to a shuddering halt at each newly discovered cul-de-sac. A casual reader drawn into the subject might well spend many hundreds of pounds, and many hours, to be left with nothing more than a bewildering array of competing ideas.

Like many, I began my 'quest' with one of these popular theories, Geoffrey Ashe's, *The Discovery of King Arthur*, which proposes a certain Riothamus in fifth-century Gaul. It was an enjoyable read and I found it rather convincing. Yet I had the same reaction to the next book, the third and then the fourth. So it went on. Several books later I smelled a rat. I began noticing contradictions between them. While they couldn't all be correct, it was possible they were all wrong. Seeking clarification, I turned to the experts.

In 'the matter of Arthur', historians tend to fall into one of two camps. First, there are those that dismiss him completely. Their argument is that trusted sources don't mention Arthur because he is not there. He is a mythical figure. A character from folklore whose name has been connected to geographical features in the land from Arthur's seat near Edinburgh to various halls, quoits and 'tables' all bearing his name. The subsequent literature which boomed in the middle ages are therefore little more than fan-fiction. Each building on the previous one and adding new elements. We can see when these aspects of the tale were added from the sword in the stone to the Holy Grail. It must be acknowledged there is nothing unreasonable about this position. It is quite possible Arthur was purely a mythical figure brought into historical narratives by poets and scribes in the centuries following the end of Roman authority in Britain.

The second group of historians argue simply that, on the balance of probabilities, there may well have been a historical figure. Unfortunately, there is simply not sufficient evidence to enable us to say anything about him. On this point I will quibble. There is evidence. It is late and unreliable, but it is there. There is also a level of consistency about it and if we scrape away the later additions to the tale we can indeed say something and it is this: the first appearances in the sources concerning Arthur suggest that he was believed to have been historical when they were written. Those sources also point to roughly the same timeframe.

My first book, *King Arthur, Man or Myth*, investigated the question of *whether* he was real and leant towards our second group of historians. My second book, *The Battles of King Arthur*, focused on *where* he fought. This is a little more complicated as one must first place him accurately between the end of Roman rule, c.410, and the emergence of petty kingdoms at the end of the sixth century. Certainly by the time reliable records begin around the time of St Augustine arrived in Kent c.597.

An Arthur living nearer the former time period would have operated in a world of surviving Roman administrative and military structures. He might be able to organise and resource campaigns across post-Roman Britain. Near the end of our period, all that has been swept away. A warband culture dominated, and any semblance of central control had been replaced by competing, emerging kingdoms. This Arthur, perhaps one warlord among many, might be confined to a specific area and would be faced with a world of rapidly changing cultural identities. I will argue that a likely historical Arthur falls on the cusp of these two worlds. Far from ending abruptly in c.410, a culturally Roman Britain limped much further into the fifth century than some have suggested. The geographical spread of the battles enable us to say something quite interesting about the political, military and cultural context.

Having covered *whether* and *where*, this book intends to look at *who*. Or at least, who the later copyists and genealogists thought he was. Many have tried before but they tend to share a number of similar flaws. One method is to trawl through the sources and genealogies looking for anyone called Arthur.

No matter if there is no connection with anything remotely Arthurian or it is from the wrong timeframe. Then a square Arthurian-peg will be forced into a round historical-hole, regardless of how much damage to known history is done. Failing that, someone of the right timeframe is found and etymologies are twisted to make their name fit to Arthur. Any Arth-type name will do – even those that have nothing to do with Arthur, such as Athwrys, Anthun or Atroys. Nor do they require him to be called Arthur, as they will try to convince the reader the name in the source actually means 'high-king' or 'bear-man', all of which, allegedly, can lead back to our hero. Failing that they simply declare it was a nickname, allowing them to apply it to anyone in the genealogies.

One of those theories I analysed in my third book, *The Roman King Arthur? Lucius Artorius Castus*. Like so many theories it fell apart under analysis. We will cover this and other theories in some detail. This book will hopefully help in sorting the wheat from the enormous sea of chaff that dominates the genre.

Having read numerous theories, and the academic view, one might next turn to the actual sources. It is at this point a reader may realise the sources do not always fully support some of the claims made by various theories. Often the error is by omission as the sources are sometimes contradictory, but also late and unreliable. It is very easy to cherry-pick your way through scores of documents across hundreds of years and weave a believable narrative (I will do just that to prove my point in chapter eleven). Especially if one ignores 99 per cent of the other sources and neglects to point out the many problems with the source being used.

It must also be remembered that the surviving sources are often copies of copies. Thus we are trying to interpret several late versions of different, and sometimes contradictory, sources and place them alongside each other to create a coherent picture. This is akin to taking half a dozen complicated and similar jigsaws, removing some pieces from each and mixing them together. Even more difficult when we don't have an accurate picture of the finished article to work on.

It would be easy for a lay-person at this point to pin their colours to a mast and simply chose their favourite theory. Often geography plays a part in this decision, as does nationalism. Others may throw their hands in the air and, as many historians have decided, give up all hope of finding anything useful to say.

But there is hope. This hope is unlikely to be found in the medieval manuscripts already looked at countless times by historians and amateurs alike over many centuries. Instead, the hope lies under our feet. New finds appear all the time. Perhaps somewhere under a ploughed-field lies a coin bearing the name *Artorius* (unlikely, given the apparent ending of coin production in Britain). Or part of a manuscript lies hidden within other source in the Vatican or a monastery. An inscribed stone commemorating Arthur used as the foundations of a later church or fort. Its face waiting to be revealed. Or a burial as rich as that found at Sutton Hoo (this last also an unlikely scenario given Arthur was almost certainly Christian).

The sources do tell us something, and it is that something this book will lay out. For this work to be the definitive book on Arthur to date it must achieve a number of things. First, it must clearly lay out the historical background followed by the evidence to date, such as it is. Once again it will demonstrate that on the balance of probabilities, there was a historical figure. It will show there is a rough consensus as to the date. The book will also look at the battles, some of which can be located allowing us to place Arthur geographically.

It will demonstrate that none of the theories to date hold water and explain why. This is worth something on its own. It will leave the reader with a clear picture as to what the issues are and where to look for answers to any questions that remain. It will hopefully lead them away from pseudo-histories and hugely speculative theories. For those, like me, who cannot help themselves and continue to buy each new theory as its published, it will help the reader spot the traps and logical fallacies that abound in this genre.

This just leaves the *who*. I have implied this is a fool's errand. Any historian foolish enough to put their head above the parapet on this subject can expect nothing more than near universal criticism. Yet I am going to do just that. At least, I am going to say who the genealogies say he was. At the very least, I will suggest who they say he wasn't. The reader will notice this covers many of the candidates proposed by modern theorists. For the genealogies, admittedly late and unreliable, have an interesting level of consistency. That allows us not only to dismiss the more imaginative theories, but to acknowledge who the earliest writers believed Arthur was.

Chapter One

Overview

The purpose of this chapter is to give a very brief overview of the range of issues covered by this book. I will begin with the historical background, which will be expanded on in much greater depth in chapter two. Next will come a very brief summation of the evidence. We will then look at the *when*, *where* and *who* of Arthur, which will provide the reader with some rough and ready guide-rails to help navigate the sometimes complex world of medieval manuscripts and genealogies.

Historical background

The end of direct Roman rule in Britain is traditionally dated to c.410. The Roman Diocese of Britannia had been divided into five provinces each containing a number of *civitates* (administrative areas often based on pre-Roman iron-age tribal lands). By the early fifth century much of the population had a Roman cultural identity and Christianity was the dominant religion. At the end of the sixth century a number of petty-kingdoms had emerged. Those in the south and east had developed a largely Germanic-cultural identity. Those in the west and north retained a distinctive Romano-Brythonic culture. One key question is how this change occurred.

At some point after c.410 the diocese and provincial structures fragmented and new political structures emerged, many based on the former Roman *civitates*, along with the concept of kingship. Insular pagan religions died out but new Germanic gods arrived and later dominated in the south and east, among the Germanic elites at least. A vibrant insular Christian church survived in the west, north and, importantly, Ireland.

Roman Britain was already in economic decline before the end of Roman rule and this seems to have accelerated in the first quarter of the fifth century with a dramatic fall in economic activity and the breakdown of urban life. The end of the coin supply together with direct Roman rule are two likely significant factors.

Another contribution to this change was the increase in Germanic material culture and immigration. The amount and timeframe of this movement of people is hotly debated and a second key question. A significant increase in archaeological evidence for Germanic material and burials can be seen after c.425 and this appears to have accelerated after the mid-fifth century. A short hiatus was followed by a further expansion after the mid-sixth century. A generation later we see our first attested Anglo-Saxon kings emerge just before St Augustine arrived in Kent in 597. Traditionally, this event has marked the starting point of known 'English' history.

Between these two dates another significant change occurred: cultural identities. A sense of Roman cultural identity had fallen to one side, in many cases rejected. In its place, for both Germanic and Brythonic peoples, a new 'warband culture' emerged. The Roman villa was replaced by the mead-hall and, in the west and north, hill forts began to be reoccupied. The elites of Britain no longer listened to the words of Homer and Virgil. Instead their bards sang of the heroes of *Y Gododdin* and *Beowulf*. Centralised authority, first from Rome then the Diocese of Britain, had given way to more localised rulers. Many Roman *civitates* evolved into the kingdoms of the late sixth century, such as the *civitas* of the Cantiaci which seems to have formed the basis of the later kingdom of Kent where the Anglo-Saxon king Æthelberht greeted St Augustine in 597.

The years between the end of Roman Rule and the apparent reintroduction of Christianity into parts of the island have in the past been called the 'Dark Ages'. This is now considered an inaccurate term however, as much light has been shed on the period and what emerges are vibrant and sophisticated cultures. Modern historians tend to use phrases such as 'early middle-ages', 'late antiquity', or 'sub-Roman Britain'. It is precisely in this period that later copyists, and modern writers, place Arthur.

Rather than highlighting the end of Roman rule and arrival of Augustine, two other dates might be more useful to focus on. The first is the *adventus Saxonum*, the arrival of the Saxons, which resulted in a major shift in political power. The sources place this at least a generation after Roman rule ended, c.440–450s. The second date, the mid-sixth century, is a little more vague and controversial. First a climatic event appears to have occurred in c.536. The significance of this event is highly debatable. Less so is the reality of the Justinian plague that swept across Europe from 541–9. It is after this mid-sixth-century plague that Anglo-Saxon polities expanded, although we must remember this ethnic term had little meaning the the time. Many of the first attested kings, 'princely burials' (such as at Sutton Hoo) and new kingdoms appear after c.570.

To support this narrowing of our timeframe we do have some credible witnesses. First, St Germanus of Auxerre visited Britain in c.429 and possibly again c.437. Our first source to note a shift in political power in Britain, the

Gallic Chronicle, dates this *adventus saxonum* to c.440. The later sources place Arthur at least a generation after this event. Continental sources, such as Procopius and Gregory of Tours, reference Britain after the mid-sixth century. Needless to say, no near contemporary source mentions Arthur. For now let us tighten our timeframe for a historical Arthur from 400–600 to 425–575. As we go forward it will become apparent we can go much further.

We have one eyewitness account covering this period. Gildas, who we shall date for now as writing between c.480–550. He tells of the disastrous decision of a council led by a 'proud tyrant' to hire Saxon mercenaries to fight off Pictish and Irish raiders. A subsequent rebellion left these mercenaries in control of some regions. A fightback was led by Ambrosius Aurelianus which culminated in a victory at Badon Hill. There Gildas leaves us, with the Britons running headlong into hell with tyrant kings and civil wars. Two centuries later, Bede names the proud tyrant as Vortigern and the leaders of the Saxons as Hengest and Horsa.

An exact date for these events is impossible as the sources are contradictory. However, there is a consensus on the narrative: Roman authority ends and the Britons suffer devastating raids from the Picts and Irish; an appeal to Rome is rejected and the Britons, led by Vortigern, hire Saxon mercenaries led by Hengest and Horsa; the Saxons rebel and gain a foothold in Britain. A war between Britons and Saxons goes back and forth and there is a victory at Badon Hill. A generation of peace follows, at which point Gildas puts quill to parchment lambasting his fellow countrymen.

It is important again to note that no contemporary source, insular or continental, mentions Arthur. No earlier source hints at anything remotely Arthurian in the Roman period. No later source places him after the sixth century. The sources that do name him are all late, but there is consensus as to a rough timeframe, that is a few decades either side of c.500. Let us first look at the evidence such as it is.

The evidence

The main evidence can be summarised as follows:

1. The first reference is from an early ninth-century text, *Historia Brittonum* (HB), which mentions Arthur in two sections. The first names him as the 'leader in battle', leading the Kings of the Britons against the Saxons in twelve battles including Badon. The second connects him with two mythical topographical features in a section titled 'The Wonders of Britain'.

2. Two references in the mid-tenth century *Annales Cambriae* (AC) connecting Arthur to the Battles of Badon and Cam lann.
3. A passing reference in a thirteenth-century manuscript, that *might* be traced to an earlier seventh-century poem, *Y Gododdin*, in which a warrior is compared to another warrior called Arthur ('he was no Arthur').
4. The existence of four persons called Arthur in genealogies from the end of the sixth century, suggesting the name became popular.
5. The existence and persistence of a body of stories and legends for several centuries.

The first two examples will be discussed in greater detail later. But it is worth noting both were compiled three to four centuries after the alleged events. The HB also contains a fair amount of pseudo-history which is considered untrustworthy.

The third example unfortunately does not stand up to scrutiny. First, it is unclear whether the line in *Y Gododdin* referring to Arthur was a late addition or not. Nor can it be shown beyond doubt that the poem can be traced back to an oral poem of the late sixth century. But let us give it the benefit of the doubt and accept this is a genuine written copy of a sixth- to seventh-century oral poem. Would this support a historical Arthur? It would first have to be demonstrated that it referenced 'the' Arthur of the HB, AC and later Arthurian tradition, and not some other historical figure such as Artuir mac Áedáin of Dalriada or Arthur ap Pedr of Dyfed (more on these potential candidates later). However, it must be acknowledged it could easily be akin to someone saying 'he was no Superman'. It could just as likely be a reference to a mythical Arthur. The most we can say here is this passing poetical line *might* reference a historical Arthur, and the poem *might* have been composed within living memory of his death.

The existence of four persons called Arthur also cannot help. They are as follows: Artuir mac Áedáin of the Gaelic kingdom Dalriada, killed in battle around 596; Artur ap Bicuir, recorded as killing an Ulster chieftain in 624; Arthur ap Pedr of Dyfed (late sixth century); an Irish Artur, grandfather of Faradach recorded in a law text of 697. With Dyfed having extensive Irish settlement, it's worth noting all four Arthurs have Irish heritage (although the name itself is either Brythonic or Latin in origin). Beyond that, four persons with a similar name spread across a century isn't really the deluge of Arthur-type names many claim. The absence of similarly-named persons in Welsh genealogies in the centuries that followed is equally noteworthy, but more importantly in the generations either side of c.500. For this argument to stand, one would expect to see a plethora of Arthurs in the early to mid-sixth century, and yet we see none.

Our last category is the 'no smoke without fire' argument. The main influence for the growth of the Arthurian legend was a twelfth century pseudo-historical best-seller, *Historia regum Britanniae* (HRB), 'History of the Kings of Britain', by Geoffrey of Monmouth. This was hugely popular and spawned a plethora of works connected to Arthur. There are two main types. The first are the French Romances which developed a chivalrous Arthurian tradition and introduced various concepts that have become synonymous with the legend: the sword in the stone; round table; search for the grail; lady in the lake; and characters such as Lancelot. None of these feature in Geoffrey's earlier tale. They do, however, appear in Thomas Malory's late-fifteenth century *Le Morte d'Arthur*, 'The Death of Arthur', which forms the basis of many a modern retelling.

The second tradition is the insular Welsh tradition which presents a much darker and more mythical figure. Unfortunately none pre-date the HRB and so could easily have been corrupted by Geoffrey's tall tale. Some at least have clear influence from French Romances. However, it is thought others have their origins much earlier and thus could have influenced Geoffrey rather than the other way round. Even so, our earliest attested source remains the ninth-century HB.

The most we can say is perhaps that people in the early ninth century believed Arthur was a historical figure, and by the eleventh century there was a tradition that could be drawn on to produce a literary genre. Unsurprisingly, historians regard these later sources as little better than fan-fiction, having been written many centuries after the events. The earliest sources are seen as untrustworthy at best, and pseudo-historical at worst. This hasn't prevented theorists selectively taking bits from various sources to support their pet-theory. When these sources do suggest a date for our hero, it is interesting they point to the same timeframe.

When was Arthur?

Many of the tales place Arthur in a mythical Brythonic landscape or a timeless chivalric past. However our earliest source, the HB, does place Arthur in a very specific timeframe. 'On Hengest's death Octha came down from the north … Then Arthur fought against them in those days…'.[1] This comes directly after a section on St Patrick's life, which places the saint's death eighty-five years after he began preaching in Ireland. It then goes on to say that after Arthur's victorious battles, the English increased their numbers, 'until the time Ida, the first king of Bernicia, reigned'. Dates for Patrick's death in the Irish annals range from 457 to 493. The Anglo-Saxon Chronicle (ASC) dates Hengest's death to 488 and Ida's reign to 547. We cannot know if the author of the HB knew of, or accepted, these dates. However, he does seem to be placing Arthur somewhere between the mid-fifth and mid-sixth centuries.

The AC has two entries for Arthur:

516: The battle of Badon, in which Arthur carried the Cross of our Lord Jesus Christ for three days and three nights on his shoulders and the Britons were the victors.

537: The battle of Cam lann, in which Arthur and Medraut fell: and there was plague in Britain and Ireland.

Geoffrey's HRB in c.1138 gives only one date: after the battle with Mordred at the River *Camblam*, a 'mortally wounded' Arthur was carried off to the Isle of Avalon to have his wounds attended to. He handed the crown of Britain to his cousin Constantine, 'this in the year 542 after our Lord's Incarnation'.[2]

Arthur is also attached to various saints through hagiographies (Saints' Lives), most importantly: St Illtud; St Cadoc; St Gildas; St Carannog; and St Padarn. It is perhaps significant that all these figures are dated to the same timeframe: the late fifth to the sixth century. They all place Arthur in the same location of South Wales or the West Country. None can be trusted and were often written to justify certain land rights established by the heroic saint.

We can see that all the sources that do date Arthur allow us to reduce our timeframe further to c.450–550. Indeed we *could* tighten this even more to c.480–540. We must however proceed with caution. Dating is notoriously difficult. Errors, duplicate entries, the use of conflicting Easter tables, confusion between AP (Anno Passionis) and AD (Anno Domini), and even malicious additions all conspire to mislead us into a misguided confidence.

Where was Arthur?

While theorists attempt to pin Arthur down to one particular area, the sources allow a much wider spread. Certainly the popularity of the tradition together with topographical landmarks place him in a wide arc from Southern Scotland to Brittany, encompassing Wales and Devon and Cornwall. The battle list from the HB points to battles in Lincolnshire, to the north of Hadrian's Wall, and Chester. His association with Badon places him in the south (although this is hotly debated). The Saints' Lives place him in South Wales and the West Country.

The mid-thirteenth century Welsh poem *Pa gur* has him referencing battles near Edinburgh and Anglesey. In the poem *Culhwch and Olwen* his palace is at Celliwig in Cornwall (again, debated) and he travels to Ireland, Armorica and through South Wales. In the fifteenth century, the *Welsh Triads* name Arthur's courts as Pen Rhionydd in the north, Celliwig in Cornwall and Mynyw. The latter is the only one we can place with certainty, St David's in South-West Wales. Another Triad follows the HRB which places Arthur's principal court at Caerleon in South Wales.

This presents a curious problem. An early historical Arthur, closer to c.450, might have lived in a world of surviving Roman political and military institutions hanging by a thread. Perhaps a fragmented diocese or provincial structure. Such as a contracted Britannia Prima in the west or northern military command centred around Hadrian's Wall. Such a man might well lead a force the length and breadth of the former diocese in an attempt to hold things together. A later Arthur would be living in a world of warbands and mead-halls, amid the wreckage of the former provincial structures as petty kingdoms emerged. Such a man might be more localised, confined to one area.

Yet the Welsh tradition presents us with essentially a warband leader who is also associated with places across Britain. The HRB makes him a king of all Britain, inheritor of the Roman imperial crown. The French Romances paint the picture of a medieval king. Yet many theories try to place him in just one particular area: Wales; South Scotland; the North; Cornwall or the West Country.

The important point to make here is one can only place him in a particular area if we ignore all the other sources placing him elsewhere. If we accept the sources as they are, then a historical Arthur lived and fought across much of Britain.

Who was Arthur?

The first point to note is that none of the *earliest* Welsh genealogies mention Arthur.[3] Nor are any contemporary with the fifth or sixth centuries. Yet a number of genealogies survive and many can be associated with specific kingdoms. Into these late genealogies, copyists added Arthur. Importantly none make him a king of a particular kingdom. These king lists come from three main sources which can be seen in table 1.

This can be a confusing subject. Similar names, the same name with different spellings and the cross referencing across multiple sources can make a reader's head spin. Additionally, it is often forgotten we are dealing with sources, copies of copies, that were compiled many centuries after the

Table 1: Genealogies of Welsh kings and saints.

Genealogy	Date	Kingdoms	Comment
Harleian	Compiled tenth century, earliest copy c.AD 1100	Various Welsh kingdoms from the fifth century, such as Gwynedd, Powys, Ceredigion	Descendants of Cunedda. Includes Welsh kings and saints. British library (MS 3859) also contains *Annales Cambriae* and *Historia Brittonum*.
bonedd gwyr y Ogledd (Descent of the Men of the North)	Earliest manuscript thirteenth century	Various northern Brittonic kingdoms from fifth century, such as Rheged, Alt Clud, Elmet	Descendants of Coel Hen
Jesus College (MS 20)	Late fourteenth century	Various Welsh kingdoms from fifth century from South Wales	Various Welsh lineages

figures allegedly represented in the lists of kings and saints. The potential for errors, late additions or amendments and deliberate omissions or erroneous insertions abound.

In order to simplify this complex web of family trees I would suggest the reader considers two main royal lineages. The first, is that of Cunedda in northern Wales. The HB tells us he came from Manaw Gododdin near the Antonine Wall in modern Scotland. The second is the house of Coel Hen, from whom many of the kings of *Yr Hen Ogledd*, 'The Old North', stem (*Yr Hen Gogledd* is a modern version and was previously referred to as *Gwyr y Gogledd*). Cunedda supposedly married a daughter of Coel Hen, linking the two dynasties.

From these two patriarchs we get many a Welsh king and saint, who crop up in various Arthurian tales and Saints' Lives. Many are regularly touted as favoured candidates for our hero by modern theorists. As we shall see, none of the sources support these identifications. In fact the earliest genealogies (admittedly late and unreliable) place Arthur in a specific place in relation to these figures.

A daughter of Cunedda, Gwen, is said to have married Amlawdd Wledig. They had a number of children who appear in our tales, such as Goleuddydd, mother to the central character in *Culhwch and Olwen* and Rehieingulid, mother to St Illtud. A number of cousins, all great grandsons of Cunedda, also appear: St Padarn; St David; St Carannog; Maelgwn king of Gwynedd; and King Gwynllyw, father to St Cadoc.

Importantly for our story, Gwen and Amlawdd had another daughter, Eigr, who we know today as Igraine. Eigr's first husband according to the HRB is Gorlois of Cornwall (Gwrlais in Welsh tradition). Their sons, Cador and Gwyar, were thus half brothers to Arthur. Their grandsons, Constantine and Gwalchmai (Gawain in French Romances), also feature in later tales. An alternative name for Eigr's first husband comes from *Culhwch and Olwen*, in which Arthur's step-brother is called Gormant, son of Ricca, 'the chief-elder of Cornwall'. This tradition of a connection with Cornwall through his mother might be what caused Geoffrey of Monmouth to place Arthur's conception at Tintagel. Uther is portrayed as Eigr's second husband and the sources gives them two children: Arthur, and a sister, Anna. Modred is the product of Anna's second marriage to Lot.

All this might seem difficult enough to remember but it inevitably gets more complex. Some of these relationships change over time between versions of the tales, most notably with the evolution of Modred as an early nephew to the incestuous product of Arthur and his half-sister Morgause or Morgana (whose own story evolved over the centuries). Thus Arthur's family tree differs depending which source one looks at.

However, there is some consistency from the earliest Welsh sources to the French Romances. His father is Uthr, Uther or Uthyr Ben- or Pendragon. His mother is Eigr, Ygerne, Igerne, Ygraine or Igraine. His wife is Guinevere, Gwenhwyfar or Guanhumara.

Numerous sources offer different names for his sons: Llacheu, Gwydre, Amhar, Loholt and Borre. Welsh sources name his sister as Gwyar, while in the HRB it is Anna. Later French Romances turn Morgan Le Fay into his sibling and add Morgause. We will try to make sense of this kaleidoscope of changing family trees later. For now we will leave a snapshot of different versions.

Figure 1 presents a simplified version of a family tree. It is worth remembering the name of his sister(s) and cousins change along with his relationship with Medraut (here I've used the Welsh spelling from the AC). This is just one version and I have cobbled together pieces from different tales and genealogies. No doubt many a medieval scribe did exactly the same thing, just as many an amateur theorist does today. We will look at the genealogies in much greater depth later, but for now this gives a brief snapshot and prepares the reader for the coming chapters.

It is worth noting, however, the names on the far left and right of the tree. Many of the descendants of Cunedda and Coel Hen appear throughout Arthurian tradition. Many a theory rests on the identification of Arthur with one of these figures. We will look at some of these theories later. What should be apparent at this stage is that medieval scribes never associate these figures

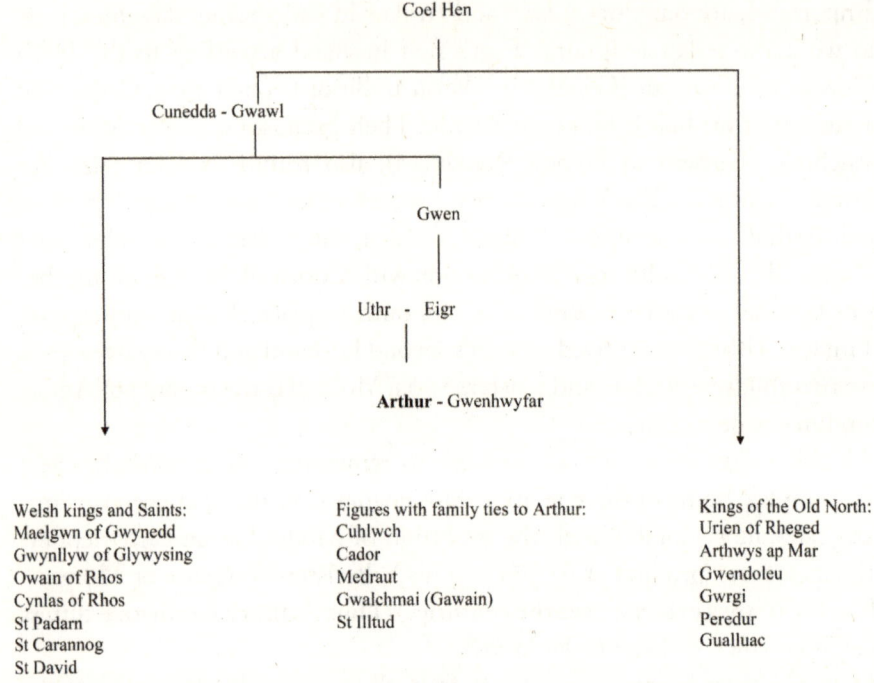

Figure 1: One version of Arthur's family tree.

with Arthur. Writers, genealogists and copyists, when they did reference Arthur, always regarded him as a separate figure, and his immediate family connections remain relatively consistent.

It is worth emphasising this figure cannot be trusted. It is a summary of a number of late, unreliable and at times contradictory sources. I provide it only to assist the reader in visualising where these late sources placed Arthur in relation to two of the main genealogies. We will see different claims about Arthur's wider family when we get to *Culhwch and Olwen* and the HRB.

The evolution of the legend

The appearance of Arthur in the ninth-century HB implies some people at least likely accepted Arthur as a historical figure, c.450–550. The entries in the AC point to the early sixth century. The HB also portrays Arthur as connected to two magical topographical features in Wales. While the earliest Welsh tales all post-date HRB, some are thought to point to an earlier insular tradition. This presents a darker, more mythical figure in tales full of magic and monsters. Academic opinion is that the Arthur of local legends and magical animals was the dominant one until the twelfth century.[4]

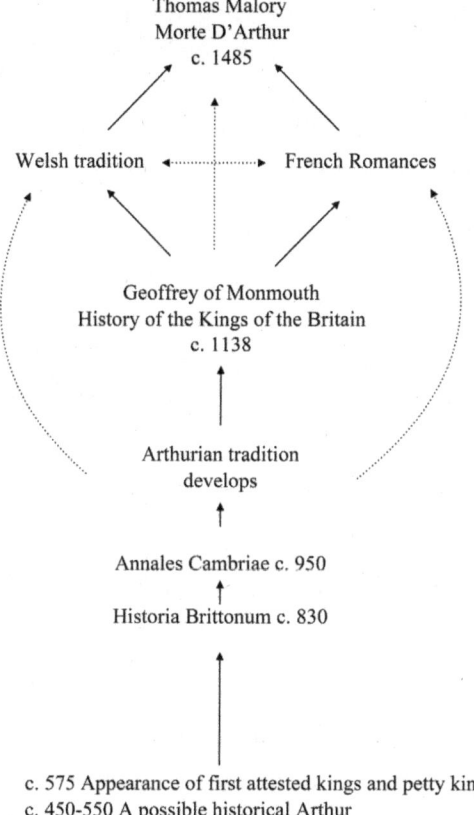

Figure 2: The potential evolution of the legend.

By c.1100, the first architectural portrayal of Arthur appeared on a doorway of Modena Cathedral in northern Italy.[5] Around the same time, the *Vitae Cadoci* refers to Arthur as the 'illustrious king of Britannia', the first time he is titled king in Welsh sources.[6] Yet Arthur is curiously absent from the bulk of early Welsh tradition. The tenth-century poem, *Armes Prydein*, calls on two Welsh heroes to deliver them from the English, but Arthur is not one of them.

However, by the twelve century Geoffrey of Monmouth was able to draw on tales and legends to produce his fantastical epic, the HRB, c.1138. This proved enormously popular and influential. A number of continental and insular authors added to the genre, most notably the French Romance writers such as Wace and Chrétien de Troyes and the French Vulgate and Post-Vulgate Cycles in the thirteenth century. The earliest Welsh Arthurian manuscripts appear from c.1250. While some tales show a clear influence from French authors, others hint at a pre-HRB tradition.

In 1485 Tomas Malory's *Morte D'Arthur* was published, which achieved two things. First, it collected the various traditions into one coherent story, and second, it provided the basis for many a modern Arthurian movie and book. Arthur's popularity, and belief in his historicity, has not always been constant, either in Wales or the rest of Britain. We will come back to this point in later chapters.

Figure 2 portrays the potential evolution of the legend up to Thomas Malory. Scraping back these layers will enable us at the very least to see what was added to the story and when. The results may surprise the reader. The last few decades has seen a huge increase in the number of books attempting to 'reveal the true King Arthur'. Chapter 11 will dismantle some of the more common theories.

Summary

We have a gap in the historical record with only one insular contemporary source, Gildas, who gives us a glimpse of events. It is precisely into this gap later literary sources place our hero. Our first attested source the HB, centuries later, references both a seemingly historical figure with a list of battles, and a mythical figure attached to topographical features in the landscape. Later sources date him, or attach him to figures or events, between the late fifth to mid-sixth century. This tradition survived in, and placed him in, a wide arc from Southern Scotland, through Wales to Cornwall. Later genealogies connected him to various Welsh kings and saints.

In the twelfth century, Geoffrey of Monmouth's medieval best-seller spawned an industry of Arthurian tales, French Romances and Thomas Malory's famous *Morte D'Arthur*, which helped formed the basis of the legend we know today. Hundreds of years later modern enthusiasts pore over these late tales, pseudo-histories and genealogies looking for clues, delivering scores of books.

Before we move on to the next chapter, let us remind ourselves of the alleged narrative and where Arthur is placed on that timeline. The ending of Roman authority we can date to c.410. Britain suffered from devastating Pictish and Irish raids. An appeal to Rome was rejected and the Britons, led by Vortigern, hired Saxon mercenaries led by Hengest and Horsa. The Saxons rebelled and gained a foothold in Britain. A subsequent fightback was led by Ambrosius Aurelianus and this culminated in a victory at *Mons Badonicus*. Tempting as it is to declare Ambrosius our prime candidate, the HB suggests he is a separate figure.

Additionally, while sources do associate Arthur with Badon it is worth noting Welsh tradition not only largely ignores this, but rarely has him fighting Saxons at all. Yet we can tentatively suggest the following timeline:

410	Roman authority ends
c.440–460	Shift in political power to Saxons
c.440–500	War between Britons and Saxons
c.480–520	Battle of Badon
c.480–550	Gildas wrote *De excidio*
c.550–600	emergence and expansion of Anglo-Saxon petty kingdoms
597	St Augustine arrived in Kent

Later sources place Arthur in the middle of this timeline, a generation or more either side of 500. The next chapter will allow us to fill in some of the gaps and tighten dates. One important factor to consider will be events in Gaul and the wider Roman and 'barbarian' world. The political, social and cultural changes which led up to the fall of the Western Roman Empire (traditionally dated to 476) may help us understand events in Britain.

Chapter Two
The Historical Background

Pre-Roman Britain was a patchwork of iron-age tribes; 350 years of direct Roman rule had a profound effect on much of the island. Roads and towns appeared across the province. Villas too, although those found to date are concentrated mainly in the south and east. Interestingly, it is largely in these more urbanised and Romanised regions that we see the bulk of Germanic material culture and burial practices in the fifth century. This is a point worth remembering when considering the political and cultural world in which a historical Arthur might have fought.

Regarding the nature of settlement or invasion, the main points of the debate can be summarised as follows:[1] 'The degree to which Roman civilisation and organisation survived ... and the size and nature of the Germanic migration to eastern Britain.' There are two main models for the nature of Germanic settlement:[2] widespread acculturation of an elite against a mass migration of settlers. The most recent evidence supports the latter but this doesn't rule out an initial arrival of elites in specific areas.

The bulk of the population, perhaps 90 per cent, remained rural. Yet urbanisation had a significant effect and transformed social and economic life. This raises important questions for our investigation. How did tribal cultural identities evolve over hundreds of years of Roman rule? How did cultural identities change between the end of direct Roman rule and the sixth century? Let us take a moment to put those timescales in perspective by equating them with our own time.

Julius Caesar fought his way ashore against an army of Britons, a century before the Claudian invasion and 642 years before St Augustine was greeted by the Anglo-Saxon king of Kent, Æthelberht. A copyist or chronicler writing in c.600 would obviously have had none of the modern aids that allow us to write an accurate history. If we apply the same timescales to our present time, looking back over 640 years, then we start our period in c.1360 as the Black Death ravaged England for a second time. A century later finds us in the Wars of the Roses. Incidentally it also finds the author of *Le Morte D'Arthur*, Sir Thomas Malory, languishing in a Lancastrian prison. A fascinating tale we will cover in detail later.

The 350 years of Roman rule applied from there takes us through the Tudor and Stuart kings, the English Civil War and the Glorious Revolution. It covers the discovery and settlement of the New World and the subsequent War of Independence of the United States from Great Britain. This same period takes us just past the Napoleonic Wars. The time between the last legions leaving and St Augustine arriving is roughly the same as between the death of Napoleon and the present. One wonders how confident the average reader would be in writing an accurate history covering the last 642 years without the aid of modern books, TV documentaries and the internet?

History does not advance in a straight line. Centuries can pass with little change and then, as in our own time, huge technological advances can alter the world massively in a relatively short time. Britain in c.410 was not the same as the one Agrippa fought across in the first century. A historical Arthur lived in a different world from the one that witnessed Roman collapse in the early fifth century. Different again a century or more later as kings such as Penda, Cadwallon, Edwin and Rædwald fought for supremacy in the seventh century. The first question to address is what did post-Roman Britain look like just after Constantine III left for Gaul in c.407?

Late Roman-Britain consisted of five provinces. Two of these were headed by Consuls: Maxima Caesariensis and Valentia. Three were headed by a *Presidii*: Britannia prima, Britannia secunda and Flavia Caesariensis. These governors reported to the *Vicarius Britanniae* who ruled the diocese of Britain under the praetorian prefect of the Gauls based at Trier. The exact position of

Figure 3: The five provinces of the Diocese of Britain c.400.

these provinces and their boundaries are not clear, although some consensus has formed over the south of the diocese. Figure 3 gives two possible scenarios for the position of Valentia, which has proved the most elusive to date.

Each of these five provinces contained several *civitates*, many based on pre-Roman tribal areas. Each *civitas* had an administrative capital such as Durovernum Cantiacorum, modern Canterbury, of the Cantiaci tribe. Some of the petty kingdoms that emerged at the end of the sixth century appear to be based on these very *civitates* or pre-Roman tribal areas, in this case Kent. Civilian posts included *Decurions* on town councils, *aediles* responsible for public buildings and services, and *quaestors* in charge of finance and magistrates. These men were supported by a town senate, *ordo*, made up of representatives from the local elites.

The main field army was commanded by the *comes Britanniarum* who reported to the *Magister utriusque militiae* in Gaul. Under the *comes* came the *Dux Britanniarum* in the north who controlled the *Limitanei* (literally, frontier troops), which included those along Hadrian's wall. A second post, *comes Litoris Saxonici per Britanniam* (count of the Saxon shore) also utilised

Figure 4: Map of late Roman Britain.

Figure 5: Map of Roman villas in Britain.

Limitanei across the forts along the southern and eastern coast. Figure 4 shows the location of the various *civitates* and military commands (although the exact location of the *comes Britanniarum* is unknown).

Britain had been a relatively prosperous Diocese, but archaeological evidence points to decline towards the end of the fourth century. Repeated incursions from Picts, Scots and Germanic raiders, together with internal political upheavals added to the economic decline. This decline was not uniform. Power seems to have drifted from towns to elite villas.[3] Onerous taxes favoured the rich as the 'middle-classes' were squeezed. Small to medium villas deteriorated or were abandoned, while grander examples were improved and enlarged.[4] Urban centres had been inextricably linked with the monetary and tax system.[5] It is worth detailing which areas may have been the most affected by this decline. One way of viewing this is to plot on a map the largest concentration of Roman villas. The reader may note the later increase in Germanic material culture and settlement occurred within this same area.

In 383, the usurper Magnus Maximus was declared emperor by the troops in Britain. He took much of the army from Britain to Gaul, killed the western emperor, Gratian, and consolidated power west of the Alps. His death in 388 is one of the few events that allow us to date the sole surviving narrative from an insular sixth-century source, Gildas. Coins under Maximus were the last to be minted in Britain. A generation later the Western Roman general, Stilicho, removed much of the coinage from Britain in c.402, which may have contributed to further economic decline and unrest.

In the winter of 406 the Rhine froze over and multiple tribes crossed into Gaul. These included Vandals, Burgundians, Alemanni, Alans, Saxons and Gepids. Stilicho had been unable to respond as he was dealing with Alaric's Goths in northern Italy. The Britons rebelled and proclaimed three leaders in quick succession. Mark and Gratian were soon killed, but Constantine crossed over to Gaul in c.407 with much of the remaining garrison from Britain. He managed to secure Gaul as far as the Alps and sent troops into Spain. The Western Emperor, Honorius, was forced to accept him as co-emperor.

In c.409, Britain suffered a devastating raid by the Saxons. The Romans often used Saxons as catchall term for pirate or raider but it is equally possible, given later events, it does actually mean what it says. The Britons rebelled once more, this time against Constantine. Zozimus, writing a century later, states that the barbarians crossed the Rhine and raided 'every province', including Britain. These provinces revolted and threw off 'Roman law'.[6] The Britons then took up arms and 'freed their cities from the *barbarians* who besieged them'. It is notable that Zozimus includes Armorica (modern Brittany in northwest France) in 'expelling the Roman magistrates or officers, and erecting a government, such as they pleased, of their own'. The Gallic Chronicle of 452 places this raid in either 408 or 409: 'The Britains were devastated by an incursion of the Saxons.'[7]

Despite this apparent break with Constantine's regime, the sources claim the Britons appealed to Honorius at Ravenna. His response, *Rescript of Honorius*, is often cited as the final end of Roman Britain, instructing the Britons to look to their own defences. It was addressed to the *civitates* and not to the provinces. Perhaps he did not trust the governors, or alternatively the governmental apparatus had been swept away. There is some debate as to whether the intended recipients were in Britain, or Bruttium in Italy. That debate won't be covered here as it makes no difference to the outcome. Later sources all accept the Romans never again held authority in Britain.

A Romano-Briton in 410 might be forgiven in believing this was just a temporary break. Britain had broken away several times before only to return under the *Pax Romana*: The Gallic Empire and break-away regimes of Carausius and Alectus in the third century; Constantine the Great, Magnentius and Magnus Maximus in the fourth. Towns, though reduced, still functioned. Perhaps not everyone shared a longing for Roman authority. Yet there is nothing to suggest Roman institutions collapsed overnight. If the provincial structure remained, what of the military?

It is estimated that by the end of the fourth century, the army had dropped to between 12,000 and 20,000 men, compared to a force of perhaps 50,000 in the second century.[8] One estimate places the army size as low as 6,000 by the year 400.[9] Constantine had taken much of what remained to Gaul in his bid for power. The question is, what skeleton force was left behind to defend the diocese? An army requires logistics and resources. Some sort of central authority has to organise these things. More importantly, it needs paying. This requires a functioning tax system and economy. It also needs coins.

The army in Britain was divided under the three main commands noted earlier: *Comes Britanniarum* (Count of the Britains), *Dux Britanniarum* (Duke of the Britains), and the *Comes Litoris Saxonici per Britanniam* (count of the Saxon shore). The first is often used to shoehorn a later description of Arthur as a *dux bellorum*. However, a *dux* in the late-Roman army has little to do with a *dux* written by a ninth-century scribe. The former is an official command of a border area, usually spread across more than one province. For a medieval writer, *dux* simply meant commander and was a general descriptor rather than an official post.

One view is that Roman Britain ended abruptly and the former province entered an economic dark-age. A defenceless people were harassed on all sides by savage barbarians who exterminated, replaced or enslaved the indigenous population. We have an eyewitness account from a generation after Constantine III that presents Britain as still essentially Roman, in character if not politically. It also suggests a functioning army existed, presumably with newly trained recruits as well as some veterans who served in the 400s. Before we turn to that, it would be useful to see what was happening in Gaul in the early fifth-century. We will finish this section with a view of the administrative and military structures that existed c.410. An early historical Arthur may have witnessed the last shadows of these fading structures.

Figure 6 presents the civil and military organisation of Britain within the wider Western Empire. We can only speculate where and how quickly fault-lines emerged. Was there friction between the military and civilian administration?

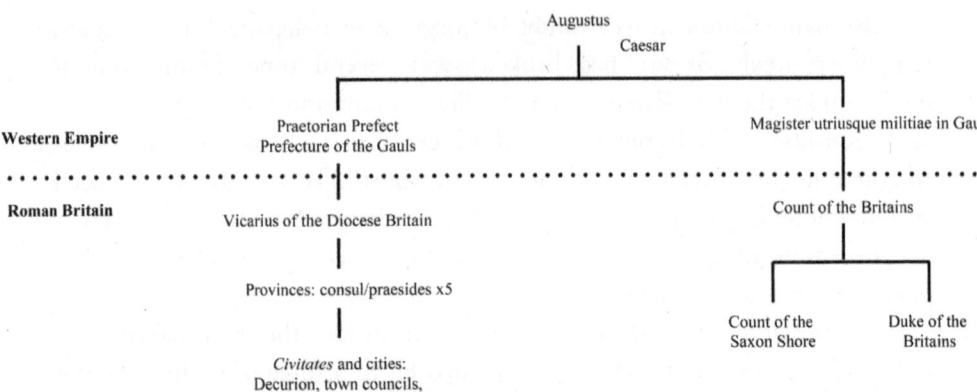

Figure 6: The Organisation of the late-Roman Western Empire.

Between provinces? Or, if provincial structures broke down, did individual *civitates* yearn for autonomy? Did pre-Roman tribal identities re-emerge?

Provincial and diocesan political structures may have continued into the fifth century, and within most Romano-British *civitates*, into the sixth.[10] It is at least possible that parts of the Diocese remained a cohesive political unit in to the sixth. The 'mutually hostile' petty kingdoms emerging only in the late sixth century. There is a marked provincial difference with large numbers of non-Romanised Germanic settlers in Flavia Caesariensis; Romanised Saxons employed as mercenaries in Maxima Caesariensis; and Britannia Secunda adopting a small number of Germanic soldiers. In the west, Britannia Prima relied on its own forces and Irish mercenaries. The evidence is against a 'free-for-all egalitarian land grab of a landscape vacated by the British'.[11]

The following sections will look at two periods: First, post-Roman Britain leading up to what some sources call the *adventus Saxonum*. This refers to the arrival of Germanic mercenaries in the mid-fifth century, who subsequently revolted against their employers. Second, the period towards the end of the sixth century when petty kingdoms emerged, both Anglo-Saxon and Brythonic, just before the papal mission of St Augustine to King Æthelberht of Kent in 597. Essentially, one of our main questions is: how did the *civitates* and provinces of Britain change to the petty kingdoms of the late sixth century? When, how, and why did the post-Roman diocese structures break down and how quickly?

Britain up to the mid-fifth century

We have seen how Roman Britain was already experiencing economic difficulties and a level of deurbanisation when Constantine left for Gaul. The end of direct Roman rule, and the coin supply, disrupted the economic cycle so severely it caused Roman life to fail suddenly and irrevocably.[12] The mass-production of goods fell off a cliff.[13] While life in some towns continued, some academics suggest 'town life' in Britain did not survive past c.430.[14] Villas too began to be abandoned and those living between 375–425 witnessed 'crippling economic and political dislocations'.[15] This collapse in the infrastructure of Roman Britain was perhaps more sudden and more complete than elsewhere in the Western Empire.[16]

Yet over 90 per cent of population remained rural and continued to till their fields.[17] The removal of the burden of taxation and a corrupt elite may have had little effect on agricultural life other than the removal of a requirement to grow a surplus in certain crops. The evidence points to a continuation of land use but also in towns such as Lindum, Viroconium, Calleva Atrebatum and Verulamium.[18] At the same time some sites show a marked contraction such as at Cirencester, where the amphitheatre appears to have been fortified.

Distinctive types of villas and socio-economic material culture suggest tribal differences persisted throughout the Roman period.[19] These cultural identities may have remained a factor in post-Roman Britain.[20] Sidonius Apollinaris writing c.471, refers to a Briton as *Regiensem*, identifying him as a citizen of the Regni.[21] An inscribed stone dated to the fifth or sixth centuries states: 'Aliortus of Elmet lies here.'[22] The importance of the *civitas* was central to cultural identity in the fifth century.[23] The *patria*, or hometown, held a significant loyalty for a leading Roman.[24]

One striking phenomenon in fifth-century Britain is the reoccupation of hillforts: South Cadbury, and Crickley Hill near Gloucester;[25] stone enclosures in the south-west such as at Trethurgy in Cornwall;[26] as far north as Dunadd hillfort, an important centre of power in Dalriada, with evidence of trade links with post Roman Southern Europe.[27] Also other strongholds such as Tintagel and Cadbury Congresbury.[28]

It is difficult to ascertain who and for what purpose such places were occupied. Dinas Powys was occupied from the fifth century, fortified in the sixth and abandoned by around 700.[29] By the sixth century, settlements in the north and west were distinctive and often could be described as 'family forts' in a well defended position such as a hill.[30] There was a clear distinction between the area north and west of a line from Tees to Exeter and the more Romanised south eastern areas.[31] Many of these locations show links to the Roman past.[32] There is a striking amount of Mediterranean and continental imports.[33] The least Romanised regions maintained the strongest links to the Mediterranean world, while the south and the east experienced significant levels of Germanic material culture.

We have a witness for this continuation of Roman life into the second quarter of the fifth century. In 429 Pope Celestine sent St Germanus of Auxerre to combat the Pelegian heresy which had taken root in Britain. This suggests that not only were lines of communication still open between Britain and Rome but someone was able to travel to, and across, the former diocese. Germanus was greeted by crowds of welcomers and debated 'richly dressed' Pelagians. Naturally he won, and then cured the blind daughter of a tribune before visiting the shrine of St Alban at Verulamium. All this we learn from Constantius of Lyon writing c.480 in *De Vita Sancta Germani*. The impression it gives is of a Diocese still culturally Roman if not politically. Christianity appears to be dominant and there are functioning towns.

Dramatically, we learn of a raid of Picts and Saxons and Germanus is called upon to save the day. The exact wording is interesting as the saint appoints himself *Dux Proelii* (leader for battle). He finds the army in camp, apparently ready and willing to fight. An ambush is prepared and the saint ordered the soldiers to shout 'Alleluia' three times which terrified the enemy so much they fled, many drowning in a nearby river.

Germanus travelled back to Gaul but the heresy returned, causing a second visit, possibly in 437. This time the Pelagians were not merely 'confounded', but 'condemned and exiled', suggesting a shifting of power towards the Roman church. Constantius describes the 'opulent island' as secure and peaceful.[34] Prosper, writing shortly after Germanus visited Britain, praises the Pope: 'while he labours to keep the Roman island Catholic he has also made the barbarian island Christian'.[35] The 'Roman island' here is Britain, the barbarian island being Ireland. He refers to Palladius, sent to Ireland in c.431, to Christian communities apparently already established: 'Palladius was sent by Pope Celestine to the Scots who believed in Christ, and was ordained as their first bishop.' Our next source is another churchman who crossed the Irish sea.

There are two reasons why St Patrick is relevant. Firstly his two surviving works, the *Confessio* and *Epistola*, provide a snapshot into fifth-century Britain. We learn his father, Calpurnius, was a deacon in the church and a *decurio*, a member of town council, and his grandfather, Potitus, was a priest.[36] Again, pointing to a surviving Roman and Christian community, perhaps similar to many Germanus travelled through on route to his debate in 429. Patrick's hometown of *Bannavem Taburniae* is unknown but likely in the west as he was captured by Irish raiders at the age of 16. He escaped some years later but returned to preach.

During his time in Ireland his community was attacked by the soldiers of a King Coroticus. Some have suggested a connection with a similarly named king of Alt Clud in the Strathclyde area in the mid-fifth century, Ceretic Guletic, but in truth we simply don't know. Patrick's letter to him gives some clues. He labels him as being neither a Christian nor a Roman citizen, implying to be called such is an insult. His men are: 'soldiers whom I no longer call my fellow citizens'. So we get a glimpse of a world where raiding is common enough to feature twice in Patrick's floruit. There is a continuation of Roman culture and Christianity and from the phrase 'fellow citizens', perhaps a sense of surviving *Pax Romana*. At the same time we have a king engaging in raiding and selling slaves to the 'apostate Scots and Picts'.

The second reason is the more important: the date. Our first attested source that mentions Arthur is the early ninth-century HB. There is a long section about St Patrick which ends with his death at the unlikely age of 120 years old. Then we get the famous Chapter 56, detailing Arthur's battles which we will discuss in more detail later. For now, it is enough to say that directly after Patrick's life and death we read that Hengest died and then his son Octha came down from the north: 'At that time the Saxons increased their numbers and grew in Britain. On Hengest's death Octha came down from the north … Then Arthur fought against them in those days….'[37]

If we take this at face value (a dangerous assumption with this unreliable source), 'at that time' refers to either St Patrick's life or his death. However, 'in those days' seems to mean *after* the deaths of St Patrick *and* Hengest. Frustratingly, we cannot date Patrick accurately.[38] Irish Annals suggest two likely floruits. The first places his death c.457. However, a more accepted date from the Annals of Ulster place his death in 493.[39] This last date ties in very nicely with later evidence. Perhaps significantly, the Anglo-Saxon Chronicles (equally unreliable for this time period) date Hengest's death to 488.

From Germanus and Patrick we get a sense of Roman life continuing alongside a thriving Christianity. They each post-date the ending of Roman rule by at least a generation. Interesting that both accounts feature raiding by Scots, Picts or Saxons, as our earliest source states Arthur was fighting specifically against the *Saxones*. Our only contemporary account, Gildas, also tells of repeated raids leading up to the *adventus Saxonum*, the major turning point in the historical narrative. If Germanus had witnessed a wide-scale revolt, one suspects it would have been mentioned. Yet Constantius leaves us with the impression of a relatively prosperous and stable Britain. As we shall see, the dates for this event are debatable. Gildas is the only insular contemporary source that helps us fill in the gap between St Germanus and the late sixth century. It is to this latter time period we will now turn.

Britain at the end of the sixth century

We left the last section with the second visit of St Germans in c.437. If we accept the account of Constantius, much of Britain was still culturally Roman and Christian. It also had a functioning army, suggesting a level of organisation, training and resourcing. We are left to wonder if the provincial and Diocese structure of Britannia survived. Given the literary sources suggest a central authority placed mercenaries in the east and north, we can accept this as a possibility.

Over a century-and-a-half later, recorded history becomes more reliable after St Augustine arrived on the Kent coast in 597. However, some sources enable us to go back a little further. In c.553 Procopius repeats what he learns from a visiting embassy of Franks and Angles to Constantinople: Britain was populated by three 'populous nations', each ruled by their own king: *Anglii*, *Frissones*, and *Britonnes*.[40] Here we have a source, in the mid-sixth century, broadly supporting the picture Gildas paints. Albeit he cites Angles and Frissones rather than Saxons.

Gregory of Tours (538–594) wrote the *History of the Franks* in the late sixth century. He named the king of Kent as Æthelberht (c.550–616), stating he married Bertha, a Frankish princess, when his father was still king. Bede names his father as Eormenric. Scholars suggest this marriage took place in the 580s with Æthelberht's reign beginning c.589.

The table below shows a list of Anglo-Saxon kingdoms along with the first alleged kings and their historically attested counterparts. For this section we are focusing on the final column, the first *confirmed* historical king. These earliest attested kings appear towards the end of the sixth century with one or two dated to c.560. It is worth noting Ida of Bernicia, traditionally dated to 547, as he is named as a king reigning after Arthur's time in the HB.

It is noteworthy that we start to see 'princely graves' from the late sixth century, such as the one at Sutton Hoo. Historians suggest the development of 'ranked societies' formed a 'transition period' between a fragmented political situation and the formation of early kingdoms.[41] Another important factor is that a sense of Roman identity, *pax Romana*, had been swept away. In its place both the Britons and Germanic peoples came to share a common institution: the *comitatus* or warband.[42] This term includes the Anglo-Saxon hearth-companions and Welsh *teulu* (family).

By the seventh century this social and personal structure gave way to one based more on territory. However, in the sixth century Germanic kingship was more about a people than a fixed territory. The warband was initially closely linked to kinship groups but came to include warriors bound to their Lord

Table 2: Earliest Anglo-Saxon kings.

Kingdom	First alleged founder of dynasty or arrival.	First alleged king	First confirmed historical king
Kent	Hengest 449	Octa 488	Æthelberht 589–616
South Saxons	Ælle 477	Ælle 477	Æthelwealh 660
Wessex	Cerdic 495 (or 532)	Cerdic and Cynric 501 (or 538)	Ceawlin 560 (or 580)
Deira	Soemel	Soemel (five generations before Aelle)	Ælle 560–600
Bernicia	Oesa (grandfather of Ida)	Ida 547	Æthelfrith 592–616
Essex	Sledd	Sledd	Sabert c.600
East Anglia	Wehha (father of Wuffa)	Wuffa 571	Raedwald 599–624
Mercia	Icel (grandfather of Creoda)	Creoda 585	Penda 626

and who, in return for their loyalty, gave them shelter and food. In the sixth century it appears to have been the dominant force. The principle function of the *comitatus* was warfare and we see many examples of endemic raiding, cattle rustling and battles in Irish and Welsh Annals and the Anglo-Saxon Chronicle, as well as heroic sagas and poems. Literary and archaeological evidence suggest that war bands of both Britons and Germanic peoples would have likely numbered less than 100.[43]

In short, the villa had been replaced by the mead-hall. Cicero and Tacitus had been replaced by Taliesin and Beowulf. The *civitas* of the Cantiaci was now the Kingdom of Kent. In the south-east, where Latin and a Brythonic language was once spoken, Old English now dominated. Yet the west and north still retained a distinctive Romano-British culture. Indeed, goods still flowed from the Mediterranean to Tintagel and as far north as Dunadd in Dalriada.

If we are correct about early sub-Roman Britain, then some sort of Diocese or provincial structure survived beyond c.410. By c.600 a number of petty kingdoms had emerged and we can see the main ones in the map below. These are not exclusive and other sub-kingdoms will make an appearance. It is precisely the genealogies of these kingdoms that countless people have scoured for clues as to Arthur's identity.

How did we get from a sub-Roman Britain with an apparent surviving Roman culture to a patchwork of petty kingdoms? How and when did the provincial structure fragment? A recent study breaks it down into three periods:[44]

Figure 7: Map of early kingdoms c.600.

400–475 – Migration period: Evidence of Irish and Pictish pressure and 'dispersed settlement by English.' At the same time evidence from cemeteries is mainly one of continuation.

475–550 – Land-claiming period: Evidence of burials south of the Humber suggest settlement increases after 450 but 'becomes more marked' after 475. Accompanied by appearance of Anglo-Saxon presence north of the Humber.

550–630 – Rise of warlords: Emergence of a 'flourishing aristocracy' and 'insular equestrian class' by the late sixth century.

An alternative study suggests two phases for Western areas:[45]

Early phase, 350/370 to 430/470: Late Roman material culture. Villas and urban centres still important.

Late phase, 430/470 to 550/600: Reoccupation of hill forts; decline in importance of urban centres; change of use of villas; increase in Mediterranean material culture.

In the first phase, elites governed through 'economic relationships' such as tax collectors or landlords.[46] They shared a *paideia* or social identity formed through education, speech, material culture, world view and built environment. There was an acceptance of a 'civilian ideology'. However the second phase involved a shift to a more martial power. Material culture and symbols reflected a more individual and paramilitary world view.

In summary, the *adventus Saxonum* proved the catalyst for change across Britain. Whether you were a Romano-British elite, a Germanic settler or mercenary or a peasant. As a young child you might have been in the crowd that welcomed St Germanus to your very Roman-looking villa or town, albeit much reduced from its heyday in the fourth century. If you survived the Saxon revolt, your son might have fought in the subsequent war. Your grandson's world would have been unrecognisable, perhaps feasting in a mead-hall with his warband in the early sixth century. Just maybe he fought at Badon, but let us not assume what side he would have been on.

A historical Arthur is most likely placed in the 'land claiming period' above. In the context of increased Germanic settlement expanding north and west. In a period where hill forts were being reoccupied as urban centres contracted. Just as a warband culture was flourishing in both Brythonic and Germanic elites.

Fifth-century Gaul

Too often theorists look at fifth- and-sixth century Britain in isolation. It is vital for our investigation to have a good understanding about what was happening just over twenty miles away across the channel. The fall of Rome to the Goths in 410 rocked the empire. While the emperors had long since moved to Ravenna in northern Italy, the symbolism was strong. Yet the Western Empire survived this shock. The Goths were later settled in south-west Gaul and other barbarian groups were given similar *foederati* status. These arrangements often involved the granting of settlement rights, land, and tax exemptions. As we shall see, the sources hint at a similar arrangement in Britain leading up to the events involving Arthur.

It is important to note the picture is not one of hundreds of thousands of barbarian hordes displacing the Roman population. Instead it is one of various groups, mostly in the low tens of thousands, being accommodated within Roman society and law.[47] In the early examples, some groups were granted not land, but the tax revenues from that land. This is an important distinction. In return, they gave military service. Importantly, this made little difference to the indigenous population. The Romano-Gallic population was largely Christian and still had a Roman cultural identity.

We have seen how Britain and northern Gaul broke away from Rome under Constantine III. After his death in 411 the Romans were able to regain Gaul under Constantius, later Constantius III. A decade later the general Aetius continued with this policy, using Germanic mercenaries extensively, playing one barbarian group off against another. This culminated in the defeat of Attila at The Battle of the Catalaunian Plains in 451.

Gildas, our sixth-century source, references the death of Magnus Maximus, allowing us to date the crucial part of his narrative from 388. He also mentions a rejected appeal to 'Agitius thrice consul', thought to be Aetius. As he was consul for the third time in 445 and died in 454, this would give us a second important date to note. The arrival of the Saxons, subsequent revolt, fightback and victory at Badon all come after this appeal.

Meanwhile in Gaul, the military successes in the first half of the fifth century papered over the cracks of a dysfunctional central authority. At the beginning of the century we see the rise of the *bacaudae*, a colloquial term meaning bandit, synonymous with rebel.[48] Many of these 'rebels' were peasant freeholders, but contemporary reports suggest the 'lesser aristocracy' were also forced to flee from ruinous taxation and corruption.[49] Contemporary sources make little distinction between *bacaudae* and barbarians, viewing both as being outside of Roman law.

Heavy taxation, economic contraction, the arrival of significant barbarian peoples, and warfare all contributed to social unrest.[50] By 431 tax revenues had dropped by an estimated 50 per cent.[51] Social mobility, which 'energised the imperial administration in the fourth century dried up'.[52] One contemporary writer in mid-fifth-century Gaul, Salvian of Marseilles, provides a vivid picture of a society in turmoil: Romans living in areas settled by 'barbarians' desired to never again 'pass under Roman authority';[53] even those of 'not obscure birth' chose to live among them, fleeing to the Goths or, notably, the *bacaudae*, to avoid Roman 'iniquity and cruelty'; freeborn Roman citizens found themselves branded as *bacaudae* and subject to 'vicious campaigns of repression'.[54]

Salvian had fled the Rhineland to escape repeated raids and now witnessed Roman citizens fleeing to the barbarians: 'the *Romana respublica* is now dead

... strangled, as if by thugs, with the bonds of taxes'.[55] He described how high taxation led to impoverishment, this in turn led poor farmers to hand the titles of their farms to the rich and eventually become little more than slaves. The blame, according to Salvian, lay with local elites such as town councillors, *principales*. He helpfully described the process:[56] high taxation led to impoverishment causing poor farmers to hand the titles of their farms to the rich and eventually become little more than slaves. The Roman order hung on by a thread: 'dead or at least drawing its last breath'.[57]

Power became more localised. Salvian references *tyranni* and *curiales* in municipalities who 'glory in this name of *tyrannus*'. Indeed there is evidence linking *decurions* to the word 'tyrant' in the fifth century.[58] Perhaps relevant to our investigation the Celtic words for 'lord' reflects how provincial people would refer to the local *decurion* or *curiale*.[59] Forms of the word *tigernos* can be seen in names from Ireland to Breton charters. In Old Welsh, for example, Vortigern means 'overlord'.

If the same processes were occurring in Britain, then we might expect to see similar social conflicts. A significant percentage of the population disillusioned not just with Rome but with their own local elites: the rich, absentee landlords, onerous taxes and a shrinking economy. Yet Rome clung on in the West past the mid-fifth century. After the death of Aetius in 454, Rome went through a number of short-lived emperors and powerful Germanic generals. One of these emperors was called Avitus, possible alternative interpretation of Agitius to Aetius. A second, and more likely alternative, was Aegidius who had served under Aetius and became the *magister militum* of Gaul. As the Western Empire fragmented he established the kingdom of Soissons in 464.

We now come to an important point which many have attempted to tie in with Arthurian theories.

A century later, Gregory of Tours tells of Britons fighting in the Loire valley and being expelled from Bourg-de Deols.[60] There followed 'a great war' between Saxons and Romans supported by Frankish allies. The Saxons lost and were pushed out of the Loire. It would appear Britons were now north of the Loire in significant numbers, settled in parts of what is now Brittany. Where and when did this influx occur?

Gildas tells us that after the Saxon revolt some 'made for lands beyond the sea'.[61] One historian places this migration as early as the 440s.[62] The largest concentration of Britons in the sixth century was in the west in the *civitas* of the Ossimi, suggesting this could have been the core of initial settlement in the fifth century.[63] By the year 461 we hear of Mansuetus, 'bishop of the Britons', at the council of Tours.[64] It is at this point we hear of one of our many candidates. But first let us look at figure 8, which places various peoples in

Figure 8: Map of Roman Gaul c.460s.

Roman Gaul in c.460s. It is worth noting the appearance of Brythonic place names and the presence of Britons and Saxons in the Loire Valley.

Jordanes, in *The Origin and Deeds of the Goths*, writing in the mid-sixth century adds a little more detail to Gregory of Tours' account of the Roman wars in the 460s. Emperor Anthemius (467–472) requested help from 'King Riotimus of the Brittones' to fight the Visigoth king Euric. Riotimus arrived with 12,000 men 'by way of the ocean ... to the state of the Bituriges'. This simple line has been used as evidence of a king travelling from Britain with a vast army to do battle in Gaul.

However, this could just as easily mean he travelled from Armorica around the west coast of modern Brittany and into the Loire, or further south to Aquitania, where the Goths were settled. This would avoid Saxons north of the Loire and bring the force close to Bourg-de Deols, where Gregory of Tours said the Britons were defeated. Jordanes tells us the Britons were beaten and Riotimus fled east towards the Burgundians. Tellingly, letters from the fifth-century Roman diplomat and bishop, Sidonius Apollinaris, to Riotimus suggests he came from north of the Loire rather than Britain.[65]

The map in figure 9 shows the various routes by which Britons might have accessed central Gaul. If Riotimus did come from Britain this would suggest

Figure 9: Possible routes for army of Riothamus.

the former province was stable enough in c.470 to allow a sizeable force to cross the channel to assist the Romans. Yet no insular source mentions him.

The Western Empire limped on for a few more years, finally ending in 476 when the Germanic general Odoacer deposed the last emperor, Romulus Augustus, sending his imperial regalia to the eastern emperor in Constantinople.

The Saxons had been driven out of their settlements in the Loire Valley and the Franks were now in the ascendency in northern Gaul. Here we have evidence, independent of British sources, for migration of Germanic peoples away from Gaul and towards Britain.[66] Interestingly, the Anglo-Saxon Chronicle dates the arrival of Ælle in Sussex to 477.

The Franks, led by Clovis, were able to wipe out the last Roman rump state in Gaul when Soissons fell in c.486. The Visigoths were pushed further south. This brought the Franks up to the border of Armorica. There is no record of any early conflict between Franks and Britons, indeed there is evidence of a treaty around 497.[67] Later Procopius describes the Bretons (used now to distinguish from Britons) fighting off the Franks so that they were forced to make them 'their companions and relations by marriage'.[68] The same source records the Frankish embassy as claiming a level of sovereignty over part of Britain.

Clovis established a powerful dynasty, succeeded by his four sons after his death in 511. Importantly, the history of sixth-century Frankish-Gaul is well attested, and later claims of a Arthurian-Roman War in this period cannot be supported. There are three main options for this scenario, none as grand as Geoffrey of Monmouth's epic war against Rome. The first places Arthur in the war of the 460s, which might support the Riothamus theory. The second places him assisting Bretons in the war between Clovis and Syagrius of Soissons in the 480s. The last option has him fighting border clashes alongside Bretons against either Clovis (reigned 481–511) or his sons (the last of which died in 561).

In summary, the Western Empire held together for a few decades. As in Britain, the mid-fifth century proved a pivotal time. After the death of Aetius, Roman Gaul began to fragment and a major war was fought in the 460s between the Romans, Franks, Visigoths and Britons. After the abdication of the last western emperor in 476, it was the Franks who proved dominant, expanding across Gaul and finally given their name to a new kingdom. A historical Arthur may have lived through the last two decades of the Western Roman Empire. However it is more likely his floruit was a decade or more after the last emperor abdicated.

Germanic immigration

Let us now return to events in Britain. We noted that in fifth-century Gaul many people had grown disillusioned with Roman rule just at the time various Germanic settlements were increasing. Indeed, our eyewitness Salvian stated many actively preferred life with the 'barbarians'. It is interesting to consider if similar social and cultural changes were taking place in Britain, even before the *adventus Saxonum*.

Germanic troops had been present in Britain from the time of the invasion in 43. Over the centuries, veterans had settled near their posting after their service but the numbers were relatively small. The Roman army in Britain at its height was approximately 50,000 while the population of post-Roman Britain has been estimated at 1–4 million.[69] Recent estimates suggest it rose to 3 million, before falling in the fifth century due to famine and disease.[70] Given over 90 per cent of the population remained rural, we can estimate that the Roman military and civilian administration, coming from all over the empire, made up less that 5 per cent of the population in Britain. Germanic troops and their descendants would have been a fraction of this slither of the population.

The numbers of barbarians in the Roman army, and Germanic troops in particular, increased over the centuries. The Edict of Caracalla in 212 extended Roman citizenship and removed the distinction between the largely non-Roman auxiliaries and the legions, the latter of which had previously been restricted to Roman citizens. Examples of various Germanic troops in Britain include the following: Emperor Probus (276–82) posted captured Burgundians and Vandals to Britain to deal with rebellions.[71] A decade later, the usurper Carausius removed the fleet and significant numbers of Germanic mercenaries to Britain. The field army of his lieutenant, Allectus, was largely made up of Germanic mercenaries, most notably Franks, in his defeat in Britain in 296.[72] When Constantine was declared Emperor at York in 306 he was supported by Crocus, a king of the Alemanni. Alemanni troops were still based there in the 370s and were said to be 'distinguished for their numbers and strength'.[73] Lastly the late fourth century title, *Comes Litoris Saxonici*, suggests Saxon *foederati* or settlers were present in the area, as Roman defensive systems were not generally named after an enemy.[74]

This last example could point to raiding by Saxon pirates. Such raids became prevalent from the late third century.[75] Ammianus Marcellinus describes multiple raids involving Saxons in the late fourth century. The *Gallic Chronicle* refers to a major Saxon raid in c.409. Evidence of Saxons in the Loire and Saxon pirates on the coast in the 460s can be seen in both the archaeological and literary record.[76] In the last quarter of the fifth century, Sidonius Apollinaris wrote of Saxon pirates off the Gaulish coast. Frustratingly, the Romans often used the label *Saxones* as a catch-all term meaning pirate or barbarian, and might not indicate ethnicity.

The first references to Angli, Frisii and Eudoses (Jutes) appear in Tacitus, *Germania* AD 98. The *Saxones* appears in Ptolemy in the following century. The phrase Anglo-Saxon first appeared on the Continent in the eighth century and in Britain in the ninth. In reality the settlers were a variety of different peoples. Despite this, contemporaries such as Gildas and the *Gallic Chronicles*, viewed them as *Saxones*. The Britons may have viewed settlers collectively as *Germani*.[77] Pope Gregory referred to them as Angles, despite sending Augustine to Saxon or Jutish Kent. A little over a century later Bede used *Angli* and *Saxones* interchangeably, while other times making an interesting contextual distinction: *Saxones* and *Angli* appear in military and religious contexts respectively.[78]

We see a marked increase in Germanic material culture from the second quarter of the fifth century. This early settlement appears to have been confined to coastal areas and rivers and marginal areas. Evidence from sites such as Mucking in Essex point to Saxon settlement and burials before the end of the fourth century.[79] Similar evidence from Caistor-by-Norwich involve cremation burial vessels dated to the late fourth century.[80] The indications are that Germanic troops or settlers were deliberately placed, or allowed to settle, in marginal areas, or possibly a grant of land peripheral to existing

Romano-British communities.[81] One historian describes it as 'patchy and opportunistic'.[82] Settlement was inconsistent and irregular with complex and different timescales.[83]

Fifteen sites suggest the presence of Germanic settlers prior to 450, with the earliest occurring in the Thames Valley c.420.[84] There is also archaeological evidence for the presence of Germanic soldiers at Corbridge in the fifth century. A burial site at West Heslerton in Yorkshire for the period found one in six came from Scandinavia and were all female.[85] The rest were indigenous Britons but interestingly, a majority of these came from west of the Pennines.

The Germanic material culture dated to the early to mid-fifth century was relatively homogenous.[86] It is often difficult to tell if the presence of certain goods indicates ethnicity or simply the adoption of new fashions or practices. Yet burial practices do indicate a marked increase in Germanic presence. For example, cremation, more associated with Angles, was prevalent in the east with inhumations which included grave goods more common in areas later associated with Saxons.[87] These early finds are confined to the east and south of a line roughly from Southampton to the Humber. Early settlements are found in East Anglia and the Thames Valley towards Dorchester and Oxford.[88] The earliest finds in Wessex are confined to the east of the later kingdom and begin around 425.[89] The evidence for increased presence of Germanic culture and peoples increases markedly after the mid-fifth century, corresponding to an *adventus Saxonum* in the middle of the century. This ties in with the literary sources that claim a significant movement of Germanic people into Britain.

If we map evidence for fifth century Germanic burials we note a number of important things. First, they are found in the most Romanised regions in the south and east. Second, they are confined to specific areas. For example cremations, associated with Angles, are predominately found in the former province of Flavia Caesariensis. Here they seem to form rings around former *civitas* capitals at Lincoln and Leicester suggesting they were placed there deliberately by some surviving polity. Third, they are relatively sparsely spread out.

The distribution of burials and material culture point to provincial differences.[90] While East Anglia was one of the earliest areas to be settled, Saxon *laeti* predominate in the province of Maxima Caesariensis. Anglian *foederati*, accompanied by significant numbers of settlers, in Flavia Caesariensis and across the Humber in the *civitas* of the Parisii within Britannia Secunda (or Valentia). The densest areas appear to have been Angles in Lincolnshire and the West Midlands and Saxons along the Thames Valley. The earliest burials in the south point to Germanic soldiers employed 'within the existing late

Figure 10: Map of fifth-century Germanic burials.

Roman structures of the early fifth century'.[91] In contrast, the evidence from eastern Britain suggests the large scale immigration of whole communities.

DNA evidence has provided some clues, although it is difficult to separate it out from later Viking contributions and so must be treated with caution. Ancestry can be seen through studies for men of the Y chromosome and for females through mitochondrial DNA. One study suggests 'continental influences' account for up to 38 per cent of DNA content in specific areas.[92] Another estimates the male immigrant population of 10 per cent in the Wessex area compared to 20 per cent in East Anglia.[93]

A summary of multiple studies states 'a significant level of immigration into south-eastern England during the fifth century in the order of between 10 and 20 per cent'.[94] Interestingly, a study found a warrior elite of only 10 per cent, spread over many decades, could account for up to 50 per cent towards the gene pool within five generations due to reproductive advantages.[95]

Importantly, the archaeological and DNA evidence does not support a one-off military invasion and widespread population displacement.[96] There appears to have been significant levels of assimilation and integration rather than displacement by force.[97] There are no widespread signs of destruction. No burnt layer such as in London with Boudicca's rebellion. Instead we have a movement of people in the tens of thousands, perhaps low hundreds of thousands, spread across many decades.

This does not mean there was no bloodshed or a violent take-over of specific areas. The movement of people in this period has been described as a 'substantial migration event'.[98] The Norman invasion of 1066 involved as little as 7,000 troops and had enormous ramifications. The process might be unclear but the outcome was not: several kingdoms whose rulers saw themselves as culturally Germanic and different to the indigenous Britons.

A recent study (2022) involving 460 medieval north-western Europeans (including 278 from England) found 'a substantial increase … [in] migration across the North Sea into Britain during the Early Middle Ages'. They found a close relationship with present-day inhabitants of Germany and Denmark. Those analysed from England derived 76 per cent of their DNA from the continental North Sea zone. The study makes the following points:[99]

- Strong evidence of large-scale early medieval migration across the North Sea zone.
- The results suggest a continuous movement of people from across the North Sea to Britain from the later Roman period into the eleventh century.
- The results overwhelmingly support the view that the formation of early medieval society in England was not simply the result of a small elite migration but that mass migration from afar must also have had a substantial role.
- The lack of genetic evidence for male sex bias, and the correlation between ancestry and archaeological features, point to women being an important factor in this migration.
- The combined genetic and archaeological analysis point to a complex, regionally contingent migration with partial integration that was probably dependent on the fortunes of specific families and their individual members.

The next question to ask is who were these people arriving in Britain? The archaeological evidence can be summarised as follows:[100]

- Saxons from west of the River Elbe in Germany settle in the Thames Valley and the South from the early fifth century.
- Jutes from Jutland in the mid-fifth century settle in East Kent.

- Angles from the Schleswig-Holstein region between modern Germany and Denmark and the island of Fyn settled in central, eastern and north of England with some Saxons.
- Further late fifth-century influx from western Norway into Norfolk and Humberside.

A century later, in c.553, Procopius repeats what he learns from a visiting embassy of Franks and Angles to Constantinople – Britain was populated by three 'populous nations', each ruled by their own king: *Anglii, Frissones,* and *Britonnes*.[101] Gildas, writing slightly earlier in Britain, regards the *Saxones* as barbarians and separate from his fellow countrymen. Looking back from the eighth century Bede famously describes the 'three Germanic tribes': Saxons in Wessex, Sussex and Essex; Jutes in Kent and Hampshire; and Angles in East Anglia, Mercia and Northumbria. The archaeology broadly supports this up to a point.[102] Evidence points to a significant depopulation of the region between the Weser and Jutland in the second-half of the fifth century.[103] Bede describes their original homeland of Angeln as still being unpopulated in his day.[104] However it is often forgotten Bede lists several other peoples who settled in Britain: Frissians; Rugians; Danes; Huns; Old Saxons; and Bructeri.[105]

Figure 11: Map of Angle, Saxon and Jute settlement in fifth-century Britain according to Bede.

A number of brooches suggest Germanic women may have been present as early the fourth century.[106] The distribution of fourth-century continental military belt-fittings centres on Kent and Dorchester.[107] Kent may well have been the main area of command for the *Comes Litoris Saxonici*. With the *Dux Britanniarum* likely at York, it is possible the *Comes Britanniarum* was stationed, if not at London, further west down the Thames Valley. There is evidence of sixth-century Anglian burials near or in a number of northern forts:[108] Benwell, Winchester, Corbridge and Piercebridge. The earliest evidence from Wessex shows mixed British and Germanic burial practices beginning in the east of the region.[109] In addition, Hampshire shows a continuity of Romano-British to Anglo-Saxon cemeteries.

The marked increase of Germanic material culture and burials appears to come to halt around the end of the fifth century and this hiatus lasts a few decades. At first sight this coincides with historians' rough estimate for the date of the Battle of Badon. We also have a number of literary sources hinting at the same; for example, Bede names a number of Germanic leaders holding *imperium* in Britain, south of the Humber. The Anglo-Saxon Chronicle titles these kings *Bretwalda*, 'wide-ruler'. Bede's first such ruler is Ælle of Sussex, who the ASC dates as arriving in 477. The second is Caewlin of Wessex, dated to the last quarter of the sixth century. There then follows several more in quick succession, Æthelberht of Kent and Rædwald of East Anglia, followed by the Northumbrian kings. The question arises why is there a significant gap between the first and second of his rulers?

Gregory of Tours records the Frankish king Theuderic I, son of Clovis I, using Saxon emigrants from Britain being used as mercenaries in the Thuringian War of 531. Procopius reports the following information from the Frankish and Angle embassy in 553: 'So great apparently is the multitude of these peoples that every year in large groups they migrate from there [Britain] with their women and children and go to the Franks.'[110]

So far we have an increase in Germanic material culture after c.425 and a significant increase in settlement after the mid-fifth century. This coincides with the literary sources which date the arrival of Germanic mercenaries. The most recent studies support the theory of a mass migration in the fifth century, although the process and timescale is open to debate.

The shift in language provides the strongest support for a mass migration. The adoption of Old English by a British population should have affected the development of the language. However, there was very little contribution of Brythonic to Old English. In contrast, 280 Lombard words are found in Italian, 520 Frankish words in French, and ninety Gothic and 4,000 Arabic words in Spanish.[111]

Old English is most closely related to Frisian, part of a number of north-west Germanic languages such as Dutch, Swedish, Danish and German. Fifth-century settlers would have had a variety of dialects and linguistic forms. The growth of a unified language may have developed alongside political consolidation and the emergence of kingdoms ruled by a Germanic elite with a substantial Germanic speaking immigrant population.

Different dialects of Old English may have developed distinctive features on the Continent. There is some suggestion Anglian and Saxon areas retained and developed separate dialects in Britain.[112] This may have influenced Æthelberht in writing his law codes English rather than Latin.

Place-name studies suggest large-scale immigration in the same areas we find the highest levels of Germanic material culture and burials.[113] Name endings often refer to topographical features: *burna* (stream); *dun* (hill); *eg* (island); *feld* (open pasture); *ford* (river crossing); *wella* (spring) *ham* (estate); *bury* (fortified site); and *wich* (from the Roman *vicus* meaning settlement). Latin words in English place-names could suggest some settlement took place within a functioning Roman administrative structure:[114] *Campus* (plain), *castra* (fort), *ecclesia* (church), *fons* (spring), *portus* (harbour), *strata* (road) and *vicus* (village, township).

Place names can be linked with a number of tribal groups:[115] Alemanni (Almondbury); Angles (Englefield, Engleton); Swabians; (Swaffham and Swavesey); Saxons (Saxton, Saxham and Saxondale); and Frisians (Frisby, Frieston, Friesthorpe, Freston, Friston, Firsby, Freezingham, French Hay and Frenchhurst).

What then of the Britons? They were likely still the majority even in areas under Germanic authority. In Cornwall it took 600 years for Cornish to all but disappear as English advanced westward.[116] Brythonic place-names are rare in the east and confined to topographical features, although it is feasible Brythonic lasted into the eighth century in this area.[117] They become more common the further west one travels until one finds a dominance of Brythonic place-names alongside topographical features in Wales and Cornwall.

It could be the two peoples kept relatively separate. There seems to have been little attempt to convert the Germanic settlers to Christianity. Bede castigates the Britons for just this neglect although that may be more about highlighting the importance of the Augustine mission.

A number of factors may have contributed to this mass movement of people and varied between regions and across time:[118] overpopulation in the those areas of north-western Europe, soil erosion, a rise in sea levels and economic collapse of the Western Roman Empire. Britain may have offered opportunities with land becoming available and offers of military employment. The siting of early cemeteries around Venta Icenorum (Caistor) and Eboracum (York) support this. There are two models for employment of Germanic soldiers. The first involved the granting of land by landowners the second the granting of a proportion of the tax receipts from that land. A revolt of the Alemanni occurred for a similar reason in c.365.

Evidence suggests the population in Britain suffered a marked decline from 3–5 million to perhaps 2 million during the migration period.[119] This may be due to a worsening climate (both colder and wetter) during the fifth and sixth centuries, however we do not see a regeneration of woodland. The next question to address is how did these Germanic settlers arrive into this landscape?

John Haywood's *Dark Age Naval Power, A Reassessment of Frankish and Anglo-Saxon Seafaring Activity* is an invaluable source of information on Anglo-Saxon boats.[120] One example from c.350 was just over 70 ft long and held thirty oarsmen. Some examples held just fourteen men. The poem *Beowulf* describes a sail-powered boat with a crew of fourteen. The Sutton Hoo ship, c.600, was 89 ft in length, 14 ft wide and over 4 ft in depth. It likely held forty oarsmen. A Herul raid in Spain noted 400 men from seven ships.

A crew rowing at 3 knots for twelve hours could make thirty-six nautical miles. In contrast, a sail could increase this distance by a factor of four. The journey across the North Sea might take three days, although if they 'hugged' the coast the final leg across the channel would only be a day's rowing. Early settlers or raiders would have put to sea March to October and likely avoided the winter months to make best use of prevailing winds and tides.[121]

We can thus speculate as the to numbers involved. The Vandal migration to North Africa involved 80,000 people. The Visigoths settled in fifth-century Gaul numbered 200,000. Carver describes the *adventus Saxonum* as a 'game-changing demographic event'.[122] Germanic immigration of between 24.4 and 72.5 per cent in specific areas. In terms of numbers, the estimates are of between 250,000 and 500,000 men, and 100,000 women into a population of between 1–4 million.

Let us consider a movement of 300,000 people into a population of 1 million in just the Romanised south and east of the former province (with the rest of the Brythonic population spread across the west and north). This would take 7,500 ships carrying an average of forty people. Spread over 150 years this would equate to fifty ships a year. Just one a week, or two during the calmer sailing months between March and October. A steady trickle of settlers over many decades could thus have a significant affect on demographics. Alternatively, consider a similar sized movement as the Vandals migration. This would require just two ships a week over a generation. It is likely this steady trickle was interspersed with arrival of larger groups at different times and places. Some looking for land to settle but others perhaps for plunder or conquest.

In summary, descendants of Germanic troops and settlers were already in Britain prior to the end of Roman rule. Signs of an increase in Germanic material culture and burial customs increase after 425. This first phase of settlement, before the *adventus Saxonum*, was confined to the east of Britain between the Humber and the Thames, although stretching out to the west down the Thames Valley.[123]

This seems independent of the general economic decline and deurbanisation Britain experienced in the first decades of the fifth century. These Germanic peoples were no more homogeneous than the Britons, but it is worth noting their presence is predominantly in the areas that had experienced the greatest levels of Romanisation.

A further increase in settlement from the mid-fifth century appears to have slowed down by the beginning of the sixth century. Recent studies point to a mass movement of people – but importantly, not a displacement of the indigenous population. Germanic kingdoms emerge in the second-half of that century and we get our first historically attested kings. The Anglo-Saxon Chronicle, though unreliable for this period, also records further expansion of Wessex and the establishment of Bernicia from the mid-sixth century. Coincidently it is in this apparent hiatus, late fifth to mid-sixth centuries, that the earliest sources will place Arthur. It is also when our first insular contemporary witness put pen to parchment. Before we come to Gildas, there is one early continental source that refers to a major political shift in Britannia just before the mid-fifth century.

Gallic chronicle

An anonymous author, possibly in southern Gaul, chronicled events up to the year 452, in a document known as *Chronica Gallica CCCCLII*. The earliest surviving copies can be dated to ninth or tenth century.[124] A later copyist added entries up to the year 511 in *Chronica Gallica DXI*. The content is considered authentic and generally accepted to have a contemporary origin.[125] We thus have two manuscripts, both apparently recording the same event for Britain:

> **Gallic Chronicle 452 – Entry for the year 441:** 'The Britains [i.e. the five provinces], which to this time had suffered from various disasters and misfortunes, are reduced to the power of the Saxons.'

> **Gallic Chronicle 511 – Entry for the year 440:** 'The Britains, lost to the Romans, yield to the power of the Saxons.'

We recall an earlier entry from the same document for 409/10 stated: 'The Britains were devastated by an incursion of the Saxons.' This led to the revolt against Constantine III and the appeal to Honorius in Ravenna. While some have suggested the later entry could be a duplicate, the chronicle is considered fairly accurate. Although prior to the year 446 some dates are slightly out. For example, the fall of Carthage, dated to 444 in the GC, was captured by the Vandals in 439 and officially ceded in 442.[126] The GC gets less accurate the further from Gaul and further in time the event occurred. Thus the entry for Britain may be slightly earlier, perhaps shortly after the second visit of Germanus in 437.

For the GC the actions of barbarians are central to events; however, for Prosper of Aquitaine writing in c.433 they are peripheral.[127] The GC appears to have little to say about northern Gaul or the Franks. This leads us to wonder what was meant by yield or reduced 'to the power of the Saxons'? It certainly cannot be taken literally as parts of the north and west held back Anglo-Saxon expansion for centuries. This leaves us with a number of options.

The copyist could have been mistaken, either by a duplication of the earlier entry or an error from bad information. It could be an exaggeration if Britain was temporarily cut off by pirate raids in the Channel, or part of the Diocese broke away such as the south-east including the former Diocese capital, Londinium. A copyist in southern Gaul receiving second-hand information a few years after the event, with lines of communication cut, might make assumptions. Alternatively, it could be an accurate entry recording a temporary military situation.

Finally, the last option is that it refers to a political event such as the appointment of a Saxon *magister militum*, *dux* or *comes*, giving the impression a powerful Saxon elite had 'taken over'. This is not such an extraordinary suggestion, given the number of Germanic officers who did just that in the Western Empire in the fifth-century from Stilicho, Ricimer to Odoacer. A marriage might give the same impression. Such as when the emperor's sister, Galla Placidia, married the Gothic king, Ataulf, in 414. As we shall see, our earliest source for Arthur records a similar marriage between Vortigern and Hengest's daughter. The HB claims the British king made Hengest his advisor and ceded Kent in return for his daughter's hand.

A Gallic monk receiving this information a few years later might indeed feel Britain had been lost to the Saxons. This explanation would at least fit in with other sources such as Bede, who place the *adventus Saxonum* slightly later than 440. At the very least we have one reliable source which dates a significant political change in Britain c.440. If the second visit of St Germanus can be dated to 437, then the GC entry for 440 could pinpoint the moment when fifth-century Britain ceased to be culturally Roman in any real sense. Our next source comes decades, or even a century, later – but importantly, it comes from Britain.

Gildas

There are a number of reasons why Gildas is important to our study. First, he gives one of the few contemporary eyewitness accounts of fifth- or sixth-century Britain. He also provides a narrative from the end of Roman Britain to the present in which he references Ambrosius Aurelianus and the Battle of Badon, both of interest to our study.

Unfortunately there is uncertainty about when Gildas wrote, with dates ranging from c.479 to 550.[128] To confuse matters further, various sources seem to point to two separate figures, one recorded by Irish Chronicles as Gildas dying in 570, and another by William of Malmesbury (c.1095–1143) dating his death to 512 and connecting him to Glastonbury. Two Saints' Lives contribute to this confusion, with one pointing to the fifth century and the other the sixth. Later sources also give him a number of different epithets: Gildas Sanctus; Gildas Sapiens; Gildas Historiographus; Gildas the Confessor; and Gildas Auctor.[129] The second Saint's Life connects him with Arthur, which we will come to later.

He was known for other works as later churchmen called on his authority. Columbanus, in a letter to Pope Gregory in c.600, referred to Gildas' advice to Finian on monastic life. Indeed it is a 'monastic model of authority' that Gilda emphasises in the text we are most concerned with.[130] This work is *De Excidio et Conquestu Britanniae*, 'On the Ruin and Conquest of Britain' (DEB). There are two broad schools of thought concerning dating the document: some place it in the second quarter of the sixth century;[131] others suggest the last quarter of the fifth.[132] The writing style, rhetoric and content point to cultural links with late fifth-century Gaul, supporting the early date.[133] However, the narrative and implied timespans within may point to a later date.

The Latin is 'classical' rather than 'insular' and demonstrates a good level of training.[134] This suggests the survival of Roman culture later than first thought.[135] Importantly, it was written in the context of an 'organised church influenced by the respect for *romanitas*'.[136] The text offers the following clues about the author:[137] He was 43 years old at the time of writing; a cleric, possibly a deacon and a monk; well-educated in rhetoric and Latin; a member of the Romano-British elite; he likely had a previous secular career or training; was located in the south-west; and saw Britain as a 'nation', supporting a *romanitas* although one outside direct Roman rule.

It is important to note it is a sermon and not intended as an accurate historical account. He begins by stating he has waited ten years to write his 'warning'. And a warning it is, full of fire and brimstone, in broadly three sections. The first describes Britain and offers a narrative which describes the history between the end of Roman Britain and the time of writing. The second castigates five tyrant kings, thought to reside in the former province of Britannia Prima: Constantine, 'whelp of the filthy lioness of Damnoniae'; Aurelius Caninus, 'lion-whelp'; Cuneglasus, 'Bear ... Red butcher'; Maglocunnus, 'dragon of the island'; and Vortipor, 'bad son of a good king ... tyrant of Demetae', Dyfed in South West Wales. We will meet these figures in the genealogies and various theories connecting some to Arthur. The final section is aimed at the clergy.

Before we get to the narrative leading up to Badon it is useful to note certain comments. Gildas seems to be talking over the heads of his five tyrant kings to one people, citizens or countrymen, in one country, *patria*. Britain has rulers and 'watchmen' (*habet britanni rectores, habet speculatores*); kings, but they are 'tyrants'; judges, but they are 'ungodly men' (*reges habet britannia, sed tyrannos; iudices habet, sed impios*); priests, but they are 'unwise'; ministers, but many are 'impudent'; clerks, 'deceitful raveners'; and pastors, 'wolves prepared for the slaughter of souls'.

We will hear of a war that resulted in a *lugubri divortio barbarorum*, a 'grievous divorce from the barbarians'. This could mean a physical border or simply refer to the breaking of an arrangement such as a formal *foederati* treaty. Yet at the time of writing, Gildas is unable to access the shrines of the martyrs, specifically St Alban at Verulamium and *Aaron et Iulium Legionum urbes cives*. The location of *Legionum urbes cives* has been much debated with Caerleon a leading contender as a later medieval tradition attests. However, it is the location of their shrines to which Gildas refers, not their hometown. Additionally, Gildas says they have been deprived of these which could equally mean destroyed rather than prevented access to.

Britain is 'ornamented' with twenty-eight cities, castles, towers, gates and houses, well equipped with fortifications.[138] These cities are not populated as they once were, deserted, in ruins and unkempt.[139] Important to note the archaeological evidence does not back-up wide-scale destruction and this could be poetic licence. We take up the text when Magnus Maximus 'had his evil head cut off at Aquileia', one of the few events in Gildas we can date accurately, 388.

The Britons 'groaned aghast for many years' due to two exceedingly savage, over-seas nations', the Scots (Irish) and the Picts. The Britons send envoys to Rome and a legion is despatched. A turf wall is built from sea to sea which appears to be an attempt to explain the Antonine Wall (in reality built c.142).

A second incursion results in another appeal and once more the Romans send help, this time building a wall of stone. If this is Hadrian's Wall Gildas is again hopelessly wrong by many centuries (built from c.122). The Romans tell the Britons they must stand alone and leave them 'manuals for weapons' and place towers overlooking the sea at intervals on the south coast. They say goodbye, 'meaning never to return'. Frustratingly, Gildas does not mention Constantine III so it is difficult to date these raids. There were major raids in 398 and 407. There is no record of Roman intervention after 410.

The Picts and Scots then return, the wall and towns are abandoned and the barbarians seize the 'whole of the extreme north of the island right up to the wall'. We must assume the reference to the abandonment of the 'high wall' and towns means Hadrian's Wall. Much looting and bloodshed follows. Interestingly, we have an entry in the Anglo-Saxon Chronicle for 418: 'This year the Romans gathered all the gold-hoards there were in Britain; some they hid in the earth, so that no man might find them, and some they took with them to Gaul.' We also recall St Patrick's account of being captured by Irish raiders, which, if he was back in Ireland in the mid-fifth century, could be dated to the first quarter of the fifth century.

We then come to an important milestone, the third appeal to the Romans. It is clear Gildas regards this appeal as in response to the Picts and Irish, not the Saxons. The Britons send a letter: 'To Agitius, thrice consul: The groans of the British.' The Britons complain that they are caught between the sea and the the barbarians and either drowned or slaughtered. Agitius has traditionally been identified as Aetius, Roman general in the west. Just to complicate matters, other contenders include Avitus, western emperor in 455–6, and Aegidius, *magister militum* in the west (458) and king of the breakaway kingdom of Soissons (461–4).

However, only Aetius was consul three times. This has led some to date this appeal to his third consulship, 446–454. Unfortunately, it is possible the epithet '*thrice consul*' was added later, perhaps by Gildas himself, meaning the appeal could have occurred earlier. Aetius came to the fore in the mid-420s but he wasn't the sole dominant military commander until 432–3 when he was consul for the first time and made *magister militum* in the west. We must remember, Gildas is rather hazy about the events many decades before his lifetime. The *Life of St Germanus* recorded none of these dramatic events in neither 429 or 437.

The appeal is rejected, followed by a notorious famine. The Britons fight back alone and 'for the first time' defeat their enemies. The Irish return home and the Picts settle the northern part. There followed a period of truce and 'a period of abundance'. The Britons turned from truth and welcomed Satan.

Neither Pelagius or Germanus is mentioned directly, but could this be a veiled reference to Pelagianism? We then read: 'Kings are anointed', suggesting the beginnings of kingship and fragmentation of provincial structures.

Then disaster struck: a rumour of further raids is followed by a plague killing so many the 'living could not bury the dead'. There is a record of pestilence in 442 that 'spread over almost the entire world'.[140] In general, climatic changes, plagues, famines, civil wars and raids put downward pressure on population in the west in the fifth century.[141] We then come to the event that later sources use to build a narrative that leads to Arthur.

A council led lead by a 'proud tyrant' invite Saxon mercenaries to deal with the Irish and Picts. Three warships arrive and they 'first fixed their dreadful talons in the eastern part of the island'. Next, a larger contingent joins itself 'to their bastard comrades'. The language Gildas uses implies strongly that this was an arrangement typical of Roman *foederati* being employed. They receive provisions, *annonas*, within a treaty, *foedere*.

The arrangement 'for a long time shut the dog's mouth', although how long is not detailed. The barbarians ask for more and gave 'false colour to individual incidents'. Eventually they revolt and 'fire from sea to sea … burned nearly the whole island … licking the western ocean with it's fierce red tongue'. All the major towns were 'laid low', many were killed, enslaved or forced to emigrate. The 'cruel plunderers return home', presumably to their bases in the east. We are left to guess how many years between the arrival of the first group and this devastation.

Once again, after a time, the Britons fought back. They are led by Ambrosius Aurelianus, the 'sole survivor of the Roman race', whose parents had 'worn the purple'. This could mean they were part of an imperial, consular or episcopal family, all of which wore clothing with the colour purple. Indeed, the HB refers to Ambrosius as the son of 'a consul of the Roman people'. Gildas states the Britons win an initial victory and then the battles go back and forth. This war carries on up to a most crucial point on which many an Arthurian theory hangs its date.

The war goes back and forth 'up to the siege of Badon Hill, pretty well the last defeat of the villains and certainly not the least. That was the year of my birth; … one month of the forty-fourth year since then has already past.' Taken at face value this seems to read as Gildas was born in the same year as Badon, and he is now writing forty-four years later. Additionally, as it follows on from the previous paragraph, Ambrosius Aurelianus is the likely victorious general. This wouldn't negate a younger warrior being present, or indeed Ambrosius Artorius Aurelianus being our hero, although the sources concerning Arthur are clear they are two different figures.

It is worth emphasising the phrase: 'pretty well last defeat of the villains and certainly not the least'. Rather than the final climatic battle, this indicates it was neither the final or largest battles. Why Gildas chose to highlight it is unclear. Perhaps it was the last Ambrosius fought in? Or perhaps it was simply that it was fought in the year of his birth? It's significance being overstated by later writers such as Bede.

Bede, writing in 731, follows Gildas closely yet interpreted this forty-four years rather differently. Instead of the forty-four years being *since* Badon, he dates Badon as forty-four years *after* the *adventus Saxonum*. Given he places their arrival to 449–456, this dates Bede's Badon to c.493–500. Surviving copies of Bede's *Historia ecclesiastica gentis Anglorum* (eighth century) pre-dates the earliest copy of *De Excidio* (ninth – tenth century).[142] This might lead us to accept Bede's calculation.

Using annals and chronicles for dating events raises difficulties. Two different Christian dating systems relating to Easter tables might account for the different obits recorded for figures such as St Patrick.[143] In this case as much as a thirty-odd year discrepancy. We must bear this in mind when trying to date events related to Arthur or when comparing different sources. Bede used Gildas to place the date of the *adventus Saxonum* in his *Chronica minora* to between 451–7 and in another work, *De temporibus ratione*, to between 450–5.[144] However, we do not have the version of *De Excidio* from which Bede was working.

A more literal translation of Gildas does not make things clearer:[145] 'now citizens now the enemies were victorious … up to the year of the siege of Mount Badon almost the last defeat of the rascals and by no means the least one month of the forty fourth year as I know having passed which was of my birth.'

This allows two possible interpretations. First, Gildas is writing forty-four years after Badon. Second, he is writing forty-four years after some other event, either the initial arrival, the revolt, or more likely, the initial victory under Ambrosius Aurelianus, given that passage directly precedes the information about Badon. In this scenario, Badon occurred in the intervening period. At the time of writing, the generation who experienced the wars have died out. An exasperated Gildas writes the age that succeeded them are 'ignorant of that storm' and are racing headlong into hell. The adult grandchildren of Ambrosius Aurelianus are alive yet 'inferior' to their forebear. Perhaps one of his five tyrant kings, Aurelius Caninus, is one of them.

The difficulty in interpreting and dating this has obviously caused a headache for historians and Arthurian theorists alike. Taken at face value, one could place the appeal to Aetius in c.446, the *adventus Saxonum* to c.449,

Badon to 493 and have Gildas writing in c.437. Having one's forty-four-year cake and eating it twice, once with Bede's interpretation and again with forty-four years between Badon and *De Excidio*.

One historian has attempted to place the narrative chronologically;[146] this places the appeal to Aetius in 446–54 and allows a long period for the Britons to fight back, suffer famine and abundance and appoint kings. The mercenaries don't arrive until c.480 and Badon is dated to c.500, with Gildas writing in c.544. Another places the appeal to 426–9, equates the revolt with the GC entry for 440 and places Badon 483–5.[147] The AC dates it over thirty years later to 516. Geoffrey of Monmouth gives only one date: Arthur dying at Camlann in 542, the text implying Badon was c.520.

We have one piece of evidence from an unusual source that might help: an extreme climatic event c.535.[148] Tree rings and ice core studies show a marked reduction in growth and evidence for a drop in temperatures. Literary sources seem to refer to this event; Cassiodorus in Italy, c.536, described a dust veil or fog darkening the sky for about a year. Procopius in Constantinople, also 536, records a 'most dread portent', the sun giving forth light 'without brightness'. John Lydus in c.540s in Constantinople states clouds 'dimmed the light of the sun' over Europe and the produce was destroyed'. The Annals of Ulster in 536 records a 'failure of bread', the Annals of Inisfallen dating it to 536–539. Widespread crop failures are reported from China to Europe.

Gildas states: 'a dense cloud and black night of their sin so loom over the whole island', and uses many images of light and dark throughout the text. One historian argues it is possible that Gildas is alluding to this and thus likely writing in 537 having taken this as a sign from God.[149] Interestingly, a forty-four year period before 537 would place Gildas' birth, and possibly Badon, in 493. I would suggest if Gildas saw such things he would have made far more of it which would date *De excidio before* 537.

We can say a number of things at least. An eyewitness writing between c.480–540s is able to give a contemporary account. It may be biased, hyperbolic and confused. Possibly even in parts wrong, such as the building of Hadrian's Wall. But we learn a number of crucial things. After the Romans left the Britons suffered major raids from the Picts and Irish. Germanic mercenaries were hired and they subsequently rebelled. The Britons fought back under Ambrosius Aurelianus and won an initial victory. A subsequent war went back and forth with one victory (not the last or the least), a siege at Badon Hill, *Badonici montis*.

Later sources will associate Arthur with this battle. It's important to note that the earliest Welsh tales do not, and don't even involve fighting Saxons. Gildas doesn't mention Arthur at all although later tradition will bring them together. For now we shall leave a wide timespan for Badon, perhaps a generation either side of c.500.

Lastly Gildas viewed Britain as a discrete unit, morally and historically, and the Britons as distinctive from others, such as Romans and Saxons.[150] This may have been a view shared by many others. Clear cultural divides certainly evolved centuries later between Anglo-Saxons and the Welsh. However we should not assume this was universally accepted at the time. Cultural identity is often multi-layered and loyalties can be divided. There are a number of elements to ethnicity:[151] tradition, customs and manners, language, law, descent, a common proper name, common ancestry, shared historical memories, common culture, a link with a homeland and sense of solidarity. One key feature is a definition in relation to others.

A word of warning

Before moving on to our next source it is worth reminding readers that while Bede follows Gildas, the earliest copy of the *Historia ecclesiastica* pre-dates that of *De Excidio*. We do have references to the existence of *De excidio* from the seventh century so we can confirm it was known and used before Bede. For example the Leiden Glossary, c.800, references the teachings of Theodore of Tarsus and Adrian of Canterbury who taught at St Augustine's Abbey in Canterbury in the seventh century. It includes references to *De excidio*, but not details of the entire content or narrative.

Bede makes the following comment regarding Gildas: 'To other unspeakable crimes, which Gildas their own historian describes in woeful words, was added this crime, that they never preached the faith to the Saxons and Angles who inhabited Britain with them.'[152] What he doesn't do is say exactly which parts of the narrative came from Gildas. Our reliance on a later copy of *De excidio* raises an intriguing possibility.

We have already noted Bede's interpretation of the forty-four years before or after Badon suggests he had access to a different version of *De excidio*. It is just possible that later copies of *De excidio* were constructed using Bede's *Historia ecclesiastica* rather than the other way round. Suspicions are raised further by Bede's use of a 150-year cycle and a prophecy of the same length in *De excidio*.[153]

Gildas tells us the Saxons arrive in 'three *keels*, as they call warships their language', using both the Germanic word and a common trope of three ships used in other legends (see the Anglo-Saxon Chronicles and the Arthurian tale *Preiddeu Annwfn*). The omens favoured the Saxons and Gildas is somehow aware of their portents: 'they would live for three hundred years in the land towards which their prows were directed, and that for half that time, a hundred and fifty years, they would repeatedly lay it waste'.[154] Bede alludes to this towards the end of *Historia ecclesiastica* when he states 285 years have passed since the coming of the English to Britain stating what comes after 'a later generation will discover'.[155]

It has been suggested this short but important passage was added sometime between 672–747.[156] In contrast, others accept the text stating: '*De excidio* makes more thematic sense as a prophecy responding to a crisis in *romanitas* and Roman Christianity in western Europe in the last quarter of the fifth century.'[157] The point of this is not to undermine *De excidio*, but rather to apply caution. The reason for this caution is that some theorists have suggested Gildas can be trusted word for word and the text can be use to find hidden clues. One theory uses the number of words in specific sentences or paragraphs to reveal hidden meanings or dates. Another claims Gildas was using acrostics, in which hidden words or meanings can be found by using letters in each line. Often this uses the first letter of each word. While early medieval religious writers did use acrostics, in this case it relies on our fifth- to sixth-century text surviving intact and being copied accurately time after time over several centuries.

To accept this I would suggest two things need to be shown. First, the choice of sentences or paragraphs can't just be chosen randomly or arbitrarily. Secondly the text has to be traced back to it's original. Otherwise, in the case of *De excidio*, it can be suggested a ninth-century scribe added his own glosses using Bede's *Historia ecclesiastica*, and embedded numerology or acrostics. However, it is generally accepted that much of the content of *De excidio* was faithfully copied by Bede.

Bede

Around 200 years after the British cleric Gildas wrote his scathing sermon, an Anglo-Saxon monk in the north of England began his most famous work: *Historia ecclesiastica gentis Anglorum*, 'The Ecclesiastical History of the English People' (HE). Completed in c.731 it provides the point of view of the descendants of the very people Gildas had described as heathens and barbarians. Bede was born near Jarrow around 673, admitted into the Monasteries of Wearmouth and Jarrow aged 7, and was ordained aged 29. Considered by some as the 'Father of English History', his methods are respected even today. He was one of the first to date events from the birth of Christ, a method that influenced later writers, which is a great help to modern historians.

He had access to an enormous library at the monastery which contained many of the sources we've already mentioned: Orosius, Eusebius, Gregory of Tours, Constantius' Life of St Germanus and Gildas to mention just a few. He also lists who helped him compile the recent history of the Anglo-Saxon Kingdoms: Abbot Albinus from the Kentish church; Nothhelm, a priest from London; Daniel the Bishop of the West Saxons; the brethren of the monastery of Lastingham in Mercia; Bishop Cyneberht of Lindsey; and his own knowledge and connections in Northumbria. An extensive body of evidence.

By the time of writing in 731, the larger Anglo-Saxon Kingdoms had expanded further westwards from Gildas' day. Many of the British enclaves and small kingdoms had been swallowed up. As with *De excidio*, the first few chapters are a description of Britain and the history leading up to the end of Roman Britain. As a historian he is fairly well respected and where he is unsure of a fact he says so.[158] For example, he says the first leaders of the Angles 'are said to have been' the two brothers, Hengest and Horsa.[159]

Bede follows the same series of raids, appeals and responses as in Gildas. He helpfully dates the appeal to the Romans to the twenty-third year of the reign of Theodosius, 445/6, and the year after the death of Attila's brother, Blaedla (died, c.444). He names Aetius as the 'thrice consul' (446). The 'proud tyrant' is also named. The early version of the name, *Uuertigerno*, suggests a fifth-century source.[160] Famine, a period of abundance and plague were followed by Vortigern seeking help from the Angles and Saxons.

They arrived in three ships in the time of Marcian and Valentinian (449–456) and settled in the 'eastern part of the island'. Bede singles out 'three powerful Germanic tribes', forming the origins of the kingdoms in his day: Jutes in Kent and the Isle of Wight; Saxons in Essex, Sussex and Wessex; and Angles in East Anglia, Mercia and Northumbria. Interestingly, he claims *Angulus* remains deserted to his day, as evidence points to parts of northern Europe being depopulated.

The mercenaries rebel and 'lay waste to every part of the island'. The Britons fight back, defeating them under Ambrosius Aurelianus, 'the sole member of the Roman race' who had survived. His parents bore a 'royal and famous name'. Victory then goes back and forth up to the siege of Mount Badon which he dates to forty-four years *after* their arrival, thus 493–500. He describes the visit of St Germanus as being 'a few years before' the arrival of the Saxons, and follows Constantius of Lyon's account in *The Life of St Germanus*.

Bede finishes with the same picture of ruined cities, civil wars and the Britons turning away from 'truth and justice'. For Bede the Britons received their just deserts for God had chosen 'worthier heralds of the truth to bring this people to the faith'.[161] In the following chapter he takes up the arrival of

St Augustine, which he makes a point of stating is about 150 years after the Angles arrived in Britain. Like Gildas, Bede makes no reference to Arthur or anything remotely Arthurian.

Anglo-Saxon Chronicle

The chronicle (ASC from now on) is thought to have been commissioned by Alfred the Great around 891. A number of manuscripts survive and the version used here is Swanton's translation unless others stated.[162] It roughly follows Bede's dates, though not exactly, and with additional information. The appeal to the Romans is dated to 443. Then the Britons turn to 'the princes of the Angle race'. During the reign of Martianus and Valentinian (449–456) we read: 'Hengest and Horsa, invited by Votigern, king of the Britons sought out Britain.' They land at Ebba's Creek (Thanet, Kent) and are given land in the 'south-east' in return for fighting the Picts. It then repeats Bede's description of three tribes. Their numbers increase but there is no mention of a revolt.

The entries for the fifth and sixth century focus mainly on the south. If we separate out the entries, we can see the echoes of three foundations stories. The first is in Kent and some of these battles can be equated with those in the HB (see next chapter), which perhaps significantly records battles going back and forth and British victories under Vortigern's son, Vortimer. In one of these battles the HB records Horsa is killed alongside Vortigern's second son, Cateyrn. We can see below this can be equated with a battle in the ASC dated to 455:

- 455 Hengest fought Vortigern at Agelesford (Aylesford, Kent?), Horsa is killed. Hengest and his son Æsc 'succeeds to the Kingdom (Kent?).
- 456 Hengest wins the victory, killing 4,000, at Crecganford (Crayford, Kent?). Britons flee to their stronghold at London and 'abandon Kent'.
- 465 Hengest and Æsc fought the Welsh at Wipped's Creek (unidentified) and twelve Welsh chieftains killed along with 'one of their thegns' called Wipped.
- 473 Hengest and Æsc fought the Welsh and they 'fled from the English like fire'.
- 488 Hengest dies and is succeed by Æsc who rules for twenty-four years.

This last entry is worth noting as the HB places Arthur firmly after Hengest's death. The next three entries all relate to Sussex:

477 Ælle and his three sons land at Cymen's shore (probably Selsey, Sussex) with three ships. He fights a battle driving the Welsh into the Weald.
485 Ælle fought the Welsh near the 'margins of *Mearcred's Burn*' (unidentified).
491 Ælle besieges Anderitum (coastal fort at Pevensey, Sussex). He kills 'all who live there'.

No more is heard of the South Saxons until 607. They appear to be confined to the *civitas* of the Regni, yet Ælle is described by Bede as the first to hold *imperium* south of the Humber, or Bretwalda (wide-ruler) in the ASC. Our next example involves Wessex, who Bede states were originally called the *Gewisse*.

495 Two *ealdormen* Cerdic and Cynric arrive with five ships at Cerdic's shore and fight the Welsh.
501 Port and two sons, Bieda and Maelga, arrive with two ships at Portsmouth and kill a 'noble British man'.
508 Cerdic and Cynric kill a British king, Natanleod, along with 5,000 men (near Charford and Netley in Hampshire).
514 West Saxons Stuf and Whitgar arrive with three ships at Cerdic's shore and fight Britons putting them to flight.
519 Cerdic and Cynric succeed to kingdom of West Saxons, fight the Britons at Cerdic's Ford.
527 Cerdic and Cynric fight Britons at Cerdic's Wood.
530 Cerdic and Cynric take the Isle of Wight.

Academic analysis has revealed that the regnal dates at the start of the Chronicle do not add up and that there appears to be duplicate entries. Thus there is a consensus the more likely date for Cerdic's arrival would be 532.[163] Having said that, Asser's ninth-century *Life of Alfred the Great* adds a Creoda, son of Cerdic and father to Cynric, into the list of kings. While none of the above entries or dates in the fifth to sixth centuries can be trusted, there is evidence to suggest some at least can be. Two entries for eclipses are dated to 1 March 538 and 20 June 540. In fact, there were indeed eclipses on 15 February 538 and 20 March 540.[164]

The earliest battles are confined to the New Forest and Isle of Wight areas. The next expansion comes from the Thames Valley, where the archaeological evidence places the earliest settlement. Importantly just before these entries the ASC provides a date for Ida, first king of the Berncians, which the HB firmly places after Arthur. There then follows victories for the West Saxons

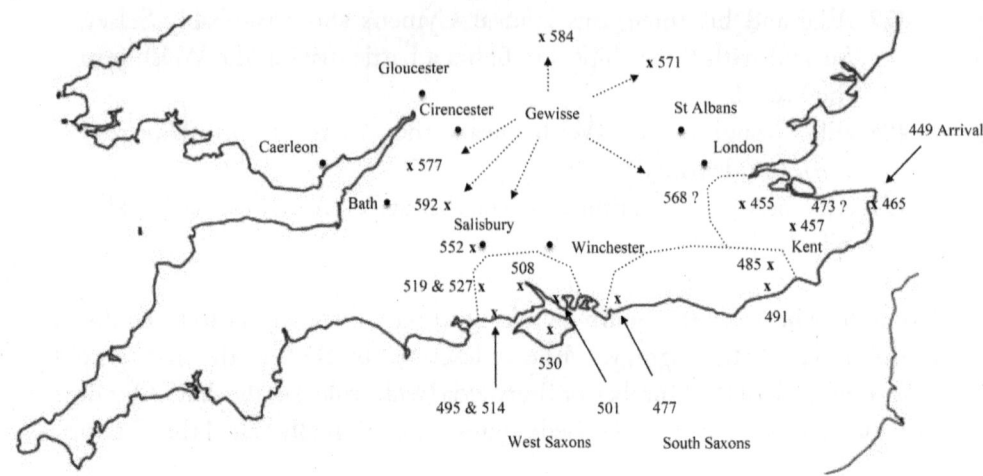

Figure 12: Map of early battle sites in the Anglo-Saxon Chronicles.

in 552 at Salisbury and in 556 at Bera's stronghold (Barbury in Wiltshire). They are powerful enough to defeat Æthelberht of Kent in 568. There is then a further expansion:

- 571 Battle at Bedcanford and taking of settlements of Limbury, Aylesbury, Benson and Eynsham
- 577 Battle of Dyrham against 3 British Kings and taking of three cities: Gloucester, Cirencester and Bath.

The ASC then moves into known history and figures appear that match up with later genealogies. The map in figure 12 plots the locations mentioned above. It is interesting to note that prior to the mid-sixth century they are confined to the south coast. A significant expansion occurs after this period. This offers a similar gap to the one suggested by our first two Bretwaldas, Ælle at the end of the fifth century and Caewlin towards the end of the sixth. It is tempting to place Arthur there but the ASC makes no mention of him or Badon.

Summary

After direct Roman rule ended c.410 Britannia limped into the fifth century with evidence of surviving Roman and Christian institutions and culture. A severe economic shock coincided with deurbanisation in the first quarter of the fifth century. Villas were abandoned or modified, towns contracted or were given over to agriculture and hill-forts were reoccupied. The second quarter was marked by a significant increase in Germanic material culture and burials in the south and east.

In Gaul the Western Empire held together for half a century. After the death of Aetius, the situation worsened up to the last emperor in 476. A decade before that, a war between Romans, Franks, Goths and Britons place Riothamus in Gaul and Britons, or Bretons, north of the Loire in modern Brittany. Perhaps importantly, Saxons were driven out of the Loire in c.460s. By the end of the fifth century the Franks were dominant in Gaul, led first by Clovis and then his sons after 511. There is no space for a grand Arthurian war against the Romans in Gaul as described by Geoffrey of Monmouth.

A major change caused a Gallic Chronicler in 440 to record Britain as 'lost to the power of the Saxons'. What this means is debatable as Bede dates the revolt to after 449. Yet it is important to note the sequence of events remains remarkably consistent with Gildas. Roman rule ends; Picts and Irish raid; an appeal to Agitius (Aetius) is rejected; Vortigern invites Germanic mercenaries; they rebel, Ambrosius Aurelianus leads a fightback; war goes back and forth up to the siege of Badon Hill; and Gildas looks back on these events and writes *De excidio*.

None of our sources, insular or continental, make any reference to Arthur, historical or mythical. Yet into this narrative our later sources will place him and it is important to note which generation each figure belongs to. Vortigern is an adult when the Saxons arrive, as are the parents of Ambrosius Aurelianus. Ambrosius is portrayed as a child under Vortigern but one who grows up to defeat him. Geoffrey of Monmouth claims the brother of Ambrosius is none other than Uther. If we accept this chronology, Vortigern–Ambrosius–Arthur, then it becomes important to date Vortigern accurately. As with most things Arthurian, this will prove difficult.

However, we can confirm the rough timeframe for our hero's floruit at this point. Certainly after the mid-fifth century. More likely towards the end of the fifth or in the early sixth century. We will narrow this down more tightly as we go forward. We also have a tentative timeframe for the fragmentation of the provincial structure and emergence of petty kingdoms.

Gildas places 'anointed kings' after the appeal to Agitius but before the *adventus Saxonum*. The ASC proved foundation legends for Kent, Sussex and Wessex, but major expansion only from the mid-Sixth century. Archaeology points to a significant increase in Germanic settlement through the second half of the fifth century only to slow down or stop around c.500. Cultural identity had also changed. While a sense of *romanitas* can be heard in Gildas, at the same time we see signs of a warband culture with petty tyrants engaged in civil wars.

The next chapter will provide an explanation for the discrepancies between the GC and Bede concerning the date of the *Adventus Saxonum*. This will enable us to place Arthur a little more accurately in our timeline. We will see if the earliest Welsh sources portray Arthur as a mythical or historical figure. If the latter, perhaps he is trying to maintain a culturally Roman Britain alongside men like Ambrosius Aurelianus. Alternatively, he could be one of Gildas' tyrants, leading a warband of 'bloody, proud and murderous men'. If Arthur was historical, then our first attested source comes about 300 years after his time. But there is one piece of evidence which might point to a reference made much earlier. We will begin our next chapter in a world of warbands and mead-halls, and a warrior who fought in the sixth century, perhaps within living memory of Arthur.

Chapter Three

The First Whispers of Arthur

The first attested reference to Arthur in any literary source comes in the HB, c.830, 300 years after the alleged events. There is another source often used to support the theory of a historical figure however: the Welsh poem *Y Gododdin*. The earliest manuscript dates to the thirteenth century in the *Book of Aneirin*. It is claimed to be a copy of a genuine early seventh-century account of the battle, which would make it the closest contemporary account of a battle between Britons and Saxons. While the poem was known about in the middle ages it only became popular in the nineteenth century with a renewed interest in Welsh nationalism. Exactly when, where and who composed it is unknown.

It is not a narrative poem but a series of eulogies praising various warriors. These men, 300 in all, were gathered together and feasted for a year by Mynyddog Mwynfawr, the king of the Gododdin, at Din Eidyn (Edinburgh). Travelling from all over Britain, only eighty of the heroes are named. Their target was the Angles of Deira and Bernicia, although the earliest version of the manuscript only mentions the former. The battle was at Cattraeth, which some have identified with Catterick, others further north, nearer the borders of Gododdin. The battle is generally dated to c.600, but this too cannot be confirmed and I will argue a possible connection with Urien of Rheged might place it a little earlier.

The key passage refers to the warrior Gwawrddur, who fought 'in the front rank' leading the 300 in a charge, cutting down enemies in both the centre and the wing:[1] 'He fed black ravens on the rampart of a fortress, though he was no Arthur.' There is no guarantee this one passing reference was not a late addition. Nor does it prove Arthur was historical. It could easily be similar to someone today saying someone was no Superman. Even if it is a genuine reference to a real warrior there is no certainty it refers to *the* Arthur. In this northern context it could easily refer to the historical Artuir mac Áedáin of Dalriada who died in battle towards the end of the sixth century (we shall deal with this candidate later).

On its own, this passing reference in a thirteenth-century copy, of a possible seventh-century poem, doesn't count for very much. Yet some argue the sheer innocuousness of its appearance suggests the figure of Arthur was well known relatively early. If we are generous we can accept the oral composition of the poem occurred in the third quarter of the sixth century.[2] Written down decades later, perhaps when Gododdin fell to Bernicia in 638.

Taken at face value the poem provides some vivid imagery and we can imagine a sixth-century bard singing a lament for the fallen heroes in mead-halls across Britain. A small troop of 300 valiantly charged against a force many times their number, all but one falling in battle. The warriors rode out in dark-blue-coloured mail coats over crimson tunics. Bearing round, white shields and yellow spears with square spearheads. The battle begins with javelins and spears as the Britons try to break the 'stronghold of shields' (surely a shield-wall) of the 'crafty Deirians'. Shields were broken, spearpoints 'splintered and shattered'. The battle may have started with the Britons on horseback; casting 'spears in battle from a bounding, wide tracked charger', or from a 'steaming slender bay horse'. But elsewhere it is a 'spear-fight' and they 'formed a battle pen against the spears', shield-wall against shield-wall.

Because of the problem with dating both this battle and Badon, a century could separate the two events. If this battle was earlier than thought, and Arthur can be placed in the early sixth century, it is possible a young man alive when Arthur fought at Camlann might still be active by the time the Gododdin rode to glorious defeat, However this picture of heroic Britons fighting hordes of Anglo-Saxons might be a little too simplistic.

One study looks at other early Welsh poems and may reference the same battle from the other side.[3] In the Welsh heroic poem *The battle of Gwen Ystrad*, Urien is said to lead the 'men of Cattraeth. Elsewhere he is named the 'Lord of Cattraeth'. In the *Eulogy of Cadwallon*, 'fierce Gwallawg' is said to have caused the 'mortality at Cattraeth'. In later Welsh Genealogies, Urien and Gwallawg are cousins and kings of Rheged and Elmet respectively. Implying it is possible the kings of these two Brythonic kingdoms, Rheged and Elmet, were fighting on the side of the Angles of Deira against the Britons of Gododdin.

The HB has the same men fighting in alliance against the Angles of Bernicia. Besieging them on the island of Lindisfarne for three days and three nights, a timeframe repeated for one of Arthur's battles. This battle is dated to the time of Theodoric who reigned for seven years, twelve years after Ida, the first king of the Bernicians. None of this can be relied upon, but it would place the siege of Lindisfarne in the years c.571–8. Urien is murdered by an ally, and fellow Briton, Morcant. The Bernicians survived and a generation later become the dominant force in the north under Æthelfrith.

As an aside it is Æthelfrith's successor Edwin (616–633) who, according to the HB, is baptised (c.627) by Rhun, a son of Urien, and Paulinus, Archbishop of York (Bede only mentions Paulinus). One manuscript copy of the HB names

Rhun as its author which, if true, would provide a much earlier provenance than previously thought. The same source also claims that Oswy (King of Northumbria 642–670) married Rieinmellt, a granddaughter of Rhun. Could this be the same man? If so it is a marriage between a princess of Rheged, a great-granddaughter of Urien 'Lord of Cattraeth', and the king of Bernicia and Deira. We also read in the HB that Æthelfrith gave Din Guaire (Bamburgh) to his Brythonic-sounding wife, Bebba, from which, according to Bede, it was named Bebbanburg.

Taken together this tells us two things. First, late sixth- and early seventh-century politics was not neatly divided along ethnic, cultural or religious lines. The early to mid-seventh-century wars between Cadwallon of Gwynedd, allied with Penda of Mercia and the kings of Northumbria, attest to this. It is thus likely at the time a historical Arthur lived, between c.450–550, the situation was just as complex and nuanced. Indeed, two battles recorded in the tenth century AC, Camlann (537) and Arfderydd (573), are portrayed as civil wars with no involvement of Angles or Saxons at all.

Second, if Urien and Gwallawg were involved then it forces us to reconsider the date for Cattraeth. This scenario would place it a generation earlier than c.600, within the lifetime of someone who had lived through Camlann and Arfderydd. We will cover this latter battle when we come to the genealogies. At this point it is worth noting another figure that appears at the siege of Lindisfarne and at Arfderydd. Rhydderch Hael was a king of Alt Clud, a Brythonic kingdom in the Strathclyde area. Many of these figures appear in the genealogies and traditions of *Yr Hen Ogledd* (the old north).

In summary, we have a potential early Welsh poem that makes a passing reference to Arthur. If we take this, and other Welsh poems and traditions, at face value then the following scenarios can be suggested. In the second-half of the sixth century a complex political situation bisected ethnic differences. Brythonic kings of Rheged and Elmet fought alongside the men of Deira against the Britons of Gododdin and their allies. In the same period, the Britons came together to push the Bernicians back into the sea. Only for one of those kings, Urien of Rheged, to be treacherously murdered by his fellow Briton, Morcant. Also around the same time (c.573) the AC records a bloody battle at Arfderydd between Brythonic kings of the north.

This is important for two reasons. First, it shows the political reality of the sixth century was more complex than a simple Romano-Britons vs Anglo-Saxons. This might reflect the world Arthur was living in more accurately than the one presented by Gildas of fellow countrymen against barbarian Saxons. Second, many of the figures above feature in the later genealogies. This will be worth remembering when trying to date Arthur as he is placed a roughly a generation or two before these figures.

Figure 13: Northern kingdoms and battles of the late sixth century.

The map in figure 13 shows the kingdoms and battles in the late sixth century. The exact location, boundaries and battle sites are speculative. It is a very different situation from the days of the last *Dux Britanniarum* and the provinces of Britannia Secunda and Valentia. Some forts along Hadrian's Wall and across the north show signs of continued occupation throughout the fifth century. Additionally, many of the proposed locations for Arthur's twelve battles are in this region. That battle list appears in the HB, written just over 200 years after the Gododdin made their fateful charge into the shield wall at Cattraeth.

Historia Brittonum

Around forty manuscripts of the HB survive, the earliest of which can be dated to c.828. It is often attributed to a monk, Nennius, although this only appears in a later version.[4] It is thought to have been written in northern Wales, although some have suggested the south-west, in Dyfed. The text begins with the ages of the world and the origins of Britain with an unlikely tale of Trojan immigrants. It then covers Roman Britain before reaching the main part of the book with which we are most concerned.

Some historians view the source with scepticism: the structure is 'a mess' and the fifth-century dates 'worthless';[5] it is 'synchronised history' written for political purposes in a ninth-century context;[6] and the author is 'actively manipulating his text to create a synthetic pseudo-history'.[7] Others state: 'if such history is unhistorical, so also are all the major histories of the early middle ages'.[8] Vortigern is possibly the most important figure in the text. While some academics are sceptical, others state there is 'no reasonable doubt' he is historical.[9] It also features Ambrosius Aurelianus as Emrys (Emrys is simply the Welsh version of Ambrosius), undoubtedly the same figure Gildas mentions as leading the fightback against the Saxons. Later used by Geoffrey of Monmouth to construct his figure of *Merlinus*.

The various recensions usually referred to appear to derive from an archetype dated to c.829.[10]

However, one version, the Chartres manuscript, may be as early as the mid-eighth century. Tantalisingly, this version claims Rhun, son of Urien, as the author.[11] This would still date the earliest manuscript to a hundred years after Rhun allegedly baptised Edwin of Northumbria (627), but only shortly after Bede had completed his *Historia ecclesiastica gentis Anglorum* (731). As such, it could be a riposte against Bede's English version of history. Where the text impinges on known history it is wrong or 'distorts the evidence'.[12] Instead it weaves together 'strands of traditions' to create a 'well crafted literary construction'. Yet the Arthurian battle list shows signs of being poetic in nature and uses Old Welsh rhyming structures. It is this battle list most theories focus on, and we will certainly come to it. We will begin with the part of the text often ignored or glossed over, *The Wonders of Britain*.

Historia Brittonum – The wonders of Britain

This section includes a number of 'wonders' including springs and whirlpools. Three of these wonders are connected to our study, two of which mention Arthur. These are important because they tell us something about this first Arthurian source. The battle list might suggest people in the ninth century viewed Arthur as a historical figure. Yet at the same time a parallel tradition existed of a more mythical figure, tied to the land in specific locations.

The earliest copy of the Wonders, *Mirabilia*, are found in Harleian 3859 with a copy of AC and Welsh genealogies separating it from the HB. They are not found with manuscripts of the Vatican rescission. They therefore can not be relied upon to date the HB and 'should be treated as a separate text that had been associated with the HB by the early twelfth century'.[13] It is likely the *Mirabilia* was added during the migration of the documents from north-west Wales to south-west Wales via south-east Wales. A number of 'Wonders' are in mid- to south-east Wales. Both of the Wonders attributed to Arthur are in southern Wales.

The first wonder is in the 'country called Builth' and describes a heap of stones with the footprint of Cafal, Arthur's dog. Arthur was hunting the great Boar, Twrch Trwyth (also found in the later legend of *Culhwch and Olwen*). Cafal, Arthur's hound, impressed his footprint on the stone. At this spot Arthur brought together a pile of stones 'under the stone in which was his dog's footprint'. This pile was called Carn Cafal. Men can come and take the stone for a day and a night, but on the next day it is miraculously found back on the stone pile.

Some theorists try to historicise this. The great boar is transformed into a barbarian king and his piglets into his sons or warriors. Perhaps Arthur really did bury a beloved dog and it would be quite plausible for it to be marked with a pile of stones. But this is be pure speculation and it would be difficult to explain how stones, once removed, could magically reappear on the pile.

The second is the tomb of Arthur's son, Amr, in the country of Ergyng, South Wales. Arthur himself is said to have killed and buried him by a spring, since called Llygad Amr. The circumstances of his death are not recorded. Men come to measure the tomb and 'whatever measure you measure it on one occasion, you never find it again of the same measure'; be it 6, 9, 12 or 15 ft. The author claimed he has seen this for himself.

Here, Arthur is described as 'Arthur the soldier'. A following wonder also tells of a tomb of changing length, in Ceredigion. This time it changes to match the man visiting it and if one kneels three times it removes 'weariness ... to the end of his death'. Amr's tomb has no other powers beyond changing in size.

These are not the only topographical features that have attracted Arthur's name. There are many such sites all over Britain: twenty-two Arthur's stones, thirty Arthur's Quoits (discuss shaped stone); five tables and three round tables; eight seats; six Halls, camps or other types of residence; five graves; and fifteen other sites referring to Arthur.[14] There is no evidence connecting any of them to Arthur beyond local myth and legend. Nor can we date the names back to the fifth or sixth century. In fact, our earliest attested documentary evidence of an Arthurian-named topographical feature in Wales is c.1100.[15]

As we can see in the map in figure 14, these features are spread across Britain. Interesting to note where they are not found. None south and east of the line from Middlesborough to Southampton. A small number in

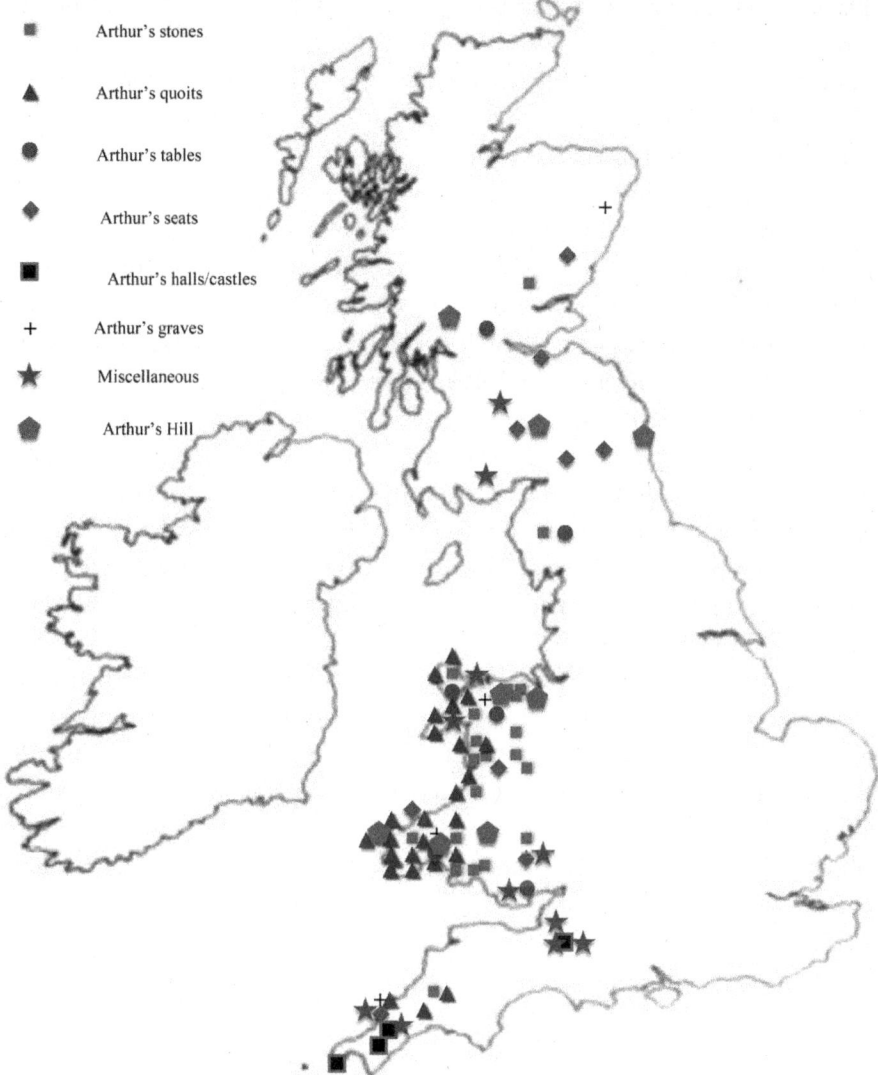

Figure 14: Map of Arthurian landmarks.

Cumbria, the lowlands of Scotland and interestingly, further north. A cluster in Somerset but a more significant number in Cornwall. The largest number by far are spread throughout modern Wales. This has emboldened some theorists in selecting just a few of these to bolster a case for one specific area. The fact none can be traced back to Arthur's alleged floruit is brushed aside. The dozens of other locations scattered across Britain are ignored. A similar methodology is used with the battle list or with locations that pop up in later tales, such as Avalon or Camelot. In short, one could choose an area and weave a plausible theory placing Arthur there, surrounded by half a dozen Arthurian topographical features.

One example involves a Neolithic stone ring called King Arthur's Round Table near Penrith in Cumbria. Some have linked this to the fifteenth-century Welsh Triad which lists Arthur's courts: Celliwig in Cornwall, Mynyw at St David's in Wales and Pen Rhionydd. This latter one has been associated with the Penrith site. It is an uninspiring site, one which can be walked across in a few seconds. Smaller than a football pitch. It dates to the late Neolithic period (2000 to 1000 BC), and forms a simple, low, circular platform surrounded by a wide ditch and earthen bank. There is evidence that two standing stones were originally placed at one entrance. English Heritage notes it may have acquired its name in the seventeenth century.

A similar investigation into other locations and we see the various theories collapse. The fact Arthur's name has been attached to so many locations might suggest a more mythical figure. All we can say is the HB provides our earliest evidence that Arthur had acquired a mystical tradition and been attached to specific geographical locations, in this case Wales. There is one other 'wonder' that is relevant to our study.

The third wonder on the list is 'the hot lake, where the Baths of Badon are, in the country of the Hwicce'.[16] Surrounded by a wall made of brick and stone men can visit and, 'at any time', have a hot or cold bath. In the past this convinced me that Bath was the very likely location for the battle of Badon. While we can't trust Geoffrey of Monmouth's twelfth century pseudo-history (which places Badon on a hill outside the town), here at least we had an early source pointing to Bath.

Unfortunately, this only proves how careful one needs to be even when looking at apparent original sources. The above translation came from John Morris' 1980 edition and translation of the Latin text. Yet the words in the text are not found in any manuscript. Instead these were added by Morris from the contents page.[17] This 'helpful' addition would not be so bad if the contents page itself was part of an original ninth-century copy. Instead, that contents page comes from a thirteenth-century manuscript and thus post-dates Geoffrey of Monmouth, who was the first person to associate Bath with Badon.

The 'Wonder' actually reads: *tertiary miraculous stagnum calidum quod est in regione huich*, 'the third wonder is the hot baths found the region of the Hwicce'. This might be Bath, but it is far from certain, as is the association with Badon. Interestingly, the fourth wonder is described as 'the salt springs found there, from which salt is boiled, wherewithal various foods can be salted; they are not near the sea but rise from the ground'. This is very likely to be Droitwich, which is north of Worcester and sixty miles north of Bath. Salt was a valuable commodity in Roman times. The question arises: are the salt springs from the fourth wonder found with the hot baths of the third wonder? Or does the word 'there' simply mean in the country of the Hwicce?

This is a big problem. For although we have a good early source for Badon from Gildas, we have nothing prior to Geoffrey of Monmouth that locates it. Not only can we not trust the multitude of modern theories or pseudo-historical sources from the middle-ages, but we can't always trust translations of original sources. All the earliest manuscripts of Welsh traditions and French Romances post-date Geoffrey of Monmouth and thus we cannot trust they have not been influenced by him.

While the inclusion of magical graves and stones point to a mythical Arthur, the main narrative of the HB places a very real-sounding Arthur in a historical narrative. It also provides a plausible explanation for the discrepancy in dating the *adventus Saxonum* between the GC and Bede.

Historia Brittonum – The narrative

The HB begins with a description of Britain and an origin story involving Brutus, a descendant of the Trojan prince, Aeneas. A garbled history of Roman Britain ends with the death of Maximus, three Roman generals (possibly Marcus, Gratian and Constantine III in c.406–7) and the end of Roman Britain (409–10?). We then read the Britons 'went in fear for forty years', although from which date isn't clarified. At this time, Vortigern ruled in Britain but he was under pressure from Picts and the Irish, fear of Roman invasion and from the 'dread of Ambrosius'. Confusingly, Ambrosius is met later as a small boy.

Hengest and Horsa arrive in three ships, driven from their homeland by exile rather than invitation, and are settled on an island which in 'their language is called *Tanet*', and the British call Ruoihm (traditionally accepted as Thanet off the east coast of Kent). The text then has a section on Germanus, although none of the content is in the *Life of St Germanus* by Constantius of Lyon, or vice versa. Some have suggested this is a different figure, such as St Garmon, active in fifth-century Britain, who died c.474 on the Isle of Man. He removes a tyrant king called Benlii and installs Cadell Ddyrnllug, from whose 'seed the whole country of Powys is ruled to this day'. Our author is very keen to portray Vortigern as the villain of the piece, and here he offers a rival genealogy and foundation story to counter another tradition that connects Vortigern with Powys.

The text returns to the *Saxones* who increase their numbers and then demand more supplies and threaten to break the treaty. Again we note the narrative is one of the hiring of mercenaries and not an invasion. But a deal is struck and sixteen more *keels* arrive packed with warriors and, crucially, Hengest's daughter. Vortigern is smitten and Hengest agrees to the marriage, receiving the kingdom of Kent as reward, as well as becoming the king's advisor. Now we see a situation where a Gallic Chronicler might view Britain lost to the Saxons, which might explain the discrepancy with Bede. Another deal is struck and forty ships arrive with Hengest's son and nephew, Octha and Ebissa, to fight the Picts. Octha is given land 'in the north about the Wall that is called Guaul' – surely Hadrian's Wall. More and more ships arrive until they leave the islands they came from uninhabited. (Interestingly, a village called Wall in Northumbria is very close to Hexham, once called *Hagustealde*, meaning 'young warriors enclosure'. Nearby Bardon Mill is one of many candidates for Badon, although this requires a copyist neglecting the macron above the 'a' which would indicate a long a sound).

Meanwhile scandal hits the British court. Vortigern is accused of 'taking his daughter to wife', and a child is born. It is Germanus who confronts him in front of 'the whole council of Britain'. Vortigern fled to Snowdonia and was advised by his 'wizards' to build a fortress in the 'furthest borders' of his kingdom. Tradition places this at Dinas Emrys near Beddgelert in Gwynedd. Three times he tries to build his fortress and three times it collapses. His 'wizards' advise him he must sacrifice a fatherless-child and sprinkle his blood on the spot.

Envoys are sent out across Britain and in Glywysing, South Wales they find a young boy 'playing ball'. Hearing his mother claim she had 'never known a man', they drag him off to northern Wales. On hearing of his fate the boy protested and claimed to know what the wizards did not. He went on to explain that beneath the foundations of the castle was a lake containing two vessels. Within each was a cloth containing two 'worms', one white, one red. The boy is proved correct and the 'worms' fight, the red eventually successful.

The boy explains that this represented the red dragon of the Britons finally defeating the white dragon of the invaders. Centuries later, Geoffrey of Monmouth would use this tale and fuse it with the story of a much later figure, Myrddin Wyllt. But this earliest tale has nothing to do with Merlin, or indeed Arthur, at all. Instead the boy tells Vortigern exactly who he is when asked: 'I am called Ambrosius', also known as 'Emrys the Overlord'. Just to confirm the association with Gildas and Bede's Ambrosius Aurelianus, we are helpfully told (temporarily forgetting his mother's claim he has no father): 'My father is one of the consuls of the Roman people.' Vortigern then travelled to the region of the Gwynessi and built a city called Caer Gwrtheyrn, leaving Ambrosius at the hill fort that would bear his name, Dinas Emrys.

Meanwhile Vortigern's son, Vortimer, is busy fighting to drive Hengest and Horsa out. Three times they besiege them at Thanet. Hengest sends envoys requesting more ships and a 'vast number of fighting men'. In a phrase used by Gildas the battles go back and forth as do the borders or 'frontiers'. Then we read Vortimer fought four 'keen' battles. The first at Deguentid (River Darent in Kent?); the second at Episford (Aylesford, Kent), where Cateyrn, Vortimor's brother, died along with Hengest's brother Horsa; and a third, a victory, in 'open country by the inscribed stone on the shore of the Gallic Sea (south east coast?). The fourth is not given.

The first battle could be equated with the entry in the ASC for 457: 'Hengest and Aesc fought the Britons at Crecganford, killed 4,000 men. Britons abandoned Kent and fled to their stronghold of London.' The River Cray runs from Crayford feeding into the Darent a mile to north. The second battle has an even clearer connection. The ASC entry for 455 states Hengest and Horsa fought Vortigern at *Agelesford*, Horsa was killed and Aesc succeeded to Kingdom. The final battle has the Saxons fleeing to their ships. But Vortimer dies soon after and Hengest returns with the encouragement of his daughter, Vortigern's wife.

A peace conference was called during which the English treacherously turned on their hosts, killing 300 nobles and taking Vortigern prisoner. He is forced to cede Essex, Sussex, Middlesex and other districts, which sounds very much like the former south-eastern province of Maxima Caesariensis. The Saxons were accused of a similar massacre on the Continent against the Thuringians (presumably during the Frankish-Thuringian War of 530s) by Widukind of Corvey in *Res gestae Saxonicae*, written c.980. The HB may be an earlier source referring to an earlier massacre, but we must doubt a recurring trope just as the arrival of three ships is suspicious.

Back to the narrative, we find Vortigern in Gwerthrynion, in hiding with his wives. Germanus follows him and he flees to his fortress on the River Teifi in the country of the Demetians in south-west Wales. Germanus finds him again and after a biblical-sounding three days and nights, fire reigned down from heaven and destroyed all within. The author is unsure as to Vortigern's fate and offers alternatives, from being swallowed by the earth to wandering friendless until his heart broke. Needless to say, none of this resembles the *Life of St Germanus* by Constantius.

Vortigern's four sons are listed: Vortimer, Cateryn and Pascent, the latter ruling in Builth and Gwerthrynion by permission of Ambrosius, who is now described as 'the great king among all the kings of the British nation'. His fourth son, allegedly by incest, was called Faustus. Germanus baptised the boy and took him to Gaul where he founded a monastery at Riez. There was indeed a

Bishop Faustus of Riez in 432 who died c.490s. Intriguingly, his contemporary Sidonius Apollinarus states he was born in Britain. This Faustus seems too early for a mid-fifth century Vortigern or Germanus visiting in 429–437. A genealogy is provided for Vortigern to which we will return.

There follows a lengthy section about St Patrick. Significantly, it also references Palladius being sent by Celestine (431) and appears to conflate the two arrivals. Perhaps the author genuinely thought he was sent at the same time. However, it is important to note no contemporary continental source mentions St Patrick, and as we have noted his floruit seems to have been a generation after Palladius. It goes on to say Patrick preached in Ireland for eighty-five years before he died. A point that is important to remember for later.

We then come to the crucial part of the text, Chapter 56. We must remind ourselves that this is the first attested reference to Arthur, dated to roughly 300 years after the alleged fact. Attached to the same manuscript we have two entries in the 'Wonders of Britain' that connect him to mythical places in the landscape. Immediately after the author ends with St Patrick we read the following.[18] After Hengest's death, his son Octha came from the north of Britain to Kent and it is from Octha, rather than Hengest, that the kings of the Kentishmen trace their lineage: 'Then Arthur fought against them in those days, together with the kings of the British; but he was their *dux bellorum*.' There then follows the famous list of twelve battles, including Badon. The English, defeated in all their campaigns, send for help from Germany. Their numbers increased and they brought over their kings from Germany to rule over them in Britain, 'until the time Ida, the first king of Bernicia, reigned'.

There is a bit to unpack there before we look at the battle list. First, the author describes Arthur as a *dux*, a word used by medieval writers to mean general, commander or simply leader. Centuries before, it was often used to denote a temporary command in the Roman army, but by the fourth century it had become an official title denoting a military command, usually on a border area and often across more than one province. In Britain we recall the post of *Dux Britanniarum* in northern Britain. This fact is often used by modern theorists to portray Arthur as a late Romano-British commander, or to place him in the north.

However there is no evidence that these military posts survived into sub-Roman Britain. Additionally, the exact wording in the HB is '*dux erat bellorum*' (leader in battle) which is more likely a description than a title. In fact, we recall Germanus described as *Dux Proelii* (leader for battle) and in *Y Gododdin* at Cattraeth, Ywain is named the 'battle leader' in charge of what appears to be various war bands and warriors from around Britain who have come together.

This leads on to a second point. He is described as neither a king nor British. This doesn't of course mean he wasn't. As we shall see, we also cannot be sure his name is Roman or Brythonic. All we can say is the text portrays him as a trusted military commander who leads an alliance of British kings against the English.

But which English and where? This too is not clear. Are the campaigns directed at Kent where Octha is now the first king? Or in the north where Octha came from to drive out the remnants of his mercenaries? Or perhaps it simply means the enemy in general wherever they may be found. An analysis of the battle list will show it is not at all clear where exactly these campaigns were.

What is a little clearer is *when* the author places Arthur. Sometime after the death of Hengest but before the reign of Ida. If we accepted the dates for these figures from other sources we could speculate Arthur fought his battles between c.488–547. Unfortunately we cannot trust these sources and, coupled with scribal errors and difficulties in computing Easter cycles, we are forced to return to a broader range. But let us be generous with our source and speculate, taking it at face value. The author believes St Patrick was sent by Pope Celestine (431) and preached for eighty-five years before dying (thus 516). It then tells us Hengest died (488 from the ASC) and Octha succeeded him. It is not clear if Arthur is fighting in his time or with the kings that came after. The last paragraph may be instructive as it reads as though sometime has past between the victorious campaigns and the English increasing their numbers.

It is worth briefly noting what else the HB tells us. There are a number of genealogies for Anglo-Saxon kingdoms: Kent, Bernicia, Deira and Mercia. King Maelgwn of Gwynedd is mentioned, who might be equated with one of Gildas' five tyrant kings, Maglocunnus. We also get the reference to the siege of Lindisfarne and assassination of Urien of Rheged, followed by events in the seventh century. Taken as a whole the most important figure isn't Arthur at all but Vortigern. He is the villain of the piece, together with the treacherous Saxons. Three men are named as fighting the English: first Vortimer, then Arthur and finally Outigirn, at a time when 'Aneirin and Taliesin ... were famed in British verse'. Interestingly, there is no figure from the part of the text from Maximus onwards that can be shown to be mythical. It seems reasonable to suggest that in a ninth-century audience, some at least viewed Arthur as historical.

Vortigern

One important point to note is that all of the events involving Vortigern personally occur in the south and west of Britain. He is able to place mercenaries in Thanet and later by the wall, suggesting he has authority across much of the former Diocese. He cedes Kent and later Essex, Middlesex and Sussex. This suggests someone (Gildas says there was a council headed by a 'proud tyrant') still exercised authority over much of the former Roman Diocese. I would therefore propose that post-Roman Britain maintained its integrity and provincial structures up to the mid-fifth century.

Vortigern's power base is in Wales, first in Gwynedd and finally in Demetae, where he meets a fiery end. His great-grandfather, Gloiu, supposedly built Caer Gloiu on the river Severn, Gloucester (which we know was actually founded by the Romans as a *colonia*). It is unfortunate that the text gives us a number of contradictory dates for the *adventus Saxonum*:[19]

- Chapter 16: 'From the year when the Saxons first came, to the fourth year of King Mervyn, 429 years are reckoned', i.e. 399.
- Chapter 31: 'the British went in fear for 40 years'. It is unknown if this is from the death of Maximus (388), killing of the 'generals' (407), or end of Roman Britain (410). Thus pointing to 428, 447 or 450.
- Chapter 31: 'When Gratian ruled for the second time with Equitius, the Saxons were received by Vortigern, 347 years after the Passion of Christ', i.e. 375.
- Chapter 66: 'Vortigern, however, held empire in Britain in the consulship of Theodosius and Valentinian and in the fourth year of his reign the English came to Britain, in the consulship of Felix and Taurus, in the 400th year from the the Passion of our Lord Jesus Christ', i.e. 428.
- Chapter 66: From the year when the English came to Britain and were welcomed by Vortigern to Decius and Valerian are sixty-nine years. Unidentified figures and unknown date.
- Chapter 66: From the reign of Vortigern to the quarrel between Vitalinus and Ambrosius are twelve years, that is Guoloppum, the battle of Guoloppum (possibly Wallop in Hampshire), an unknown date.

With this last entry it is rather confusing to have Ambrosius, a boy when Vortigern meets him, fighting Vitalinus, recorded as Vortigern's grandfather in his genealogy. The dates above are clearly contradictory, allowing theorists to pick the one they prefer, usually choosing between 428 and 447.

The earliest manuscripts of *De excidio* refer to him simply to *superbo tyranno*. Bede names him: *Vurtigern*, *Uurtigern* or *Vertigernus*, the earliest being *Uuertigernus*, a form which points to an early authentic origin. In Welsh sources he is Gwrtheyrn, the Irish equivalent being *Foirtchern*. We also have a

Saint Guirthiern. Thirteenth-century manuscripts of *De excidio* give a name to him: *superbo tyranno Vortigerno* or *Gurthigerno Brittanorum duce*.

The name Vortigern is a compound of ver/wor/wer, meaning 'over', and -tigern, meaning 'lord'. Here it is clearly a name rather than a title. Indeed Welsh sources, including the HB, add the epithet *Gwrtheyrn Gwrteneu* – Vortigern the Thin, suggesting perhaps a more rotund namesake or predecessor. One historian argues there is 'no reasonable doubt that Guorthigirn (Vortigern) is historical'.[20]

A version of a possible genealogy is found on The Pillar of Eliseg in Denbighshire, North Wales, erected by Cyngen ap Cadell, king of Powys (died 855). Raised to honour his great-grandfather Elisedd ap Gwylog, it included the following words: 'Britu son of Vortigern, whom Germanus blessed, and whom Sevira bore to him, daughter of Maximus the king, who killed the king of the Romans.' A number of different genealogies for Powys exist and while they differ significantly, neither Vortigern nor his sons appear.[21] The HB itself makes a point of providing an alternative founding king of Powys, Cadell Ddyrnllug.

If we take all this together we can estimate a floruit, although we must dismiss the 375 date from chapter 31. A Vortigern born in c.380s might well marry an otherwise unknown daughter of Magnus Maximus (who died in 388). Such a man may well have led a council in 428 and met St Germanus in 429 and 437. If he lived to the age of 80, he might have met St Garmon in the 460s.

This has also led some to suggest two Vortigerns, one born in the late fourth century and a thinner namesake active in the mid-fifth century. Also two men called Ambrosius Aurelianus, an earlier one fighting Vitalinus, a subsequent one fighting the second Vortigern. This is possible for Ambrosius, given Roman naming conventions. Many theories also propose two 'Arthurs', providing a veritable Noah's Ark of Arthurian characters. I would argue that the sources point to a single figure for Arthur at least.

I would also state the author of the HB intended his words to be taken seriously. He expected his early ninth-century audience to believe what they read. It follows it is likely some viewed Arthur as historical and would accept the battle list attributed to him placed in that part of the narrative. It is to the famous battle list we will now turn.

The battle list

Arthur's battle list is one of the most discussed and controversial sections of the text. Many a theory is based on a highly selective interpretation built on layers of flawed etymologies and logical fallacies to identify favoured locations to support the preconceived theory. These are then shoehorned into whatever geographical location the author has placed their version of Arthur.

Many historians have decided the only safe conclusion is that the list is 'the author's own work';[22] 'impenetrable and cannot be treated as historical'; or 'at best unproven at worst implausible'.[23] The possibility of it being an authentic battle poem is described as 'an assumption' by some academic commentators and rejected by others.[24] Those that do entertain the possibility go only so far as to say the prospects of useful information from the list as 'poor ... but cannot be ruled out', and if it is based on such a poem the date is entirely uncertain.[25]

In contrast, other academics argue that 'if such history is unhistorical, so also are all the major histories of the early middle ages'.[26] Indeed, the battle list has been 'perhaps rightly' suspected of being a welsh battle poem[27] or an 'early bardic poem'.[28] In fact 'the battle list appears to fossilise an Old Welsh rhyming structure'.[29] Given that, the best course is probably to accept it *could* be an authentic battle poem, but proceed with caution.

Here then are the twelve battles, together with the variant spellings. The etymologies and various options have been dealt with in greater depth in my previous book, *The Battles of King Arthur*.

Battle 1: The mouth of the river *Glein* (*glem* in some twelfth-century versions).

Battles 2–5: On a river called *dubglas* in *regione linnuis* (*duglas* or *dubglassi*)

Battle 6: On the river called *Bassas* (*Bassa*)

Battle 7: In *silua celidonis* 'that is the battle of *cat coit celidon*'.

Battle 8: *castellum guinnion*, 'and in it Arthur carried the image of the holy Mary, the everlasting virgin, on his shoulders...'.

Battle 9: *urbe legionis* (*urbe leogis cair lion*).

Battle 10: The bank of the river called *Tribuit* (*Treuroit* or *Ribroit*).

Battle 11: On the hill, *monte agned* (*monte breguoin, bregion* or *monte agned cat bregomion*).

Battle 12: *Monte Badonis*, 'and in it 960 men fell in one day, from a single charge of Arthur's, and no one laid them low save him alone; and he was victorious in all his campaigns'.

The locations are described by some academics as 'unknown and unknowable',[30] claiming 'safe identification is impossible'.[31] As early as the twelfth century Henry of Huntingdon in *Historia Anglorum* (c.1129) noted 'none of the places can be identified now'. This didn't stop Geoffrey of Monmouth a few years later confidently having his Arthur fighting across Britain and from Norway to Gaul. Nearly 900 years after Geoffrey's pseudo-history, and 1,500 years after a historical Arthur, a huge number of theories have placed these battles in every corner of these islands. Higham lists some of the best known from the North, to the South-West and everywhere in between.[32]

Despite the scepticism of modern historians there is hope. The oft-quoted and well-respected Guy Halsall states: 'The locations of all these battles are unknown and unknowable.'[33] But he precedes this emphatic statement by saying: 'With the exception of the battle of the Caledonian Forest, which ought to be somewhere north of Hadrian's Wall and Linnuis which *might* be Lindsey.'

In fact, there exists a general consensus from academic historians that we cannot improve much on the analysis of the eminent linguist and historian, Kenneth Jackson.[34] The point is often forgotten that academics frequently caveat their scepticism with two or three locations that can actually be identified on the balance of probability. Here then is what Jackson found:

1. *Glein*, Possibly River Glen in Northumberland or Lincolnshire but 'highly uncertain'.

2–5. *Duglas regione linnuis*, 'probably' Lindsey.

6. *Bassas*, unknown.

7. *silua celidonis, cat coit celidon*, 'Certainly' *silva caledoniae* in Strathclyde.

8. *Castellum Guinnion*, unknown.

9. *Urbe Legionis, cair lion*, 'certainly' Chester.

10. *Traht treuroit*, unknown.

11. *Monte breguoin, bregion*, 'probably' High Rochester.

12. *Monte Badonis*, 'somewhere in Wessex'.

If we accept the above then we have two that are almost certain: Chester and *silva caledoniae* in southern Scotland. A further four battles are likely in Lincolnshire. Let us look at these battles a little more closely.

Battle one: The River Glein; the Brythonic *glanos* or *glano* (*glân* in modern Welsh) means pure, clear or holy. This could evolve into *glein* or *glain* (and possibly glen). This is not connected linguistically to the old Welsh glinn (valley), Irish glenn or Scottish glen. There were likely lots of similarly named rivers, but only two survive today. The first is in Lincolnshire and is a clear river compared to the dark, peaty rivers of the nearby fens. The second is in Northumberland near Yeavering Bell, and runs into the River Till and from there the Tweed. Bede references a baptism there in the reign of Edwin, 616–633.

Battles two to five: On the 'river, called the *Dubglas* which is in the country of *Linnuis*'. Dubglas derives from the Brittonic *duboglasso-* 'black blue/black green'.[35] There are many rivers still named similarly today: black, dark, devil, dawlish, and douglas. However, historians have identified *regione Linnuis* with some confidence.[36] Indeed, historians view this as 'beyond reasonable doubt'.[37] Interestingly, archaeological evidence points to a surviving pocket of Romano-British dominance centred on Lincoln into the sixth century. In addition, it was surrounded by a ring of Germanic settlements that appear to have been placed there deliberately to provide protection. Alternatives at Ilchester or Lennox require scribe errors or have little to support them.

Battle six: On the river called *Bassas*. Could be related to Welsh basso- (shallow), or Latin bassus, for low. There are a number of Bas- type place names such as Basford, Old Basing, Bassingbourn, or Bassingthorpe, with a Germanic etymology. There is only one known Brythonic candidate: Baschurch in Shropshire. There is a reference in the ninth-century Welsh poem *Canu Heledd*, referring to *Eglwyssau Bassa* (Churches of Bassa), and it appears in the Domesday Book of 1086 as Bascherche. In reality, it could be any shallow river whose name is now lost.

Battle seven: *silua celidonis*: generally accepted as 'wood of Celyddon', derived from *Calidonia*. Pliny the Elder (c.23–79) referred to *Silua Caledonia*, and Ptolemy (c.100–170) placed it north of the Antonine Wall. However, later sources place the wood a day's march north of Hadrian's Wall. Kenneth Jackson is 'certain' it is the forest known to the Welsh as Coed Celyddon, which in turn is a memory of the older *Silva Caledoniae*.[38] There is a figure named Celyddon in Welsh legends (*Culhwch and Olwen*), but it is considered unlikely it is personal name.

Battle eight: *Castello Guinnion*. Castello suggests a Roman fort rather than a hill-fort. Temporary forts were called *castella*.[39] Gwen or Gwyn means white, holy or pure. The Brittonic uindo-, or old Welsh guinn-, suggests it means 'fort of the white people' rather than 'white fort'. Guinnion would certainly have become Gwynion in later Welsh and changed to Wen- or Wan- by Germanic speakers. The most common suggestion is the Roman fort at Binchester near Durham, Vinovium (Uinouion in Brythonic). This was refortified and still in use in the fifth century. Alternatively, there is Uindocladia, near Badury Rings; Uindonio at Neatham, East Hampshire; and Uindolanda at Chesterholm on Hadrian's Wall.

Battle nine: *urbe legionis*: In the *Historia* Chester is called *Caer Legion*, while Caerleon in South Wales is *Caer Legion Guar Usic*. Bede gives both the English name for Chester, *Legacaestir* and, as he puts it, the 'more correct' British name *Caerlegion*. Caerleon thus requires a scribal omission. The tenth-century AC refers to a syncd in 601 at Chester, *urbis legion*, and a battle at *Caer Legion* in 613. Many theories will attempt to locate this battle, rather conveniently, anywhere a legion was posted. One popular example, York, has a well attested history: Brythonic *Eburakon*, Roman *Eboracum* to Norse *Jorvik*. However Chester is the one location on the battle list we can be most confident of linguistically;[40] its identification has been described as 'certain' by an eminent linguist.[41]

Battle ten: On the bank of the river *Tribuit*. One of the most difficult to locate, it has been linked to a battle at *Tryfrwyd* or *Trywuid* in the thirteenth-century poem, *Pa Gur yv y porthaur*. Arthur praises Bedwyr at a battle on the 'strands of *Trywuid*'. Further references in the poem, such as Eiddyn (Edinburgh) hint at a northern location but it is very uncertain.

Battle eleven: at *Monte Agned* or *Breguoin*. Possibly Bremenium, the Roman fort at High Rochester in Northumberland, close to Hadrian's Wall.[42] A Welsh source records *kat gellawr brewyn*, 'the battle of the cells of brewyn', attributed to Urien of Rheged suggesting another northern location. Geoffrey of Monmouth equates Agned with Edinburgh. One later manuscript has an amendment to the margin, Cathbregyon, identified as Catbrain in Bristol.[43] Bremenium seems the most likely but again it is very uncertain.

Battle twelve: *Monte Badonis*, 'and in it 960 men fell in one day, from a single charge of Arthur's, and no one laid them low save him alone; and he was victorious in all his campaigns'. It is thought likely that Gildas was writing in the south, somewhere in the province of *Britannia Prima*, which might indicate the battle was there.[44] The linguist Kenneth Jackson agreed, placing it 'somewhere in Wessex'.[45] Other experts agree and locate it in the south, 'likely in Wessex'.[46] This is hugely debated with theorists proposing sites in every part of Britain. We will go into more detail later, but for now I would suggest a southern location is more likely.

Camlann: Unlike our next source, the HB does not mention Camlann. However, it is useful to briefly mention the most popular options. Variant spellings include *Cam lann*, *Camlam*, *Camblan* or *Gamlan*. The name Camlan consists of two elements: *Cam* meaning 'crooked', and *lan* or *glam* meaning river bank, or *Llan*, a scared enclosure or church.[47] Suggestions have included Camboglanna, a Roman fort on Hadrian's Wall, and further north near the Antonine Wall: Cambuslang, south of Glasgow, and Camelon near Falkirk.

In Wales we have the following:[48] Camlan near Mallwyd on the River Dyfi and Afon Gamlan. Camlann Isa, Camlan Uchaf, Bron Camlan and Maes y Camlan all survive on modern maps but unfortunately can only be traced back to the sixteenth century. In Welsh some letters mutated under certain circumstances, G often disappeared, and C (earlier K) can mutate into G. So Camlan and Gamlan are not alternative names, but rather the same name mutated.

Unlike Badon there is a very strong Welsh tradition associating Arthur with this battle. Medieval Welsh Triads make a number of references to it.[49] Indeed, in a fourteenth-century code of Welsh laws it states when the queen wills it, 'let the bard sing a song respecting Camlann'.[50]

The battles: A discussion

Figure 15 is a map of the most likely locations for the twelve battles in the HB. I have added the likely former provincial boundaries along with the two former northern Roman walls. If we look at these a number of things jump out. Even if we were to include many of the alternatives, as I have done in my previous book, the same significant patterns emerge. First, none of the most likely sites are in Kent where we are told Octha came down from the north and became the first king. Some of the battles are close to where we might expect a border to be, the 'unhappy partition' of Gildas. However, many of the battles are in places well away from early Germanic settlement.

This has caused some scholars and theorists to dismiss the linguistically most obvious sites such as Chester or the Caledonian Wood. However, there is nothing preventing raiders by land or sea from accessing these sites. Chester, for example, is only three days' march and two days' hard riding from the Germanic settlement around Lincoln, as well as being easily accessed from the sea. We have plenty of evidence that Saxon and Frankish raiders from the fourth century were every bit as adventurous as later Vikings.

We must also bear in mind what the sources all say. Mercenaries were hired and more than one group arrived. Gildas places them in the east, Bede 'in their [the Britons'] midst', and the HB says Kent and the north, near the wall. The

The First Whispers of Arthur

KEY
1. Mouth of the River Glein
2. 2-5. River Duglas in the regione linnuis.
6. River Bassas.
7. silua celidonis, cat coit celidon.
8. Castellum Guinnion.
9. Urbe Legionis, cair lion.
10. Traht treuroit, tribuit, ribroit.
11. Monte breguoin, bregion.
12. Monte Badonis.

Extent of Germanic settlements c. 500

Figure 15: Map showing most likely locations of Arthur's battles.

HB gives relatively small numbers, Octha's forty ships equates to between 1,200 to 2,400 troops (thirty to sixty per ship). Roman auxiliary forts held 500 or 1,000 men. Military sites along Hadrian's Wall, even the Antonine Wall, or at Chester are just as likely as the Germanic settlement ringing Lincoln. Nor can we assume a surviving Romano-British polity centre on Lincoln would be on the same side as our hero.

I would suggest an Arthur mopping up small pockets of Octha's men at various locations within British-held areas is quite plausible. As is fighting off raids from areas now controlled by Germanic settlers or mercenaries. A defensive war might fit the traditional narrative, but an aggressive ethnic cleansing of the north and west by the 'kings of the Britons' might be hard to swallow for some. An alternative scenario has Arthur attempting to hold together a fragmenting provincial or *civitas* structure.

Another point one notices is the geographical spread. First, it is very difficult to support theories that attempt to confine Arthur to a small area, although it is noticeable that many of the sites are in the north. Indeed, if Camlann was in the north as well this would leave a southern Badon as a bit of an outlier. A good case could be made for a northern Arthur operating in the former northern province of Britannia Secunda (and possibly Valentia) in the former role of the *Dux Britanniarum*. One could easily place most of the battles on the northern and southern borders which might involve fighting Picts as well as Germanic mercenaries or raiders.

As ever with Arthur it is not that simple. As we shall see, the Saints' Lives point to a different area, and the later genealogies another region again. Taking the evidence so far at face value we have an Arthur fighting along a wide arc from Wessex to the north. The question arises, was he leading a rump Diocese of Britannia, or was he one warlord or petty king among many in patchwork of emerging kingdoms?

Annales Cambriae

The earliest manuscript of the *Annales Cambriae* (AC) is a twelfth-century copy of a mid-tenth century text dated to 954–5.[51] It is thought to derive from Dyfed, south-west Wales, but was also likely influenced by Irish Chronicles and possibly a northern source.[52] It is argued the earliest date of composition of the earlier part could be in the late-eight century, although the Arthurian entries are likely to be mid-tenth century.[53] Whereas the HB was written during a period of threat from the Mercians, the AC was compiled in the middle of the Viking age in an area relatively protected from Anglo-Saxon expansion. It is the first source that attempts to date Badon and also the first that mentions Camlann.

Table 3: The Annales Cambriae.

Year	Entry
457	St Patrick goes to the Lord.
458	St David is born in the thirtieth year after Patrick left Menevia.
516	The battle of Badon, in which Arthur carried the Cross of our Lord Jesus Christ for three days and three nights on his shoulders and the Britons were the victors.
537	The battle of Camlann, in which Arthur and Medraut fell: and there was plague in Britain and Ireland.
547	A great death in which Maelgwn, King of Gwynedd died. Thus they say 'The long sleep of Maelgwn in the court of Rhos.' Then was the yellow plague.
565	The voyage of Gildas to Ireland.
570	Gildas wisest of the Britons dies.
573	The battle of Arfderydd between the sons of Eliffer and Gwenddolau son of Ceidio; in which Gwenddolau fell; Merlin went mad.
580	Gwrgi and Peredur, sons of Eliffer die.
665	The first celebration of Easter among the Saxons. The second battle of Badon, Morgan dies.

The early date for Patrick's death might be a confusion with Palladius as might the entry concerning St David. Elsewhere, David's death is dated to 589. We must take these saintly long-lives with a pinch of salt as an entry for 501 has Bishop Ebur dying at 350 years old. Gildas is placed firmly in the sixth century and we also note the first mention of Merlin in the battle of Arfderydd in 573. Many of the combatants at this battle will feature in our genealogies, and so I have included the entry recording the death of two of these in 580 (Gwrgi and Peredur, sons of Eliffer). Equally important is to note the death of Maelgwn (possibly the Maglocunnus of Gildas) in 547 for similar reasons. This will all become important later when we see where exactly Arthur is placed in relation to these figures.

The two principal entries give us our first date for a historical Arthur. To be of fighting age in 516, Arthur would have had to be born in the 480s–90s. Geoffrey of Monmouth in the twelfth century would have us believe Arthur was crowned at 15 and fought at Badon early in his career. Yet we must acknowledge that Bede places the battle sometime between 493–500. We could put this discrepancy down to a scribal error or confusion over Easter tables. Camlann is dated to 537 which ties in closely with the only date Geoffrey of Monmouth gives us – the end of Arthur's reign in 542. Of course Geoffrey could simply have copied the AC date, but here at least we have two sources that place an adult Arthur c.510–40. Let us look at the entries more closely.

First, note that the entry for Badon is very similar to the eighth battle in the HB for *Castello Guinnion*:

AC 516: The battle of Badon, in which Arthur carried the Cross of our Lord Jesus Christ for three days and three nights on his shoulders and the Britons were the victors.

HB eighth battle: The eighth battle was in Guinnion fort, and in it Arthur carried the image of the Holy Mary, the everlasting virgin, on his shoulders and the heathen were put to flight on that day, and there was a great slaughter upon them....

HB twelfth battle: The twelfth battle was on Badon Hill and in it 960 men fell in one day, from a single charge of Arthur's, and no one laid them low save him alone; and he was victorious in all his campaigns.

The discrepancies between the texts are significant.[54] In the AC Arthur carries a cross at Badon, whereas in the HB he wears an image on his shoulders or shield. Also in the AC Arthur fights for a biblical three days and nights just as Urien of Rheged did at Lindisfarne. There may have been a confusion between *ysgwyd*, 'shield', and *ysgwydd*, 'shoulder' – in Old Welsh *iscuit* and *iscuid* respectively. However, it is thought unlikely the same mistake would appear twice in two different sources which suggests 'shoulders' is correct.[55]

It should also be acknowledged that the earliest Welsh sources associate Arthur far more with Camlann than Badon. The Welsh tradition paints a far darker and more mythical figure with little to do with fighting Saxons, let alone Badon. In contrast, Camlann is presented as a disaster even though it is not clear here that Mordred is considered the enemy. We recall Gildas references civil wars and perhaps this was one example he had in mind. Also interesting, this is supposedly one year after the climatic event recorded in 536. The second part of the entry for 537 often gets forgotten: 'plague in Britain and Ireland'. The Justinian plague swept across the West after 541 and may have reached Britain a year or two later. If there is a connection, then perhaps Geoffrey's date for Camlann is actually more accurate, a thought we will leave for the moment.

We can suggest a number of possibilities: first, the AC is correct and Arthur fought at Badon and Camlann in 516 and 537 respectively, meaning Bede's date is in error. Second, Bede was correct with dating Badon and the AC wrong, which pulls Camlann back to c.514–521. Alternatively, Arthur was erroneously connected to Badon by the HB and other sources simply followed suit. This would leave Arthur able to fight Camlann in 537 and allow the likely victor at Badon to be Ambrosius Aurelianus in 493–500. The copyist of the AC simply moved Badon forward to fit within Arthur's presumed lifespan.

Before we leave the AC there is one last entry to consider, for the year 665: 'The first celebration of Easter among the Saxons. The second battle of Badon, Morgan dies.' Interestingly, we may have a corresponding entry in the ASC for the year 661. Wulfhere, King of Mercia, the son of Penda, raided as far as Ashdown. He then stood as godfather to Aethelwald, King of the South Saxons. He raided Wight, placed it under Aethelwald's authority and then stood as godfather to the Sussex king when he 'received him at Baptism'. It is thus the South Saxons and 'people of Wight' who receive the first celebration of Easter at this time.

There is no mention of this second battle of Badon in the ASC (or indeed the first battle). However, the possible locations for Ashdown are all in the south. The Mercians and British were allies against Northumbria through much of the early seventh century. Penda fought alongside the British king Cadwallon a generation before. If British warriors had accompanied Penda's son, Wulfhere, in c.661, then their attack towards Wight and Sussex would have taken them through Wessex and past many of the likely sites suggested for Badon. The entry for a second Badon may refer to a similar victory or slaughter, with the news taken back to a copyist in Wales by British allies of the Mercian king. If it refers to a battle in the same location as the first this would support a southern location.

A southern location for Badon alongside battles at Chester, Lindsey, the Caledonian Forest and other northern sites suggests the possibility of some sort of surviving political and civilian structure. With Arthur leading troops across a wide area.

Summary

In the previous chapter we were presented with a fifth-century, culturally Roman Britain, which evolved over nearly two centuries into a patchwork of petty kingdoms with a warband culture. This process was accelerated by the influx of Germanic material culture and peoples. One major turning point was the arrival and subsequent revolt of mercenaries in the mid-fifth century. A fightback led by Ambrosius Aurelianus culminated in a victory at Badon Hill and a period of stability for the emerging Brythonic kingdoms. After this apparent 'gap' in Germanic expansion, Anglo-Saxon kingdoms began to emerge from the mid-Sixth century.

Into this gap the author of the HB, writing three centuries later, places our hero. By the early ninth century Arthur is associated with magical stones and tombs embedded in the landscape. Over the centuries, dozens of topographical sites are similarly linked from Cornwall to Scotland. Yet the same source also presents a very real-sounding Arthur. Not a king but a soldier, a 'leader in battle', fighting alongside the kings of the Britons against the Saxons in twelve battles. Analysis of the text places these battles sometime between 450–550 in a geographical arc from Wessex to Southern Scotland. We could narrow this further to c.480–540 if we take our source at face value.

A hundred years after the HB, a copyist used an unknown source to record two battles for Arthur in the AC. The first dates Badon to 516 and the second the deaths of Arthur and Mordred at Camlann in 537. It could be argued that by the ninth to tenth centuries people considered Arthur to be a historical figure, although one to which a certain level of mythical stories had been attached. Others can claim he was a mythical figure historicised by a Welsh monk eager to fill the bellies of his countrymen with fire to fight against the hated English who were encroaching into North-West Wales from Mercia.

Another Welsh source from the the tenth-century *Armes Prydein* (The Prophecy of Britain) is found in the fourteenth-century *Book of Taliesin*. It is thought to have been written c.940, three years after the battle of Brunanburh and the victory of Aethelstan over a combined army of Scots, Vikings from Ireland and Britons from Strathclyde. The poem is a call to arms to the the people of Britain: the Cymry; the men of Dublin (Vikings); the Irish of Ireland and Man and Scotland; the men of Cornwall and the Clydemen (Strathclyde), even *Llydaw*, Brittany. It laments the time Hengest and Horsa took Thanet 'through false cunning' when their power was slender.

Since the time of 'Gwrtheyrn [Vortigern)]of Gwynedd' the English had been the oppressors, but Myrddin prophesied that the Britons, 'friends of St Germanus', would push the English out, 404 years after Camlann. It is not Arthur who is invoked, but Cynan and Cadwaladr. The former perhaps the legendary founder of Brittany, Conan Meriodoc (or Cynan Garwyn, another hero of the Cymry) and Cadwaladr, the seventh-century scourge of the Northumbrians who fought alongside Penda. Arthur is not mentioned at all. However, by the time Geoffrey of Monmouth wrote his medieval best-seller, *De gestis Britonum* or *Historia Regum Britanniae* ('The History of the Kings of Britain)', there must have been a rich Arthurian tradition for him to look to. That insular, Welsh tradition portrays a darker, more mythical Arthur than the one we are perhaps more familiar with.

Chapter Four
Arthur, the Earliest Traditions

We recall from figure 2 in chapter one the evolution of the legend from a potential historical Arthur to the first attested reference in the early ninth century. It was also noted that early Welsh poems, such as the tenth-century *Armes Prydein*, ignored Arthur completely. The only known sources that pre-date Geoffrey of Monmouth's *Historia Regum Britanniae*, c.1138, are the HB, AC and one of the several Saints' Lives that feature him. The French Romances can all be seen to have been heavily influenced by Geoffrey's earlier work. Unfortunately, none of the surviving manuscripts containing Welsh traditions can be dated before the HRB. Yet they are sufficiently different in style, content and language to imply a separate origin. The language especially points to a pre-Galfridian (before Geoffrey's HRB) tradition. The tales and poems can be found in the following manuscripts:

- The Black Book of Carmarthen, c.1250 (*Llyfr Du* Caerfyrddin, National Library of Wales, Peniarth MS 1)
- The White Book of Rhydderch, c.1350 (*Llyfr Gwyn Rhydderch*, National Library of Wales, Peniarth MS 4–5)
- The Red Book of Hergest, late fourteenth century *(Llyfr Coch Hergest,* Jesus College Oxford MS 111)
- The Book of Taliesin, dated to first half of fourteenth century but may include material from tenth century, although not as far back as a sixth-century poet called Taliesin (*Llyfr Taliesin*, National Library of Wales, Peniarth MS 2)
- Book of Aneirin, dated to around 1265 but thought to be a copy of a ninth-century original. It contains the poem, *Y Gododdin* concerning a battle in the late-sixth century and the possibly contemporary poet Aneirin.
- The Triads of Britain, dated to the thirteenth century, containing both mythic and historical figures and events (*Trioedd Ynys Prydein*, National Library of Wales, Peniarth MS 16).
- The Mabinogion is a collection of many of the works already mentioned into an eighteenth-century compilation.

Table 4: Earliest Welsh sources.

Source with earliest manuscript	Titles (possible date of origin)
Black Book of Carmarthen c.1250	Pa gur yv y porthaur? (tenth century) Stanzas of the Graves (ninth–tenth century) Elegy of Geraint son of Erbin (ninth-tenth century)
Book of Aneirin c.1265	Y Gododdin (seventh–eleventh century)
Triads of Britain From thirteenth century	Various stanzas (eleventh–fourteenth century)
White Book of Rhydderch c.1350	Culhwch and Olwen (eleventh century) Geraint and Enid (Likely derived from Chrétien de Troyes) Owain or Lady of the Fountain (Likely derived from Chrétien de Troyes) Peredur son of Efrawg (Likely derived from Chrétien de Troyes)
Red Book of Hergest Late thirteenth century	Culhwch and Olwen (eleventh century) Geraint and Enid (Likely derived from Chrétien de Troyes) Owain or Lady of the Fountain (Likely derived from Chrétien de Troyes) Peredur son of Efrawg (Likely derived from Chrétien de Troyes) Dream of Rhonabwy (end of twelfth century)
The Book of Taliesin Early fourteenth century	Preiddeu Annfwn (tenth century) The Chair of the Prince (tenth century) The Elegy of Uther Pendragon (tenth century) Journey to Deganwy (tenth century)

Layamon's Brut c.1190–1215, known as 'The Chronicle of Britain', was the first English version of HRB. The thirteenth-century *Brut y Brenhinedd*, 'Chronicle of the Kings', was a middle Welsh version of the same. It is also worth mentioning that various other versions exist. One such example, *Brut Tysilio*, was initially thought by some to be attributed to the seventh-century Welsh saint, Tysilio. However, scholars now believe this, and all other versions, derive from HRB rather than the other way round.

We must bear in mind these tales, and the Welsh names within them, can be problematic. Even if we have a translation of a particular event or poem we have to ask if these names were the same in the original. Many seem to be copies of older manuscripts and scholars assess some elements to be archaic. However, it is also the case that late medieval poets used archaic words and phrases. Therefore a poem such as *Preiddau Annwn* is judged by some as possibly being tenth century, but could be much later. Very little is certain.

Some of the tales appear to derive from French Romance versions, for example: *Geraint and Enid*; *Owain* or *The Lady of the Fountain*; and *Peredur son of Efrawg*. These follow the traditional narrative of a heroic knight experiencing a number of adventures before obtaining some prized objective. Arthur's court is merely a backdrop to the tale. However, the other tales in table four above have a very different atmosphere. If they do derive from the ninth and tenth centuries, then they may give us a more accurate picture of the type of stories reflecting an 'original Arthur' from which Geoffrey drew inspiration. We will start with the earliest manuscript.

The Black Book of Carmarthen

Dated to c.1250, it is the earliest manuscript containing poems that reference Arthur and is thought to have been compiled at Carmarthen.[1] It contains thirty-eight poems, many of which are religious. However the most significant ones, written in the largest script, relate to Myrddin. The earliest poems are thought to derive from the ninth to tenth centuries. We will now look at three of these: *Pa gur yv y porthaur?* (tenth century); *Stanzas of the Graves* (ninth–tenth century); and the *Elegy of Geraint son of Erbin* (ninth–tenth century)

Pa gur yv y porthaur (What man is the gatekeeper?)

This Old Welsh poem features dialogue between Arthur and a gatekeeper, Glewlwyd Gavaelvawr (who himself is named as Arthur's gatekeeper in *Culhwch and Olwen*). Much of it is a monologue by Arthur, listing his followers and their prowess and deeds. We must imagine Arthur banging on the gate asking the name of the gatekeeper. Glewlwyd, apparently not recognising his visitors, asks who it is: 'Arthur and the fair Cai', comes the reply. But Glewlwyd is unimpressed causing Arthur to list the exploits of himself and his men.

Perhaps the most important figure throughout is Cai, described as fair, blessed and a 'sword in battle'. Bedwyr is also prominent, 'a defender for the good of the land'. Both are described as worth as much as an entire army in battle. Other notable characters include: Mabon, son of Modron, 'servant of Uthr Pendragon' (no fatherly connection with Arthur is made); Mabon son of Mellt, Anwas the Winged, and Llwch Llawynnog who defended Edinburgh 'at the border'.

A battle at Tryfrwyd (or Trywruid) is mentioned twice and has been associated with the tenth of Arthur's battles from the HB, at the River Tribuit. Here we read Manawyd brought back shattered spears from Tryfrwyd. Later 'Bedwyr the powerful' fights on the shores of Tryfrwyd, with sword and shield, killing by the hundred. His opponent is Garwlwyd, mentioned in the Welsh Triad (32), Gwrgi Garwlwyd, one of the *Three Fortunate Slaughters of the Island of Britain*. He was said to kill a man of the Cymry every day, but two on Saturdays so he could rest on Sunday. This killer's sons are named in a Triad as the *Three Chieftains of Deira and Bernicia*, thus associating him with the north. His name means roughly 'Man-hound', possibly linking him to another line in the poem concerning the fighting 'dog-heads' at Edinburgh, below.

Cai pleaded with his opponents as he fought, killing three at a time, when 'Celli was lost'. It has been suggested this is somehow linked to the break between Arthur and Cai hinted at in *Culhwch and Olwen*, which, is implied here, resulted in the loss of Celliwig in Cornwall.[2] The text is then ambiguous as to whether these are Arthur's or Cai's exploits: a hag is killed (a witch?) in Afarnach's Hall, Penpalach of Disethach is stabbed and a battle with *chinbin*, (possibly the *cynocephali*, 'dogheads') on the mountain of Edinburgh, kills hundreds of the enemy. This may be a link with the slaying of the Giant Gwrnach and witch in *Culhwch and Olwen*. Additionally, the 'dogheads' could represent dog-headed monsters or werewolves.[3] But there is nothing concrete.

The *cynocephali* (dog-head) were a feature of early medieval beliefs about monsters. They are mentioned in St Augustine's *De civitate Dei* and St Christopher was said to have originally been such a creature. Tim Flight in *Basilisks and Beowulf, Monsters of the Anglo-Saxon World*, explains how a whole range of monsters were said to have descended form Cain and were represented in medieval texts such as *Liber Monstrorum*.[4] We could see this reference as evidence the whole tale is fictional and supernatural, but it is at least plausible; calling an enemy dog-head is simply an insult or reference to the type of headgear some wore, such as a wolf's pelt. An interesting link between outlaws and wolves is made, albeit in later Anglo-Saxon period, where outlaws are said to 'carry a wolf's head'.[5] This expression apparently a literary relic from ancient Germanic law where the outlawed person was forced to wear a literal wolf's-head.

Back at the gatehouse, Arthur laments he used to have men and mourns their loss. He then implies the lords of Emrys were against him, which could suggest Gwynedd or perhaps a link with Ambrosius Aurelianus who is called Emrys in the HB. The poem turns to Cai the Fair fighting, either with or against, Llachau, named as Arthur's son in other sources. He 'pierced' nine witches in the uplands of Ystafnwn (unidentified but possibly linked to the nine witches referenced in other sources (*Peredur; Life of St Samson; Preiddeu Annwn*). He also 'destroyed lions' in Anglesey and stabbed Palug's Cat (also associated with Anglesey in the Triads). This ferocious animal killed 'nine score warriors', or champions.

The poem breaks off, leaving us to speculate how the exchange ended. Perhaps the porter, suitably impressed with this long list of heroic exports, relented and let Arthur and his men in. If we were to ignore the mythical elements of witches, 'dog-headed' warriors and monstrous cats, what can we say? First, Arthur is presented as leading a small band of warriors. He is associated with places from North Wales to Southern Scotland. Cai and Bedwyr are central characters and they took part in a battle on the shores of Tryfrwyd, which could be Arthur's tenth battle in the HB. Unfortunately, we can't simply ignore the mythical elements as they are central to the tale.

Stanzas of the Graves
The *Englynnionn y Beddev*, The 'Stanzas of the Graves', consist of seventy-three stanzas listing the burial places of early Welsh heroes dated between fifth to ninth centuries. Some also feature in the Welsh Triads and *Y Gododdin*. Gwalchmai, Arthur's nephew, is buried at *Peryddon*, which appears in other sources but remains unidentified. Osfran's son is buried at Camlan, and in the same stanza we learn Bedwyr's grave is on the hillside of *Tryfan*, possibly in Snowdonia. The most relevant stanza concerns Arthur:

> The grave of March, the grave of Gwythur;
> The grave of Gwgawn Gleddyvrudd
> A mystery to the world, the grave of Arthur

The word use to describe Arthur's grave, *anoeth*, has caused much controversy. Some translations use the word 'wonder' or 'treasure'. Alternatively, it could mean a thing difficult or impossible to find. The word *anoeth* could also reference the otherworld. The meaning seems as elusive as the location of Arthur's grave. William of Malmesbury in c.1125 wrote that Arthur's grave could not be found and 'ancient ditties prophesied his return'.[6]

There does seem to be number of tales in the middle ages suggesting Arthur still lived. Some place him sleeping under a mountain with his knights. Others simply leave it a mystery. In 1113 a certain Hermann of Tournai described a near-riot at Bodmin, Cornwall, caused by visiting canons from Laon. One of them expressed doubt when the Cornishmen insisted Arthur was not dead (and here Hermann comments 'as they are wont to do'). Writing twenty five years later Geoffrey of Monmouth leaves Arthur being taken to Avalon to be healed.

Elegy of Geraint son of Erbin
Geraint features in other Arthurian tales and corresponds with Chretien de Troyes' *Erec et Enide*. Geraint is associated with Dumnonia in the southwest. A

Geruntius is named as king of Cornwall in the ASC in 710 but the Arthurian tradition points to an earlier figure and a cousin of Arthur.

In a series of stanzas the narrator witnessed a terrible battle at Llangborth where Geraint led a charge on 'white, bowed, blood-stained' horses, brave warriors from Dyfnaint (Devon). A reconstruction of the poem tells us a great number of brave warriors of both Arthur and Geraint were slain. The implication is that they were allies but it's not certain that Arthur (described as 'emperor, leader of battle') was present himself.[7]

The location of Llangborth has been hotly debated:[8] some have suggested Langport in Somerset and linked it to a battle between King Ine of Wessex and Geruntius of Dumnonia in 710. To maintain a sixth-century date others have tried to place it at Portsmouth and connect it to the ASC entry for 501 were Port landed with his two sons and killed a 'young British man, very noble'. Alternatively, there is Llamborth in Penbryn, Ceredigion, which has a number of other place name links ('The Field of Massacre', 'The Field of Killing', 'Geraint's Bush').

The earliest authority to reference Geraint names him as the father, rather than son, of Erbin.[9] He appears in various other tales and poems connecting him to Arthur: *Culhwch and Olwen*; *Rhonabwy's Dream*; and one of the *Three Seafarers* in a Welsh Triad. Later genealogies name him as father to Cadwy and, importantly, married to Gwyar, daughter of Amlawdd Wledig. We recall another daughter was Eigr and this would make Geraint Arthur's maternal cousin. The tale of *Geraint and Enid*, which we will come to shortly, largely derives from Chrétien de Troyes' *Erec et Enide*. However, some elements not found in the French tale may be relevant. Geraint leaves Arthur's court to his father's lands, east of the Severn. His son Cadwy is found with Arthur, in the *life of St Carannog*, ruling in or near Devon. We thus get a repeated connection between Geraint and Arthur and the West Country.

The Red Book of Hergest

One of our most important, and possibly earliest tales, *Culhwch and Olwen*, appears in the late thirteenth-century Red Book of Hergest. It also contains three tales which likely derive from Chrétien de Troyes: *Geraint and Enid*; *Owain or Lady of the Fountain*; and *Peredur son of Efrawg*. These tales, or fragments of them, are also found in the mid-fourteenth-century White Book of Rhydderch. The Dream of Rhonabwy, possibly written c.late twelfth century, is only found in the Red Book of Hergest.

Culhwch and Olwen

The earliest version is found in the Red Book of Hergest, c.1400, although an earlier fragment is found in the White Book of Rhydderch, c.1325. The author is anonymous and it is thought to have originated in the eleventh century. The central character of the tale is Culhwch, born to Kilydd (the son of Prince Kelyddon) and Goleuddydd (daughter of Prince Anlawdd). His grandfather is thus surely Amlawdd Wledig, and his grandmother, Gwen, a daughter of Cunedda Wledig. This latter figure features in the HB and is the founding father of many early Welsh Kingdoms, as well as ancestor to various Welsh Saints. Importantly for our study, Amlawdd was also the father of Rieingulid, mother to St Illtud, and Eigyr, mother to Arthur. In many ways it is a test for a storyteller with a large array of characters and events.

Back to our tale, Kilydd and Goleuddydd have a son but the mother sadly dies soon after. Culhwch, we are told, was of 'gentle lineage' and, it is confirmed, 'cousin to Arthur'. After seven years the king decided to remarry and attacked the neighbouring kingdom. The king, Doged, is killed and Kilydd takes the widowed queen as his wife. The boy's new stepmother prophesies Culhwch will not have a wife until he obtains Olwen, the daughter of Yspaddaden Penkawr. Culhwch immediately falls in love at the mere thought of Olwen and goes to his father who advises him to seek help from his cousin Arthur.

Off he trotted on a dappled grey horse, 'four winters old', armed with two 'steel-headed spears' and a 'gold-hilted sword', followed by 'two white-breasted greyhounds'. He arrived at Arthur's palace on the first day of January. Later we are told this is Gelli Wic (also Celliwig or Gelliwig) in Cornwall. There has been much debate on the location of this, with Kelly Rounds being a popular candidate. While most scholars accept this it should be noted it is not certain. Gelliwig is only associated with Arthur in two Welsh sources: *Culhwch and Olwen* and the Welsh Triads.[10] There is also a *Gelli* in Monmouthshire and, perhaps more hopefully, a *Plas Gelliwig* near Botwnnog on the Llyn Peninsula.[11] Non-Arthurian twelfth-century references to *Kelliwyc* also point to Wales. Additionally there is a possibility Cernyw may be a mistranslation for an area in Powys (to be discussed later).

At first the gatekeeper, Glewlwyd, will not open the gate (shades of *Pa gur yv y porthaur?* here) but eventually Culhwch is brought before Arthur who offers him anything except: 'my ship; my mantle; and Caledvwlch, my sword; Rhongomyant, my lance; Wynebgwrthucher, my shield; Carnwenhau, my dagger; and Gwenhwyvar, my wife'. We see here the first version of his sword, latinised as Caliburnus by Geoffrey of Monmouth in the twelfth century.

Culhwch reveals himself as Arthur's cousin and Arthur promises to help him in his quest for the hand of Olwen. We then get a long list of Arthur's followers, many with magical and mystical powers. The first named are Kai and Bedwyr, who feature in other tales. Arthur's kin are mentioned: on his father's side the sons of Iaen, 'men of Caerdathal'; and maternal uncles (Llysgadrudd Emys, Gwrbothu Hên, Gweir Gwrhyd Ennwir, Gweir Paladyr Hir); his nephews by his sister (Gwalchmai and Gwalhaved, sons of Gwyar).

We learn of Arthur's son Gwydre, killed later in the tale in the quest for the giant boar, Twrch Trwyth. Gwenhwyvar is introduced as Arthur's 'chief lady' along with her sister, Gwennhwyach (or Gwenhwyfach). Arthur's mother is not named but his stepbrother Gormant's father, Ricca, is described as 'the chief-elder of Cornwall'.

Notable figures featuring in other Arthurian tales include: Taliesin the chief of the bards; Geraint the son of Erbin; Mabon the son of Modron; Osla Gyllellvawr; Morvudd the daughter of Urien Rheged; survivors from Camlann (Morvran, Sandde Bryd and Kynwyl Sant); and Gwyddawg the son of Menestyr ('who slew Kai, and whom Arthur slew, together with his brothers, to revenge Kai').

Also mentioned are Gildas and Hueil, two of nineteen sons of Kaw. A ninth-century Saint's Life of Gildas names this father as Caunus of Alt Clud (traditions claimed Gildas forgave Arthur for killing his brother Hueil). A later Saint's Life claims twenty-three brothers. In this tale, the hatred between Arthur and Hueil was caused by the latter's stabbing of his nephew, Gwydre whose father is named as Llwyddeu.

Arthur sends messengers out and for a whole year they search in vain for Olwen. Culhwch is all for giving up, but Kai admonishes him and declares they will go with him to determine if she is real or not. A fellowship is formed to accompany Culhwch: Kai (he could last nine days and nights under water with a single breath, and the same length of time without sleep. His sword so powerful no physician could heal its cuts. All that could be put down to hyperbole but we also read he could make himself as tall as the highest tree in the forest); Bedwyr ('who never shrank from any enterprise upon which Kai was bound'); Kynddelig the Guide; Gwrhyr Gwalstawt Ieithoedd (speaker of 'all tongues'); and Menw the son of Teirgwaedd (who could cast a charm and an illusion over enemies, so that none might see them while they could see every one).

This intrepid band come to a vast open plain and great castle. They find a herdsman who introduces himself as Custennin the son of Dyfnedig, and brother to the man they seek, Yspaddaden Penkawr who lives in the castle. As fate would have it, Custennin's wife is Culhwch's maternal aunt. Yspaddaden had killed twenty-three of her sons leaving only one alive, so she agrees to help. Olwen comes to her house and Culhwch declares his love. But Olwen refuses to go with him, saying she had: 'pledged my faith to my father not to go without his counsel, for his life will last only until the time of my espousals'. Disappointed but undeterred, Culhwch and his band follow Olwen back to the castle. They slay the nine gatekeepers and nine watch dogs, gaining an audience with Yspaddaden. He hears Culhwch's marriage request and bids them return tomorrow. On leaving, he throws a poisoned dart which Bedwyr catches and throws back, piercing Yspaddaden through the knee. They leave and return the next day. A similar thing happens, and this time it is Menw who catches the spear and, throwing it back, pierces Yspaddaden in the chest and out through his back. On the third day Culhwch pierces him through the eyeball and out the back of his head.

Seemingly unbothered by these otherwise fatal wounds, Yspaddaden sets the band a series of quests, many of which involve mystical and magical objects and animals along with various figures who must be brought along to handle these. The first task to be completed is the killing of the giant Gwrnach and they take his sword to Arthur. Among the most significant of the others involve obtaining the following: the cauldron of Diwrnach Wyddel, the steward of Odgar the son of Aedd, king of Ireland; the comb and scissors that are between the two ears of the giant boar Twrch Trwyth; and the blood of the 'jet black sorceress', the daughter of the 'pure white sorceress', from Pen Nant Govid, on the confines of Hell.

In an interesting aside we read that Arthur and Kai fell out over a song composed by Arthur which caused Kai never to help Arthur again, even in 'Arthur's troubles'. The quests continued and Arthur accompanied them travelling to Armorica, the north and the west of Ireland. To the latter, Arthur travelled with 'a small retinue' on his ship Prydwen. When Odgar refuses them the cauldron, Bedwyr seizes it, but it is Llenlleawg Wyddel who takes up Arthur's sword, Caledvwlch, and kills Diwrnach Wyddel. A battle ensues and the Irish are put to flight.

Arthur returned to Britain and summoned all the warriors from the 'three Islands of Britain', together with those from France, Armorica, Normandy and the Summer Country. With this large force he returned to Ireland to battle the giant boar, Twrch Trwyth, and his seven young pigs (Twrch Trwyth was once a king whom God had transformed for his sins). The boar refuses Arthur the comb and scissors and then crosses the sea to Wales. There follows a dramatic pursuit through South Wales, across the Severn and then down into Cornwall. Many warriors are killed, including Arthur's son Gwydre along with five of the young pigs. Arthur was finally able to obtain the comb and scissors before the boar was driven into the sea and disappeared.

The final quest was for the blood of the 'witch Orddu, the daughter of the witch Orwen, of Penn Nant Govid, on the confines of Hell'. Arthur himself kills the witch with his dagger, Carnwennan. With the tasks complete Culhwch takes the wonders to the castle of Yspaddaden Penkawr and demands the hand of Olwen. Olwen's father agrees but makes a point of stating it is Arthur who obtained the marvels. He allows the surviving son of Custennin, Goreu (another who features in the genealogies) to drag him by his hair to the castle keep and cut off his head. Arthur's men dispersed to their own countries and Olwen was married Culhwch for 'as long as she lived'.

We can map one version of Arthur's family tree from the story. I have left out the figures that don't appear in other sources and add little to our study: Arthur's maternal uncles (Llysgadrudd Emys, Gwrbothu Hên, Gweir Gwrhyd Ennwir, Gweir Paladyr Hir); and the 'sons of Iaen, Men of Caerdathal, of Arthur's kindred on his father's side' (Teregud, Sulyen, Bradwen, Moren, Siawn, Cradawc). One figure that features prominently in other tales is Gwalchmai, Arthur's nephew. It is unclear if Gwyar is Arthur's sister or her husband. I have included Geraint's father and son. There is some confusion in other sources if Geraint is Erbin's father or son and he is sometimes said to be married to Gwyar, a daughter of Amlawdd Wledig.[12] Thus Geraint was possibly related to Arthur through marriage. We get the first reference of Arthur's Gwenhwyvar and her sister Gwennhwyach (later Gwenhwyfach). Later we will see one little-known tale blames their disagreement for the battle of Cam lann.

If the tale originated pre-HRB then we have evidence of a largely mythical figure battling giants, witches and monstrous boars. It is worth noting the places that can be located are South Wales and the West Country, with Arthur's court firmly placed at Celliwig. Plus an association with Cornwall through his mother's previous husband. It may also be significant Arthur raids Ireland twice. If this has a historical element, albeit one which had been mythologised, then it is a world of petty kings, warbands and raiding. The following three tales are all rather different. Deriving from the French Romances the contrast

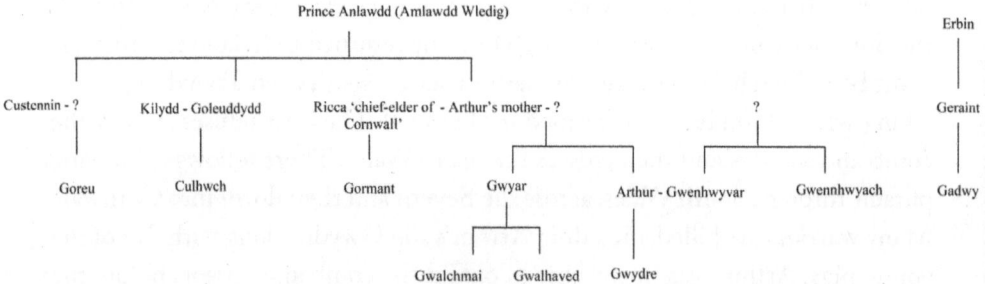

Figure 16: Arthur's family tree from Cuhlwch and Olwen.

with *Culhwch and Olwen* and *Pa Gur* should be apparent. Instead of a world of raids, cauldron thieving and giant killing it is one of tournaments and chivalry.

Geraint and Enid

The tale begins at Caerleon upon Usk where Arthur held court 'for seven Easters and five Christmases', as it had the 'easiest access to his dominions by sea and land'. We see influence from the HRB here as Geoffrey firmly places Arthur's principal court at Caerleon. Nine crowned kings arrive to pay tribute. Gwenhwyvar was present with Gwalchmai, 'the most exalted of the nine'. The Franks were also present though it is not clear if they were one of the nine.

Arthur arranges to hunt a stag the next day with various companions: Ambar, his son; Ambreu, the son of Bedwor; Goreu the son of Custennin; and Gwallawg the son of Llenawg (we will see him again in the genealogies of *Yr Hen Ogledd*). Arthur and his retinue rise early and leave for the forest. Gwenhwyvar, waking late, rides through the trees with her lady-in-waiting and meets Geraint (son of Erbin), one of Arthur's men. They ride on and come to a strange knight accompanied by a lady and a dwarf. Gwenhwyvar's lady asks the dwarf the knight's name and gets slashed with a whip for her trouble. Geraint gets the same treatment.

Lacking armour Geraint decides to follow the knight alone and leaves Gwenhwyvar to return to the hunt. He comes to a town and castle near Caerleon (later revealed to be Cardiff). Outside the town Geraint finds a ruined palace where he is entertained by an old man, his wife and their daughter, Enid. The man tells him he was once an earl who had lost his kingdom to his nephew who now lives in the castle. The next day there is to be a tournament for a Sparrow-Hawk where he can fight the strange knight he had followed, who it turns out has been champion two years running and is thus known as the 'Knight of the Sparrow-Hawk'. Geraint can only enter if he has a lady to fight for. Our hero promises to marry Enid and the old man agrees to lend him his armour.

The next day Geraint naturally prevails over the knight who reveals his name, Edeyrn the son of Nudd. The young earl who owns the castle agrees to restore the old man's (named Earl Ynywl) possessions. Geraint sends Edeyrn and the dwarf on ahead to Gwenhwyvar to atone for their treatment of her lady-in-waiting. Geraint follows, returning to Arthur's court with his new love.

The story returns to the forest where Arthur kills the stag. Arthur's dog Cavall features, as does Gildas, son of Caw. Gwenhwyvar arrives and tells Arthur about Geraint's quest. Later, back at Caerleon, Edeyrn and the dwarf arrive and are greeted by Gwenhwyvar and Arthur. The next day Geraint and Enid return to Caerleon where they are married.

Sometime later an embassy arrives at Caerleon from Cornwall from Erbin son of Custennin, 'Arthur's uncle'. He requests his son, Geraint, return to help fight off neighbouring chiefs. Geraint departs along with Ederyn, the knight he defeated, and many who appear elsewhere in tales, including: Gwalchmai the son of Gwyar; Howel the son of Emyr of Brittany; Goreu the son of Custennin; Peredur the son of Evrawc; Bedwyr the son of Bedrawd; and Kai the son of Kynyr.

In Cornwall, Geraint's rule begins well but later he mistakenly thinks Enid no longer loves him. Angered by this he decides to leave the kingdom in search of adventure and forces his wife to accompany him. Three times he commands her to ride in silence and three times she disobeys him to warn of attackers. Each time he defeats them but remains angry with his wife for breaking her vow of silence. Reaching a town the local earl offers to take Enid away. Enid refuses and warns Geraint, despite her promise to keep silent. They escape but are pursued and Geraint turns to single-handedly defeat 'four-score' knights and the earl.

Further on they come to a town and castle ruled by Gwiffert Petit, 'the little king'. Geraint defeats him in combat and travels on, now injured. He meets Kai but is not recognised by his old comrade. They fight and Kai is knocked to the ground. Kai returns to his lodgings and tells Gwalchmai of the battered knight in the woods.

Gwalchmai comes upon Geraint and during the subsequent fight he recognises him. Geraint refuses to go with him to see Arthur and so the king is brought to the woods. Arthur forces him to rest a while to be healed. But after a month Geraint insists on continuing on his way with Enid.

They meet a young woman standing over a dead knight who tells them three giants were the cause. Geraint slays the giants but is grievously wounded and collapses. The Earl of Limours enters the tale and takes them back to his castle. His mistreatment of Enid awakens Geraint who kills him and they escape. They are aided by Gwiffert Petit, the 'little king', whom Geraint had defeated earlier.

Next they come to the land of Earl Owain and Geraint enters a magical place and battles another knight. Overcoming him he was able to blow a horn that removes the enchantment from the land.

He then reconciles with Enid and returns to Cornwall.

Owain or Lady of the Fountain
The first thing to note is that Owain, son of Urien, the hero of the tale, is traditionally dated to the late sixth century and thus is unlikely to have been a member of Arthur's court. Only by stretching Urien's birth back to c.500

could we have an Owain young enough to be of fighting age towards the end of or timeframe for a historical Arthur, c.450–550. Leaving that aside the tale is as follows:

At Arthur's court in Caerleon, Cynon tells Cei a story of his defeat by a mysterious knight at fountain in a vale. The next day Owain decides to follow Cynon's footsteps. A number of adventures follows which culminates in him finding the fountain and defeating the knight. He pursues him to a city and evades capture with the help of a maiden called Luned. The knight dies from his wounds and, again with Luned's help, Owain marries the widow, the countess of the city. Owain becomes the 'knight of the fountain' and remains there for three years.

Arthur, missing his friend, sets out to look for him. They encounter the same adventures until they reach the Vale. There they are confronted by the knight, not realising it is Owain. He defeats all comers, even Cei, until Gwalchmei recognises him (one recognises the similarity with the same storyline in *Geraint and Enid*). Back in the city they feast and the countess allows Owain to accompany Arthur for three months.

But Owain forgets his promise and three years later the countess sends a messenger to take the ring from Owain's hand and declare him a false deceiver. Heartbroken, Owain leaves the court in shame and wanderers through the land encountering many adventures. One such entails him saving a lion from a servant and the lion follows, saving him several times from defeat. Owain learns that Luned is blamed for his apparent treachery in not returning and she is condemned to the fire. Owain and the lion rescue Luned and he is reconciled with the countess who returns to Arthur's court with him. One last adventure finds Owain and the lion defeating the 'Black Oppressor'. Owain remains at Arthur's court as 'captain of the warband'.

Peredur son of Efrawg

Peredur was the seventh son of Efrawg, 'earl of the north'. One day he met three knights, Gwalchmai the son of Gwyar, and Geneir Gwystyl, and Owain the son of Urien. This meeting convinced him to seek out Arthur's court. On arrival he is met by Kai who is rude to him. However a dwarf greets him with honour. Angered by this Kai strikes the dwarf. Meanwhile, a stranger has challenged Arthur's men to combat and Kai suggests Peredur take the challenge. Owain rides after him and finds Peredur has defeated the knight but he refuses to return to Arthur's court because of Kai's insult and treatment of the dwarf. Riding on, Peredur defeats another knight and commands him return to the court and tell Arthur Peredur bested him in his honour. Sixteen more knights are defeated in combat, each sent back to Arthur's court.

Peredur comes to a castle. The old man inside turns out to be his uncle. The next day he rides out and finds another castle and a second uncle. Here he is confronted with two maidens bearing a severed head on a platter (French Romances make this the Grail instead of a severed head). The next day he rides out and meets a lady who claims to be his foster-sister with the body of her husband. She tells him his mother is dead and her husband's killer is in a glade in the wood. Peredur defeats the knight and sends him back to Arthur's court.

Our hero comes to a castle and restores the lands and possessions of the lady within by defeating a whole army of her enemies. At the next castle he meets a lady who warns him the nine sorceresses of Gloucester, and their mother and father, are on their way to kill them. Peredur is able to defeat one of the nine and returns her to the palace of the sorceresses in return for surety.

He rides on and spends the night with a hermit. Meanwhile Arthur, no doubt impressed by the numerous defeated knights turning up at Caerleon, has been seeking Peredur. Arthur comes upon the hermit's cave and a knight he does not recognise. He sends a man ahead to ask his name but Peredur remains silent. A fight ensues resulting in the man's defeat. Twenty four more of Arthur's men suffer the same fate before Kai elects to try. Kai doesn't recognise his adversary and is soundly defeated, breaking his arm and shoulder (Again we have Kai being defeated by an unrecognised knight and again it is Gwalchmai who stops the fighting).

Finally Gwalchmai is able to talk Peredur into coming to Arthur's court at Caerleon. Here he meets and falls in love with a lady named Angharad Law Eurawc. Unrequited, he vows to never speak until she returns his love. Peredur rides out again and has more adventures, killing a lion and serpent along the way. Returning to Arthur's court he was met by Kai on the road. Not recognising him again, and insulted by his refusal to speak, Kai attacks him. Gwalchmai intervenes, though fails to recognise him, and sends him back to Gwenhwyvar to be cared for.

He becomes known as the 'Dumb Youth' and defeats many knights who come to Arthur's court.

Angharad falls in love with him allowing him to break his vow of silence and which point everyone suddenly recognises it is Peredur. More adventures follow: He kills a one-eyed knight and a serpent. The tale ends with Arthur and his men killing the sorceresses of Gloucester.

Dream of Rhonabwy
Set in the twelfth century, the warrior Rhonabwy falls asleep and is transported back in time. He meets Iddawg, the 'Embroiler/Churn of Britain'. So called

because he caused the battle of Camlan by passing false messages between Arthur and 'Medrawd his nephew'. They journey to Rhyd-y-Groes (on the Shropshire-Welsh border) where they meet Arthur, called here an emperor, and a great host. It is left unexplained how they can meet Arthur after the battle that killed him. Both time and place are muddled within this dream.

With Arthur are some notable figures who appear in other tales: Cei (Kai); Cadwr, 'Earl of Cornwall'; Goreu son of Custennin; Mabon son of Modron; Cadwy son of Geraint; Gwalchmai son of Gwyar; Gildas son of Caw; Rhun son of Maelgwn and Llacheu son of Arthur. They had gathered to fight Osla big-knife at the Battle of Faddon (a variant spelling of Badon) by midday (Osla Gyllellvawr is one of Arthur's men in *Culhwch and Olwen* and his knife is so broad as to be used as a bridge). Men from Denmark, Scandinavia, France and Greece also arrive.

The host set off towards Cefn Digoll (near Welshpool) and soon come to Caer Faddon (Badon). This places Badon less than a day's march from Rhyd-y-Groes, well away from where most scholars place it. It's nearly a hundred miles from Bath where the HRB places it. While they are waiting, Arthur and Owain (son of Urien) engage in a game of *gwyddbwyll*, a type of early-medieval board-game similar to the later Scandinavian game of *Tafl*. A confusing sequence follows with a vivid description of a number of events.

Eventually an embassy comes from Osla requesting a truce for a fortnight and a month. This is agreed and then Cei suggests they leave to be in Cornwall that night (an unlikely feat given it is a near 200 mile journey. Although, as we shall see, Arthur's association with Cornwall may come from a mistranslation of early placenames connected with the Cornovii precisely where this tale is placed). Rhonabwy wakes up and the author states no bard can tell the tale without a book because of the detail given to all the horses, trappings, clothing and arms. Written in c.1400 it is a playful tale not meant to be taken literally. More of a satire and perhaps a lampoon of Geoffrey of Monmouth's HRB, which had at that time just been translated in to Welsh.

Book of Taliesin

The book of Taliesin was written c.1375–1400 by a single scribe. It contains a collection of religious, prophetic and historical poems allegedly from the sixth-century poet, Taliesin. A case for an early date is perhaps best represented in various praise poems for Urien of Rheged. References to Arthur are sparse and largely incidental but two are worth noting – the first in the poem *Chair of the Sovereign*: 'To bless Arthur, Arthur the blessed.'; the second in *The Death-song of Uther Pendragon*: 'I shared my shelter, a ninth share in Arthur's valour.'

Arthur is not named as a son of Uthr although Madog is. In *Kat Godeu*, 'The Battle of the Trees', there is a reference to the prophecy of Arthur. Additionally, a triad names three horses for Gwythur, Gwarder and Arthur. However, one poem is of particular interest: *Preiddeu Annwfn*, 'The Spoils of Annwfn'.

The Spoils of Annwfn

The poem *Preiddeu Annwfn*, 'The Spoils of Annwfn', is found in the fourteenth-century *Book of Taliesin*. It refers to a disastrous expedition led by Arthur from which only seven return, one of whom is presumed to be the narrator, Taliesin himself. He begins the first few stanzas praising God and throughout the text belittles monks and priests and 'little men' who rely on books.

Gweir is held prisoner in an otherworldly castle which is given several cryptic names (Caer meaning fort):[13] Caer Sidi (a name for the otherworld), Caer Pedryvan (four-turreted/cornered), Caer Vedwyd (mead/sweet drink), Caer Rigor (stiff/hard/rigid), Caer Wydyr (glass), Caer Golud (impediment), Caer Vandwy (possibly a place named in other Welsh tales) and Caer Ochren (sides/angular or possibly a giant from other tales). The prisoner could be Gwair ap Gweirioedd (one of *The Three Exalted Prisoners of the Island of Britain* in a Welsh Triad (52) or Gwair fab Gwestyl (his father's name means hostage). It mentions Pwyll and Pryderi who feature as father and son in other tales such as the Mabinogion, associated as both Lord of Dyfed and Pen Annwn (head of the 'Otherworld/fairyland').

Men enough to fill Arthur's ship Prydwen three times over go on the raid. Three score hundred men (6,000) stood on the walls as Arthur approached. One target is the cauldron of the chief of Annwvn (head of the Otherworld), 'warmed by the breath of nine maidens'. The cauldron, we are told, will not boil the food of a coward. The cauldron is taken by one of Arthur's men, Lleminawg (named Llenlleawg Wyddel in *Culhwch and Olwen*). They also take a 'brindled ox' (named in Triad 45 as one of the Three Principal Oxen of the Island of Britain and also part of Culhwch's quest in *Culhwch and Olwen*).

It is worth noting the number of times cauldrons feature in Arthurian tradition.[14] Here the cauldron will not boil the food of a coward. In *Culhwch and Olwen* a cauldron is one of the items in a long list of things needed to complete the tasks required for Olwen's hand: the cauldron of Diwrnach Wyddel, the steward of Odgar the son of Aedd, king of Ireland, to boil the meat for the marriage feast. No magical powers mentioned here, the cauldron is simply seized and taken back to Britain full of stolen treasure. However in the much later *Thirteen Treasures of the Island of Britain*, Dyrnwch, the Giant's cauldron, boils for the brave and not for cowards just as in *Preiddeu Annwfn*. Although the *Thirteen Treasures of the Island of Britain* might be a late-medieval attempt at linking the two tales. In the tale of Branwen in the *Mabinogion* a cauldron of the king of Ireland is able to revive fallen warriors.

Attempts have been made to link this to the grail or even magical Scythian bowls. However, analysis of the different tales reveals no such links. Additionally, one would expect ubiquitous objects such as swords, cauldrons, cups and bowls to acquire traditions and stories independently across cultures.

The tale itself at first glance presents an Arthur inhabiting a mystical 'otherworld'. As in *Culhwch and Olwen* and *Pa Gur*, he leads a band of warriors and is central to the tale. This is in contrast to the tales of *Owain*, *Peredur* and *Geraint and Enid*. These three all derive from French Romances and present the adventures of a single knight with Arthur's kingdom only as a backdrop. All three involve the knight going out alone, overcoming adversaries, achieving some noble objective and marrying their love. Very different from the potentially earliest Welsh tales full of raiding and battles. One of the central figures in the warband culture was the bard and it is to one legendary example we will now turn.

Taliesin

The first mention of Taliesin appears in the HB:[15] 'At that time Outigern fought bravely against the English nation. Then Talhaearn Tad Awen was famed in poetry; and Aneirin and Taliesin and Bluchbard and Cian … famed in British verse.' This paragraph lies between the reign of Ida and that of his sons, which points to a mid to late-sixth century timeframe.

The Book of Taliesin is thought to have been written c.1275 and the poems within are written in Old Welsh and ascribed to Taliesin, 'Chief of Bards'.[16] Attempts to recreate his life place him first serving Cynan Garwyn in Powys (born c.520) before he went to the court of Urien of Rheged, with whom he has the strongest connection. A praise song, *Song on Gwallawg ab Lleenawg*, link him to Gwallawg of Elmet. The *Death-Song of Owain*, suggests he outlived Urien's son.

In the Welsh Triads he is named as one of the Three Skilled Bards of Arthur's court, the other two being Myrddin Emrys and Myrddin ap Morfryn (Myrddin Wylit). He appears fleetingly in *Culhwch and Olwen* and *Rhonabwy's Dream*. In the *Black Book of Carmarthen* there is a poem, *The Dialogue of Myrddin and Taliesin*, where the two titular figures discuss the battle of Arfderydd (which the AC dates to 573). Geoffrey of Monmouth, in his *Vita Merlini*, names Taliesin Thelgesinus, a pupil of Gildas. Here Taliesin describes how Arthur was taken to *Insula Pomorum* (Avallon) after the battle of Camlan.

A sixteenth-century text, *Hanes Taliesin*, claimed to tell the tale of his early life. This connects him to the court of Maelgwn which is just about possible for a young bard who served Urien later in the sixth century. Perhaps the earliest figure attached to him is Brochwel Ysgithrog of Powys (estimated birth c.490 and father of Cynan Garwyn above), for whom he sang 'in the meadows of the Severn'.[17]

While none of this can be confirmed, taken as a whole these late, unreliable sources point to a timeframe straddling the floruits of both Arthur and Urien. A figure living c.510–580 would make him an adult during the reigns of the figures mentioned above. We could dismiss many, or even all, these figures as legendary. Yet there is a consistency to the connections and timeframes. One gets the sense of a bard born early enough to sing to a king of Powys who was likely contemporary with a historical Arthur. One who spent his more mature years with men a generation after our hero. Who lived to see the disaster at Arfderydd and sing the death song of Owain, son of Urien, who features in many an Arthurian tale.

Elis Gruffydd

The chronicle of Elis Gruffydd (1490–1556) draws largely from the HRB but features a unique tale about Arthur and Huail (supposedly the brother of Gildas).[18] Arthur discovers Huail is in love with his mistress and is wounded in the knee in the subsequent fight. They are reconciled and Huail agrees never to mention the wound he gave Arthur, who returns to his court at Caerwys in Flintshire, northern Wales. Later, for reasons unstated, Arthur is dancing with the women of nearby Ruthin, incognito, dressed as a woman. Huail makes a sarcastic comment about the dancing being good, 'except for the knee'. Arthur claims the agreement is broken and drags Huail to a stone in the market square and cuts off his head. The stone thus became *Maen Huail*, 'the stone of Huail'. Gruffydd gives us an interesting snippet regarding how Arthur was seen in the sixteenth century; he claimed the English criticise the Welsh for their 'presumption about Arthur', when in fact it is the English that talk more about him than the Welsh.

A text from northern Wales, *Vera historia de morte Arthuri*, dated to c.1200 also links Arthur to northern Wales. It gives a unique perspective on Geoffrey's explanation regarding Arthur's death.[19] Having recovered a little from his wounds he is taken from Camlan to the Isle of Avalon in Gwynedd. There he dies and is prepared for burial in a small chapel dedicated to St Mary. The chapel was so small his body had to remain outside during the funeral. A mist descended and when it lifted the body had disappeared and the tomb that had been prepared was sealed. This is the only text that describes Arthur's funeral and places Avalon in Gwynedd.

Triads of Britain

An extensive study of The Triads of Britain can be found in Rachel Bromwich's 2014 book *Trioedd Ynys Prydein*, 'Triads of the island of Britain'. The antiquity and provenance of the early Triads, either orally or written, can be traced back to the ninth century.[20] Although our earliest manuscripts date to the the thirteenth century.[21] Perhaps importantly, up to the end of the twelfth century there appears to have been no influence from continental Romances.[22] However, Triads numbered from 47 onwards originate mostly from the White Book of Rhydderch c.mid-fourteenth century and the Red Book of Hergest c.late fourteenth century.[23] Thus only the Triads numbered 1–46 *might* have be pre-Galfridian. Below are the Triads which reference Arthur.

Table 5: Triads of the island of Britain referencing Arthur.

1	Three Tribal Thrones	Mynyw (St David's), Celliwig in Cornwall, and Pen Rhionydd in the North
2	Three Generous (Noble/Victorious) men	Nudd, Mordaf and Rhydderch: 'and Arthur himself was more generous than the three'.
4	Three Well-Endowed Men	Gwalchmei son of Gwyar, Llacheu son of Arthur, Riwallawn Broom-Hair
9	Three Chieftains of Arthur's Court	Gobrwy, Cadrieith and Fleudur Flam
12	Three Frivolous Bards	Arthur, Cadwallawn and Rahawd
18	Three Favourites of Arthur's Court and Three Battle-Horsemen	Menedd, Ludd and Caradawg
20	Three Red Reapers (Despoilers/Ravagers)	Arthur, Rhun son of Beli, Morgant the wealthy
21	Three Diademed Battle-Leaders	Drystan son of Tallwch, Hueil son of Caw and Cai son of Cynyr. And above all, Bedwyr son of Bedrawc
26	Three Powerful Swineherds	Drystan, Pryderi and Coll. Arthur tried to get a pig by deceit or force but failed.
28	Three Great Enchantments	That of Uthyr Pendragon which he taught to Menw.
30	Three Faithless (or Disloyal) Warbands	That of Alan Fyrgan who left him the night before Camlan where he was killed,
37	Three Unfortunate Disclosures	Gwrtheyrn the thin (Vortigern) revealed the bones of Gwerthefyr the Blessed (Vortimer). Gwrtheyrn disclosed the dragons at Dinas Emrys. Arthur disclosed the head of Bran the Blessed.
47	Three bravest noble Christians of the world	Arthur, Charlemagne and Godfrey of Boulogne

51	Three Men of Shame	...the third and worst was Mordred (largely repeats account leading up to Camlan from HRB)
52	Three Exalted Prisoners	Llyr, Mabon and Gwair. But Arthur was more exalted... Three nights each in the prisons of Caer Oeth and Anoeth, Gwen Pendragon and an enchanted prison under the Rock of Echeifyeint. Rescued each time by his cousin, Goreu son of Custennin.
53	Three Sinister (Ill-omened) Hard Slaps	...the second Gwenhwyfach struck upon Gwenhwyfar (which caused) the battle of Camlan.
54	Three Violent (Reckless or Costly) Ravagings	The first when Medrawd (Mordred) came to Arthur's court at Celliwig, left neither food or drink in the court and dragged Gwenhwyfar from her chair and struck her. The second when Arthur came to Medrawd's court and left neither food nor drink in the cantref.
56	Arthur's Three Great Queens	Gwenhwyfar daughter of Cywryd Gwenhwyfar daughter of Gwythyr Gwenhwyfar daughter of Gogfran the Giant
59	Three Unfortunate Counsels	Allowing Julius Caesar to land The second allowing Hengist and Horsa and Rhonwen into the island. The third the threefold division by Arthur of his men with Medrawd at Camlan.
65	Three Giants at Arthur's Court	Llywarch the Old Llemenig Heledd
73	Three Peers of Arthur's Court	Rahawd, Dalldaf and Drystan
74	Three who could not be exiled from Arthur's Court	Uchei, Coledawg and Cerenhyr
77	Three Wanderers of Arthur's Court	Llywarch, Llemenig and Heledd
80	Three Faithless (Unchaste Wives)	...more faithless than them, Gwenhwyfar, Arthur's wife
84	Three Futile Battles	...the third was the worst: Camlan which was caused by Gwenhwyfar's contention with Gwenhwyfach
85	Arthur's three principal Courts	Caerleon-on-Usk, Celliwig in Cornwall and Penrhyn Rhionydd in the North
86	Three Knight's of Arthur's Court who won the Grail	Galaad, son of Lawnslot of the Lake, Peredur and Bort

87	Three Skilful bards at Arthur's Court	Myrddin son of Morfryn, Myrddin Emrys and Taliesin
88	Three Splendid (famous) Maidens of Arthur's Court	Dyfyr, Enid and Tegau
91	Three Fearless Men	Gwalchmai son of Gwyar, Llachau son of Arthur and Peredur son of Efrog
93	Three Men who specified their sufficiency from Arthur	Culhwch, Huarwar and Gordibla

A number of interesting points stand out. First, one of the earliest triads places Arthur's courts at Mynyw (St David's), Celliwig in Cornwall, and Pen Rhionydd in the North, although a later one replaces Mynyw with Caerleon (most likely due to influence from HRB).

Arthur also features after the Three Exalted Prisoners of the Island of Britain: three nights each in the prisons of Caer Oeth and Anoeth, Gwen Pendragon and an enchanted prison under the Rock of Echeifyeint. Rescued each time by his cousin, Goreu son of Custennin. We recall Goreu featured in *Culhwch and Olwen* as the surviving son of Goleuddydd's sister and Custennin, who Olwen and his companions meet when they finally reach the castle of Olwen's father. This makes Goreu cousin to both Culhwch and Arthur. *Anoeth*, here one of Arthur's prisons, is the same word used for Arthur's grave in *The Stanzas of the Grave*. There it means a wonder or impossible to find.

The battle of Camlan also features repeatedly. It is one of the *Three Futile Battles*. But we get hints of a different version of the cause from the traditional one of Mordred treacherously stealing the throne or Gwenhwyfar or both. Although she is listed as more faithless than the *Three Faithless/Unchaste Wives*. Triad 51 does name Mordred as one of the Three Men of Shame and largely follows the HRB narrative.

Triads 53 and 54 (*Three Sinister (Ill-omened) Hard Slaps* and the *Three Violent (Reckless or Costly) Ravagings*) tell a different story. In the first we read Gwenhwyfach struck Gwenhwyfar and this was the catalyst which caused the battle of Camlan. The second expands on this: Medrawd (Mordred) came to Arthur's court at Celliwig and left 'neither food or drink in the court', dragging Gwenhwyfar from her chair and striking her. Arthur's response was to return the offence and seemingly attack Medrawd's court, this time despoiling the entire *cantref* (an administrative division of land). In Triad 84, Camlan is the worst of the Three Futile Battles and was caused by 'the contention between Gwenhwyfar and Gwenhwyfach'.

In the *Dream of Rhonabwy* it is Iddawg, the 'Embroiler/Churn of Britain', who caused the battle of Camlan by passing false messages between Arthur and 'Medrawd his nephew'. But perhaps this refers to the day of battle not the underlying cause. At the very least we have a different tradition for Camlan than the one presented by the HRB and later French Romances.

Modena Cathedral

While we cannot prove conclusively which tales pre-dated the HRB and by how much, there was clearly a tradition from which Geoffrey could draw. The earliest appearance of Arthur and his knights in art appear on the north doorway of Modena Cathedral in northern Italy. It has been securely dated to between 1099–1120.[24] Importantly, it proves the existence of Arthurian tales before the HRB. The scene depicts the deliverance of *Winlogee* by *Artus*, *Isdernus*, *Galvaginus* and *Che* from *Burmaltus*, *Mardoc* and *Carado*. Many of these characters appear in French Romances and we see variations of certain names. Artus is of course Arthur; Winlogee is a transition between the Breton Winlowen and French Guinloie, who Triads above call Gwenhwyfar; Galvaginus is a Latin form of Gawain, whom we have met in several tales as Gwalchmai.

It would appear Breton and Welsh influence had spread to Italy by the twelfth century, taking Arthurian tradition with them. A mosaic pavement in Otranto Cathedral near Bari depicts Arturus Rex bearing a sceptre and riding a goat (c.1165). Other tales existed of Arthur still alive in the bowels of Mount Etna. These two may have become linked to a late twelfth-century tale of a king visiting a subterranean realm riding a goat.[25]

The scene at Modena is reminiscent of a tale in Caradoc of llancafarn's *Life of Gildas* where Guinevere is abducted by Melvas. Chrétien names her abductor as Meleaganz and her deliverer as Lancelot rather than Arthur. Here, then, we have an earlier tradition which again suggests Lancelot was purely Chrétien's creation.

This one piece of evidence tells us something quite significant. Arthurian traditions had reached Italy independent of, and before publication of, the HRB. This tradition included a tale of Arthur rescuing Guinevere from a castle alongside his knights, one of whom was Gwalchmai, or as modern readers might know him, Gawain. The well-known Middle-English romance, *Sir Gawain and the Green Knight*, did not appear until the fourteenth century.

Summary

The earliest manuscripts of the texts discussed all post-date the HRB and were written down many centuries after the first attested reference to Arthur in the ninth-century HB. The three romance tales concerning Owain, Peredur and Geraint, have clear parallels with later French sources such as Chrétien de Troyes (to be covered later). If we put these to one side what are we left with? Tales such as *Culhwch and Olwen*, *Preiddeu Annwfn* and *Pa gur yv y porthaur?* potentially have roots as far back as the tenth century. All have magical and mystical elements. If we put aside our disbelief and imagine a historical figure mythologised, what do we see? Certainly not a high-king of Britain. At most he is one king among many. At worse he is merely a warlord, leading his warband across the land to steal cauldrons and battle enemies. In *Pa gur* he is forced to beg for entry with tales of his exploits.

There is almost an absence of fighting against Saxons let alone the siege of *mons Badonicus*. The one tale that does mention Badon, the late-thirteenth century *Dream of Rhonabwy*, is difficult to take seriously and is considered more of a satire or pastiche of Arthurian tradition. Certainly time and place are muddled within the dream sequence. Instead it is Camlan that features more prominently in Welsh tradition.

It is worth considering what view one would take if the battle list in the HB or entries in the AC did not exist. It is likely, just based on these Welsh tales, one would consider this Arthur to be purely literary and belonging to a world of myth and magic. Yet his inclusion in the HB and AC alongside accepted historical figures leaves the door open to a possible historical figure who was mythologised rather than a mythical figure historicised. Whichever the case, within two centuries of the HB, a tradition existed that Arthur was a historical figure. One who medieval writers could use to add weight to their message. How better to prove that you had certain ancient land-rights than if you could show Arthur himself had granted them.

Just 150 manuscripts written in Welsh survive from before 1540, with the earliest dated to c.1250.[26] Only a small number of these refer to Arthur: some poetic references and five prose tales, three of which are adaptions of Chrétien de Troyes. It is difficult to prove any of the Welsh material pre-dates HRB with the possible exception of *Y Gododdin*.[27] It is only after the translation of the HRB into Welsh c.1200 that it had a noticeable impact on Welsh literature.[28] Indeed it was only when Geoffrey's HRB began being called into question from the sixteenth century that Welsh authors began to give Arthur a prominent position.

Over 200 poems survive from the period after Glyndwr's revolt (1400–1415).[29] Much of pre-Tudor Welsh poetry concerned itself with the the return of Welsh sovereignty, and Welsh bards eventually looked to Henry Tudor as the man to fulfil their prophecies. While Cynan, Cadwaladr and Owain are frequently cited, Arthur does not feature. It is possible they considered his name tainted by the interest shown by their Anglo-Norman rulers. It is notable that Henry VII named his first son Arthur in 1486. The first printed edition of HRB appeared in 1508 and this prompted a new wave of criticism of its historicity, most notably by Polydore Virgil (1470–1555). John Leland (1503–1552) countered Polydore's scepticism. His most famous Arthurian claim identified South Cadbury Hill-fort as Camelot.

Before we turn to dubious clerical claims it is worth emphasising the difference between the examples above. Let us accept the three Welsh Romances were indeed entirely derived from the imagination of Chretien de Troyes in the early thirteenth century and put them to one side. If we also accept the earlier Welsh tales did indeed derive in the ninth century, then 300 years passed before they were written down. How different again might an original sixth-century Arthurian tale have been compared to say the one portrayed in *Culhwch and Olwen*?

Chapter Five

Saints' Lives

There are five insular *Saint's Lives* that directly mention Arthur: St Cadoc; St Gildas; St Carannog; St Padarn; and St Illtud. Interestingly, they are all confined to the same rough timeframe and geographical location. Two further tales, that of St Goeznovius and St Efflam, place Arthur across the Channel, although they both also make clear Arthur was from Britain. These two will be covered in a later chapter. These hagiographies are semi-biographical accounts full of miracles and wonders to demonstrate the saint's power. While they are not considered historically accurate, they do contain historical elements. They were often written to demonstrate why the church had certain rights in an area.

The earliest of our Saint's Lives pre-dates the HRB and therefore presents an Arthurian tradition independent of, and before, Geoffrey of Monmouth. This give us a rather different Arthur from the later French Romances. Here he is a petty king, one among many, living in a world of roving warbands and warring tyrants. This Arthur is rather badly behaved. A revengeful, violent tyrant, a thief of a saint's cloak, even a would-be rapist. In each tale the heroic saint, with God's help, prevails over secular kings and lords. Arthur is simply a foil to be used by the author.

It is worth noting that no other Saints' Lives mention Arthur, despite the plethora of potential candidates across post-Roman Britain. Scores of saints from all parts of the British Isles and France travelled back and forth across the land over the fifth and sixth centuries. Yet not a single northern or Irish saint is attached to Arthur. The table below lists the relevant hagiographies. Only one of them definitely places Arthur in a particular place. St Carannog, travelling from Wales, crossed the Severn River to the land where Cadwy and Arthur reigned, dwelling at Dindraithov (more on this later). The other lives have Arthur interacting with people and events *in* South Wales, but doesn't make clear where Arthur himself comes from. All the saints are dated from the late fifth century with deaths around the mid-sixth century.

Table 6: Saints' Lives connected to Arthur.

Saint	Written	Story
St Cadog ap Gwynllyw (Cadoc) c.500	c.1100 Llancarfan, S. Wales	Set in South Wales. Also features Maelgwn. St Cadoc settles dispute between Arthur and another by the River Usk in S. Wales and is granted land rights.
St Carannog c.late-fifth century	twelfth century Pembrokeshire, S Wales	Carannog travels from Wales to Somerset. Carannog subdues serpent for Arthur in return for magical altar. Carannog granted land rights.
St Gildas c.late-fifth century	twelfth century Llancarfan, S. Wales	Arthur kills Hueil, brother of Gildas but is forgiven. King Melvas abducts Arthur's wife. Arthur besieges Glastonbury but Gildas brokers peace. Abbot granted land rights.
St Illtud (AKA Hildutus) c.late-fifth century	twelfth century Pembrokeshire, S Wales	St Illtud travels from Brittany to visit his cousin King Arthur before leaving for Poulentus, King of Glamorgan. Founded a religious school in Glamorgan that later taught St Gildas, St Samson and Samson of Dol.
St Padarn c.480	twelfth century Pembrokeshire, S Wales	Defeats Maelgwn's henchmen The 'tyrant' Arthur attempted to steal Padarn's tunic and is swallowed by the earth up to his chin. Ends with a grant of land to Padarn.

The Life of Saint Cadog

The life of Saint Cadoc, *Vita Cadoci*, was written around the late eleventh century by Lifris of Llancarfan. It thus pre-dates HRB and suggests the sort of traditions Geoffrey relied on to write his book. Our tale begins with Cadog's grandfather, Glywys, in the kingdom of Glywysing, South Wales. His son, Gwynllyw, inherits part of the kingdom called Gwynlliog. Gwynllyw sets his heart on the lady Gwladus, daughter of Brychan, king of the neighbouring kingdom of Brycheiniog. Having been rejected by his bride-to-be's father, Gwynllyw leads 300 men to take the girl by force. He is pursued by the enraged King Brychan, who kills 200 of Gwynllyw's men and chases the remainder up a hill on the border between their lands.

It is at this point Arthur enters the tale. Sitting atop the hill playing dice with Cai and Bedwyr, he sees Gwynllyw approaching. Our later-chivalric hero is 'inflamed with lust' and 'filled with evil thoughts' for Gwladus. Cai and Bedwyr persuade Arthur that attacking the needy and distressed and taking the lady for himself would be a crime. Chastened by his friends, Arthur leads them against the pursuers allowing Gwynllyw's escape. The couple are married and Saint Cadog is the product of this happy union.

Certain figures crop up in other Saints' Lives, Welsh tradition and genealogies and they appear here too: Pawl Penychen; King Arthfael; St Iltud; St Gildas; St David; Rhun son of Maelgwn; and Maelgwn himself who ruled over 'all of Britannia' (likely meaning Wales). The saint travels to Ireland, Scotland, Cornwall and Armorica, and even Jerusalem. But his principal residence was Llancarfan in South Wales. Miracles occur, churches are built and land is granted.

Arthur re-enters the tale when a certain 'very brave leader of the Britons', named Ligessauc, son of Eliman (also surnamed Llaw hir, 'Long Hand'), killed three of Arthur's soldiers. Arthur is named in similar ways to Maelgwn: 'illustrious king of Britannia', perhaps the first time he is titled king in Welsh sources.[1] Cadog gives refuge to the renegade Ligessauc, in Gwynlliog for seven long years.

But he is betrayed and Arthur comes with a 'very great force of soldiers' to the River Usk en route to seize Ligessauc in Gwynlliog. Our heroic saint intercedes and suggests Arthur receives three oxen for each man killed. Arthur reluctantly agrees but makes an insulting demand: the cows are to be half red and half white. He is confounded when, by some miracle, the cows appear as requested and are driven into the ford. When Cai and Bedwyr pull the cows to the other side the cows turn into bundles of fern. Arthur begs forgiveness and predictably grants certain land rights to our saintly hero which just happens to benefit the eleventh century author's own monastery at Llancarfan. The location of Arthur's humiliation by Cadoc was Tredunnock (*Tref Redinauc*) four miles north-east of Caerleon in Monmouthshire.[2]

The Life of Saint Carannog

The *Vita Sancti Carantoci* was written in the twelfth century in south-west Wales. The genealogies make Carannog a son of Corun, grandson of Ceredig and great-grandson of Cunedda. This places him in the same generation as, as well as a distant cousin of, Arthur.[3] His birth is dated to the late fifth century.

The tale begins with the saint visiting Ireland where he met St Patrick, thirty years before the birth of St David.[4] After some time he returned to his native country of Ceredigion, performing many miracles and receiving an altar from heaven which 'preceded him whither God wished him to go'. Carannog cast the altar into the sea by the Severn river and followed it across.

It is not clear where he came ashore, but we are told: 'In those times Cadwy and Arthur were reigning in that country, dwelling in Dindraithov.' Arthur wanders by, on the hunt for a 'most formidable serpent, huge and terrible, which had been ravaging twelve portions of the land of Carrum'. The location of *Dindraithov* is uncertain, but possibly the *Cair Draithou* in the list of twenty cities of the HB.[5]

One suggestion for Dindraithov is Dunstan Castle, Exmoor, but it is frustratingly unclear. Carrum is thought to be Carhampton in Somerset, where the saint was granted land. If one travels across water from South Wales then the modern counties of Gloucestershire, Somerset, Devon and Cornwall are likely landing points. However, Cadwy is firmly connected with the kingdom of Dumnonia, which included much of the West Country from Somerset to Cornwall. We have already met his father, Geraint, son of Erbin, and the family connection is repeated across other sources:[6] a triad names Gadwy ap Geraint as one of three most courteous to guests and strangers. A late genealogy in *Bonedd y Saint* names him as Gadw ap Geraint ap Erbin. He appears in *Culhwch and Olwen* as Cadwy, one of Arthur's men; and in *Rhonabwy's Dream* as one of Arthur's counsellors.

With Carannog searching for his lost altar and Arthur seeking the serpent a deal is struck, and Arthur promises to tell him where the altar is in return for the saint catching the beast. The saint does just that. Through the power of prayer the serpent comes forward and is miraculously subdued and led 'like a lamb', raising neither 'wings or claws'. Arthur had tried to use the altar as a table but found whatever he placed on it is thrown a great distance. The altar is returned and a grateful Arthur naturally grants land rights around Carrum.

The Life of St Illtud

The *Vita Sancti Iltuti* is thought to have been written in c.1140 in South Wales. Illtud, dated to the late fifth century, was the son of a Breton prince, Bicanus. His mother was Rieingulid daughter of Amlawdd Wledig, thus making him a cousin of both Culhwch and Arthur. He was instructed in literature and other arts but turned to 'military training' and became a soldier.

Hearing of the magnificence of his cousin Arthur, he left Brittany and sailed to Britain. Arriving at Arthur's court he saw 'a great company of soldiers' and was honourably received and rewarded. He then journeyed to Poulentus, King of Glamorgan, who made him 'master of soldiers'. Frustratingly, we are not told how far he had to travel. However, it is worth noting this is the second time a Saint's Life tells us where Arthur did not rule, in this case Glamorgan.

While there Illtud met St Cadog and was persuaded to become a monk. St Dubricius, the Bishop of Llandaff, allowed him to build a church and he taught various saints: Samson, Paulinus, Gildas and David. The *Vita Sancti Sampsonis*, written in Dol, Brittany, c.600, has much to say about Illtud, including that he was a disciple of St Germanus. It is surely too early for a late fifth-century saint to have met St Germanus, so perhaps this simply means a follower of his teachings. A number of miracles occurred, most notably the arrival of the body of an unnamed man and a floating altar (one of 'The Wonders of Britain' in the HB). As well as a magical bell which appears in other Saints' Lives (e.g. Cadog, Gildas).

All we can glean from this is that Illtud sailed to Arthur's court from Brittany and from there travelled to Glamorgan. The implication being Arthur's court was elsewhere. If it was between these two places then Dumnonia is the most likely location. The other point we can speculate on is dating. Assuming he was senior to the saints he instructed, we can estimate his birth was perhaps a generation before, c.470.[7]

An interesting aside concerning dating comes from *Vita Sancti Sampsonis*.[8] The earliest date of composition is c.610–615 with this saint's birth estimated at c.480. Samson attended the Council of Paris between 556–573, so either lived to a ripe old age or was born nearer c.500. He was sent to learn under St Illtud as a young boy and was ordained, and later consecrated bishop, by St Dubricius.

It appears he succeeded Illtud as Abbot, implying Illtud had died by c.521. If this snippet of information is true *and* the life of St Illtud gives an accurate portrayal, then Illtud met Arthur at the beginning of his time in Britain. This would pull an adult Arthur back into the late fifth century.

The Life of St Padarn

The *Vita Sancti Paterni* is thought to have been written c.1120 at Llanbadarn Fawr near Aberystwyth.[9] His father was Pedrwn, son of Emyr Llydaw in Amorica. His mother was Gwen, a daughter of Ceredig ap Cunedda. This would make Padarn, like Arthur, a great-grandson of Cunedda. In his youth Padarn accompanied a number of monks to Britannia (Wales).

After a brief visit to Ireland he returned to his monastery somewhere in Ceredigion, on the west coast of Wales. There he met Samson. A confrontation with Maelgwn of Gwynedd resulted naturally in a land grant. He then travelled to Jerusalem with St David and St Teilo. Back in Britain he was visited by 'a certain tyrant named Arthur'. Arthur took a liking to the saint's tunic but Padarn refused him as it was only suitable for a member of the clergy. An enraged Arthur returned, presumably to take the cloak by force. Padarn uttered a prayer wishing the earth would swallow Arthur up – and by a miracle he was, up to his chin. He was forced to beg for forgiveness before he was equally miraculously released. Padarn moved back to Armorica where he died.

This may be linked to *Padarn Redcoat*, whose coat was one of the *Thirteen Treasures of the Island of Britain* listed in fifteenth-century texts. The *Vita Sancti Paterni* is unique in describing Arthur as a tyrant.

The Life of St Gildas

There are two versions of the *Vitae Sancti Gildae*. The first was written by a monk of Rhuys in Brittany and dated to the ninth century. In this text, the father of Gildas was Caunus, King of Alt Clud (Strathclyde) and was one of five brothers, another of whom was Cuillus (Huail), 'a man of war'. Gildas was entrusted to St Illtud to study alongside St Samson and St Paul of Leon. He travelled to Ireland and preached in northern Britain. He had interactions with St Brigit (who died c.524) and the king of all Ireland, Ainmericus (c.566–9).

Later he went to Rome and arrived in Armorica at the age of 30. Ten years after leaving Britain he wrote a book (with clear references to *De excidio*). At this point the timeframe looks in line with that of the AC, which dates his death to 570. However, his arrival in Armorica is dated to the reign of Childeric, the son of Meroveus, c.457–481. Here we must conclude the author has either conflated two figures, or confused his dates or Frankish kings.

We then get a curious tale involving a Breton king, Conomerus. This seems to be the same figure related by Geoffrey of Tours called Chonoober, count of the Bretons, who died in a Breton-Frankish war c.558–561. In this tale, the pregnant daughter of King Werocus (two Breton kings called Waroch are dated to the mid-sixth century) is killed by her murderous husband Conomerus. Gildas miraculously brings her back to life (fixing her head back in place). The child is safely born and, just to confuse matters, is named Gildas after his mother's saviour. The Bretons named him Trechmorus 'in order to distinguish him from the other St Gildas'. This first Gildas was buried in Rhuys, Brittany. Arthur is not mentioned.

The second life gives a very different version. Written by Caradoc of Llancarfan it is dated to the mid-twelfth century. Gildas is the son of Nau the king of Scotia and is one of twenty-four brothers. He studied in Gaul for seven years before returning to Britain, settling in Dyfed during the reign of King Trifinus. This Trifinus is named in the genealogies as father of Aergol Lawhir, a contemporary of St Teilo and also a father of Voteporix, possibly one of the five tyrant kings lambasted by Gildas. Again we feel the dates are being pulled in two different directions.

Gildas was preaching in Pepidiog in Dyfed when Nonnita entered the church with the future St David in her womb. The *Life of St David* contains a similar tale of his pregnant mother entering a church when Gildas was preaching during the reign of king *Triphunus*. Interestingly, the king's name derives from the Latin *Tribunus*, and is thus likely a title left over from the Roman administration. The Harleian genealogies place a Triphun as father to Aircol and grandfather to Guortepir in Dyfed (the latter possibly being Vortipor, 'tyrant of the Demetae from *De excidio*).

We read the eldest brother of Gildas, Hueil, were constantly rising up against Arthur. When the saint travelled to Ireland, Arthur killed Hueil. Gildas returned to Britain, spending some time with St Cadog. Arthur eventually made peace with Gildas and accepted the penance demanded by the other bishops. Gildas then journeyed to Rome before returning to Britain and setting up residence on an island with St Cadog as a neighbour.

Pestered by pirates from the *Orcades* (Orkneys), he travelled to *Glastonia* (Glastonbury). Here Melvas reigned, king of the summer country. This king had 'violated and carried off' Arthur's wife Gwenhwyfar. Arthur, after searching for a year, besieged the town with an army from Cornwall and Devon. Gildas interceded and brokered the return of Gwenhwyfar and peace. Both kings then grant extensive lands to the Abbot of Glastonbury. Gildas lived as a hermit nearby and was allegedly buried in the abbey.

Much of the confusion and contradiction about dates has caused some to argue for two different figures.[10] One in the fifth century c.425–512 and another in the sixth, c.520–570. The apparent connection to Arthur raises the question why did Gildas not mention our hero if he was a contemporary. He does after all devote a considerable amount of effort criticising five tyrant kings. Six hundred years later, Gerald of Wales (c.1146–1223) suggests a reason:[11] Gildas had 'many excellent books' praising the 'deeds of Arthur and his countrymen'. When he heard of his brother's murder he threw them into the sea. To accept this we must believe only Gildas possessed such books.

Discussion

It is possible to dismiss these hagiographies as medieval propaganda intended to highlight the prominence of the saint. Or to provide evidence to bolster dubious land claims. However, it may be telling that Arthur features in only a small handful of Saints' Lives, all confined to the late fifth to mid-sixth centuries, and all within the same geographical area. These saints were all active in South Wales. If a mythical figure was being used to bolster saints' reputations, then why not saints across a wider timeframe and geographical area?

Bartrum estimates the following dates for the saints in *A Welsh Classical Dictionary, People in History and Legend up to about 1000 AD*:[12] Cadog, 495;

Carannog, 470; Gildas, 490; Illtud, 470; and Padarn, 480. Other saints are connected with these 'Arthurian saints' either through the hagiographies above, or their own Saint's Lives: Teilo, 500; Samson of Dol, 480; Dyfrig (Dubricius), 465; Dewi (David), 485; and Paulinus, 470. None of these mention Arthur.

If we try to make a case for a historical Arthur through the hagiographies then the most we can say is the following. First, an adult Arthur is portrayed as interacting with saints born in the late-fifth century. One is tempted to place a historical Arthur's birth in this same range, c.470–500. If we accept Bartrum's date for Cadog's birth, any adult interaction would be more likely after c.515. Bartrum estimates Illtud's death to by 521 when Samson became bishop.[13] Arthur himself Bartrum dates to c.480.[14]

Second, Arthur is portrayed as interacting with persons in very specific geographical locations. South Wales and the West Country. Figure 17 maps these places and to it I have added the path of Twrch Trwyth from *Culhwch and Olwen*. One could argue that the poem *Pa Gur*, one of his courts in the Triads, 'Pen Rhionydd in the North', and many of the twelve battles in the HB

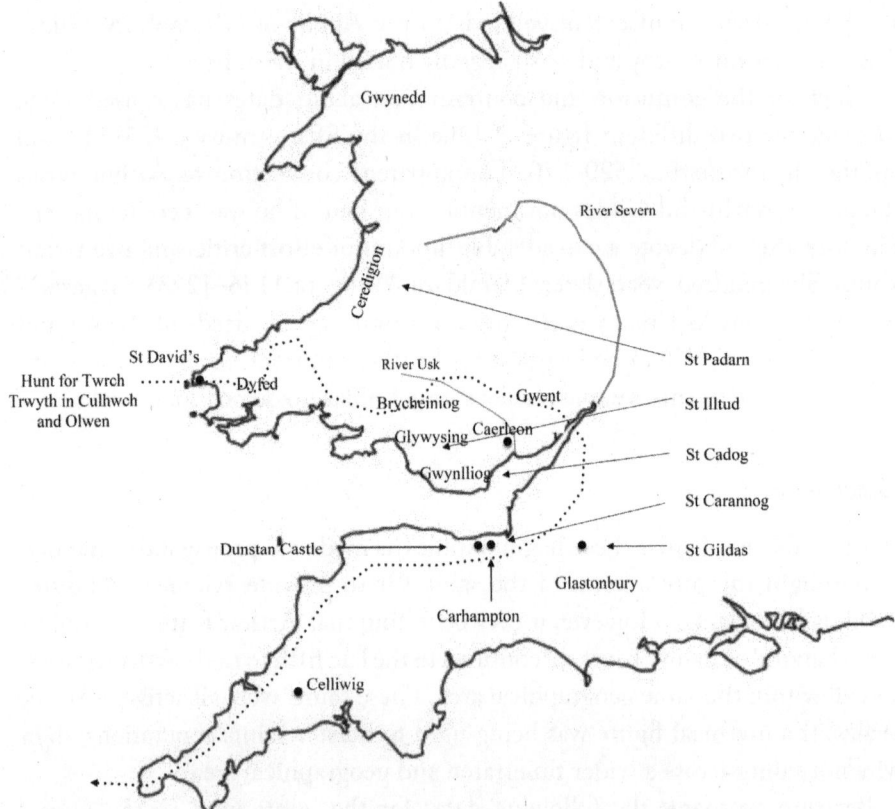

Figure 17: Arthur in the Saints' Lives and Culhwch and Olwen.

point to locations in the north. Yet here at least we see a tradition in various Saints' Lives placing Arthur in the very regions Arthur chased and fought the monstrous boar, Twrch Trwyth.

The *Vita Cadoci* c.1090 is the earliest source to refer to Arthur as *Rex*. The *Vita* Illtuti, c.1120, is the first text to depict Arthur as a king *with* a court.[15] The *Vita Paterni*, c.1120, is unique in portraying Arthur as a tyrant.[16] Despite Arthur's depictions in these tales as a tyrant, cloak-thief or revengeful pettyking, he is never portrayed as a pagan or heathen. Let us now turn to the subject of Christianity in Britain.

Religion

One theme that often crops up in Arthurian books and films is the idea that Merlin was a sort of Druid figure attempting to hold back the tide of Christianity and protect the indigenous Britons' religion. However, Christianity was already well established by the end of Roman Britain.

Christianity had been given legal status (the Edict of Milan) by Constantine I in 313. By the end of the fourth century it was the official state religion (the Edict of Thessalonica). Other creeds, such as Arianism, were deemed heretical and open to persecution. We see an example of this in action when St Germanus was sent to Britain to combat Plagiarism in 429. But what of Britain in particular?

Christianity had grown in Britain throughout the fourth century and three British bishops attended the Council of Arminium in northern Italy in 359. Records state they were so poor they had to beg for financial help. However, by the late fourth century the number of bishoprics in Britain were as high as twenty.[17] By the time Constantine III took much of the remaining military force to Gaul in 407, not only was the population 'mostly Christian', but the majority of major urban centres had large churches.[18]

There has been some debate about the survival of an insular pagan religion, with dozens of pagan shrines dated to the first half of the fifth century.[19] However, there is no evidence of pagan sites in Britain after 450.[20] This points to Britons turning away from insular paganism just as Germanic immigrants were bringing new pagan gods to Britain. When Prosper, writing c.430s, praises the Pope for 'keeping the Roman island Catholic', he is referring to the battle against Pelagiansim not paganism.

Likewise when Gildas castigates his five tyrant kings, paganism is not listed as one of their faults. It surely would have been mentioned if it was. The evidence from St Patrick also points to the survival of Roman and Christian institutions. Archaeological evidence from towns such as Lincoln and Wroxeter support this, suggesting the survival of a Roman Christian community into the sixth century. When St Augustine arrived in 597 he was met by a pagan Anglo-Saxon king in the east. Yet Æthelberht's queen was a Christian and Augustine soon made contact with the bishops of the Britons. Contact with the church in Rome appears to have broken down sometime after Easter dates calculated in Rome (c, 454) were utilised in Britain.

Christianity thrived despite the presence of the barbarians.[21] The Anglo-Saxons appeared to have retained their own religion. Bede claims Æthelberht tells Augustine his words are fair but 'new and unknown', and they cannot 'leave those things, which we have long held with all the English race'.[22] He also looks back at the crimes Gildas levels at the Britons of his day and adds this: 'they never preached the faith to the Saxons or Angles who inhabited Britain with them'.[23] The fellow citizens Gildas addresses his sermon to in *De excidio* are Christian.

Æthelberht allowed Christianity to be preached, as did later Anglo-Saxon kings such as Penda of Mercia and Edwin of Northumbria. The 'heathen tradition' of the Anglo-Saxons was a folk religion which promoted a communal identity and exclusivity. This was at odds with a 'universalist' religion like Christianity which actively sought converts. In essence, the heathen tradition may have been more tolerant and open compared to Christianity.[24] It is thus likely Christianity survived in the east and south in areas under the authority of a Germanic pagan elite.

What is certainly true is the Britons of the west and north not only maintained trade and cultural links with the Mediterranean world, but also maintained a vibrant Christianity which developed separate from the Roman church. Indeed, many of the religious problems of the seventh century, such as debates over tonsures, or dating Easter, were caused by this historical schism. The synod of Whitby in 664 did much to bring the Irish and Brythonic tradition in line with Catholic Rome, but these differences persisted for some considerable time. There is evidence of some British churches or monasteries on the sites of former Roman villas, and these in turn being linked to later Anglo-Saxon churches.[25] Roman burial rites are observed alongside early Germanic examples suggesting a level of population continuity.[26]

Arthur might well have been considered as bad a Christian as one of the tyrant kings in *De excidio* or St Patrick's King Coroticus. But a Christian none the less. The HB includes Christian imagery in his eighth battle at Guinnion fort where: 'Arthur carried the image of the holy Mary, the everlasting virgin, on his shoulders and the heathen were put to flight.' A similar image is found in the AC at Badon: 'Arthur carried the Cross of our Lord Jesus Christ for three days and three nights on his shoulders and the Britons were the victors.' We can conclude it is highly likely a fifth- or sixth-century Arthur would have been Christian.

Maelgwn of Gwynedd

Another apparent contemporary of Arthur is associated with some of the same saintly figures above. Maelgwn appears in the *Life of St Cadog*, where he is described as ruling over all Britannia (Wales). In the *Life of St Padarn* it is Maelgwn who grants land to the saint. He features in other Saints' Lives:[27] Brynach; Curig, Cybi; Mechyll; and Tydecho, where he is titled 'the great tormentor of the saints'.

However, we first meet Maelgwn in *De excidio* where he is one of the five tyrant kings Gildas lambasts, *Maglocunnus*: 'Last on the list but first in evil ... Higher than almost all the generals of Britain, in your kingdom as in your physique.'[28] He is called 'dragon of the island' who has deprived other tyrants of their kingdoms and their lives. First in mischief, malice and sinning: 'sodden with the wine of Sodom.' One of his victims was the king, his maternal uncle. Maelgwn repented and promised to become a monk. To Gildas' horror he broke his vow, but worse was to come. He discarded his lawful wife and took to bed his nephew's bride. Gildas accuses him of murdering his former wife and nephew, and berates him for the scandalous marriage of the latter's widow. It is with Maglocunnus we get the most vivid picture of a warlord culture. Surrounded by fellow 'plunderers' and 'impious men', listening to empty praises instead of the song of the church. Perhaps here Gildas is referring to bards singing praise poems and heroic tales in mead-halls.

He also appears in the HB, which places him as ruling in Gwynedd.[29] His ancestor, Cunedda (one of the two important genealogies we will come to later), is said to have came from the north, Manaw Gododdin, 146 years before Maelgwn reigned, and expelled the Irish 'with immense slaughter'.

His genealogy is given in the Harleian Genealogies as follows:[30] Maelgwn – Cadwallon Lawhir – Einion Yrth – Cunedda, and a son is called Rhun. The AC dates his death to 547:[31] 'A great death (plague) in which Maelgwn of Gwynedd died. Thus they say the long sleep of Maelgwn in the court of Rhos. Then was the yellow plague.' While we cannot confirm this entry, it is noteworthy this is within the timeframe of the plague of Justinian. The *Life of Teilo* in the *Book of Llandaff* also blames the 'yellow plague' for the death of Mailconus King of Guenedotia (Gwynedd). Scholars date his death to between 534–549.[32]

His uncle was Owain Danwyn, father of Cynlas. It is this Cynlas who, there is 'little doubt', is another of Gildas' five tyrant kings.[33] He is called Cuneglasus, 'bear ... driver of a chariot of the bear's stronghold'.[34] Like Maelgwn, he also discarded his wife only to turn to her sister. Any reference to a bear always causes at least one theorist to propose a new candidate for Arthur and this is no exception. Yet there is nothing remotely Arthurian about Maelgwn, Owain or Cynlas. Maelgwn may well have killed his uncle and taken the throne but he clearly did not fall in the same battle (as at Camlan). Gildas uses animal imagery throughout and there is no reason to take the word 'bear' to mean either Cynlas (or his father) were ever called bear-man. In Old Welsh this would be Arth-gwr. However, the ending and sounds 'ur' and 'gwr' are different and in Old Welsh poems Arthur is always rhymed with -ur words and never -gwr.[35]

It is perhaps surprising there are no traditions linking Arthur with Maelgwn. They interact with some of the same saintly figures. Both are linked to Gildas, one through a later Saint's Life and the other from Gildas himself. They are also both great-grandsons of Cunedda, Maelgwn through his paternal line and Arthur through his mother and grandmother. It might be expected their floruits would be similar. However, with eight sons, Cunedda's great-grandsons could be decades apart.

Summary

Arthur is associated, through a number of late hagiographies, with various saints all dated to between the late-fifth and the mid-sixth centuries. The five tales also place our hero in the same geographical region of southern Wales and the West Country. The inclusion of these figures and others, such as Maelgwn, in later Welsh genealogies, place Arthur in the same generation. The great-grandsons of the founding figure of Cunedda.

All this we must take with a large pinch of salt. Written six centuries after the alleged events the assertion of land rights raises suspicion. However, they do show that medieval writers viewed Arthur as someone who would add legitimacy to their narrative and claims. The logical conclusion is that some people at least accepted Arthur was historical. An abbey declaring they were granted land by Arthur centuries before hoped, if not expected, the information would be taken seriously.

So far we have seen that by the ninth century HB it is likely a historical Arthur was accepted by some. Enough to add legitimacy to late eleventh-century monks claiming land rights. The history of post-Roman Britain certainly allows the possibility of an Arthur-type historical figure. At the same time a tradition of a more mythical figure had also developed. By the early twelfth century a body of stories and tales had spread as far as Italy as can be seen in the architecture in Modena. It was at this point we get arguably the most influential Arthurian text of all.

Chapter Six

Geoffrey of Monmouth

Geoffrey of Monmouth's *Historia Regum Britanniae* ('The History of the Kings of Britain)' c.1138, had a most profound effect on the evolution of the legend. It is worth reminding ourselves of the scant pre-Galfridian sources. The ninth-century HB, which features both mystical elements in the 'Wonders of Britain' and a seemingly historical warrior leading the kings of the Britons in twelve battles between the death of Hengest and reign of Ida. The tenth-century AC, which date two battles, Badon and Camlan, to 516 and 537 respectively.

Next we have a number of poems and tales that could be tenth century or earlier, but unfortunately the earliest manuscripts are all post-Galfridian. These include: *Pa gur yv y porthaur?*; *Stanzas of the Graves*; *Elegy of Geraint son of Erbin*; *Culhwch and Olwen*; and *Preiddeu Annfwn*. To this we might add a number of early Triads and a possible passing reference in *Y Gododdin*.

Yet the tenth-century poem *Armes Prydein*, delivering a rallying cry to the Welsh and their fellow Britons, makes no mention of Arthur. Instead it invokes the spirit of Cynan and Cadwaladr. On the whole, academic opinion is that the Arthur of local legends and magical animals was the dominant one until the twelfth century.[1]

However, we know Geoffrey based his version on something. Indeed, the legend had already spread as far as Italy long before Geoffrey picked up his quill. Arthur and his knights can be seen rescuing Winlogee, shown on the doorway of Modena Cathedral in northern Italy by 1099–1120. Closer to home, two other sources demonstrate a strong tradition existed during Geoffrey's lifetime – but long before he wrote.[2] In 1113, a certain Hermann of Tournai described a near-riot at Bodmin, Cornwall, caused by visiting canons from Laon. One of them expressed doubt when the Cornishmen insisted Arthur was not dead (Hermann comments 'as they are wont to do'). Here, then, we have evidence not only of widespread belief in Arthur, but also the tradition that he still lived. In the mid-1120s, William of Malmesbury declared that Arthur's grave could not be found and 'fables' said he would return. The life of Saint Cadoc, *Vita Cadoci*, was also written in this period, c.1100.

However, these previous tales portray Arthur not as a 'High-King' type of figure, but more as a war-lord or petty king in a world of raiding and warbands. They focus on one specific story or adventure. Geoffrey was the first to create (some would say invent) a life story for our hero and place it in a longer narrative describing the history of Britain.

A number of details are known about Geoffrey:[3] He was a cleric, possibly an Augustinian canon, active in Oxford between 1129–1151. He may have worked at the Collegiate Church of St George within Oxford Castle grounds, some of which still exists. Monmouthshire is in Wales, and some have assumed Geoffrey was Welsh. However, he may have been a Breton rather than Welsh, given the prominence he gives to the Bretons. At the time Monmouthshire was controlled by a Breton family, so perhaps politics also played a part.

He knew Walter, Archdeacon of Oxford, well enough to borrow a book from him, 'a very ancient book written in the British language'. In 1151 Geoffrey became Bishop Elect of St Asaph in North Wales and was ordained the following year. In 1153 he was one of the bishops who witnessed the Treaty of Westminster between King Stephen and the son of Empress Matilda, the future Henry II. In one charter Geoffrey signs his name *magister Galf. Arcturus* 'Galfridi Arthur'.[4] The Welsh chronicle *Brut y Tywysogion* dates his death to 1154.

Politically, the HRB added valuable prestige to Plantagenet kings. Arthur takes up one sixth of the volume but in many ways his achievements are highlighted to confirm Merlin's prophetic reliability.[5] Despite some misgivings from contemporary writers it soon achieved widespread acceptance as history.[6] Originally called *De gestis Britonum* (On the Deeds of the Britons), the *Historia regum Britanniae* (The History of the Kings of Britain) was published c.1138 and dedicated to Robert, Earl of Gloucester, the son of Henry I; and Waleron, Count of Mellent, son of Robert de Beaumont.

It was the first time someone had attempted to provide a coherent and detailed story of the history of Britain. The book traced this history from its foundation by Brutus of Troy. While the book provides patriotic inspiration to the Welsh, it frequently highlights the heroic exploits of the Bretons who come to Britain and Arthur's aid on more than one occasion. He was the first to connect Arthur with Caerleon-on-Usk in South Wales which might have more to do with this connection with Monmouthshire than any pre-existing tradition.

Geoffrey claimed to have translated the Archdeacon's very old book which was 'in the British tongue'.[7] Such a claim was a common literary formula of medieval writers causing some historians to conclude Geoffrey was simply lying to cover up the fact that much of the work was his own fiction.[8]

The historical and political situation is important to note. The book was published shortly after Stephen I took the throne, and a year before open civil war broke out with Matilda. The Normans had ruled England for just seventy years. A third of William the Conqueror's army was comprised of Bretons from what was Armorica. Many were likely the descendants of the very same Britons who had emigrated in the fifth and sixth centuries. Breton lords were awarded land by the new king across England. It is perhaps no coincidence that interest in Arthurian traditions grew after the conquest of 1066. Brittany was maybe the main, if not only, route by which the legend entered the Continent.[9]

Geoffrey's Arthur is a very earthly king, recognisable in behaviour to his audience, who conquers a vast empire including Norway, Iceland and Gaul. He then engages in a battle against Rome on the Continent. These Continental adventures are a major, though often neglected, part of Geoffrey's narrative. Arthur is not the only figure to give legitimacy to the Kings of Britain. The first main character is Brutus, a Prince of Troy after that city's destruction by the Greeks. After many adventures Brutus arrives in Britain, divests the land of its many giants, and gives the island its name. A long list of kings follows, including King Lear of Shakespeare fame. Our next main characters are Belinus and Brennius, two brothers who naturally conquer Gaul and Rome.

Here, Geoffrey seems to have 'borrowed' the historical figure of Brennus, a chieftain of the Gaulish tribe the Senones. These did indeed sack Rome in 387 BC, which demonstrates our author was not averse to twisting known events to fit his narrative. More kings follow up to Magnus Maximus – or Maximianus as Geoffrey calls him. It is important to remember that while Arthur takes up a large section of the book, he is only one king among many.

The Arthurian narrative of the HRB

We take the story up with the usurper Magnus Maximus, who ruled 383–388 and remind ourselves that much of what follows is Geoffrey's distortion of known history or pure invention. The question remains: is there a kernel of truth in any of it?

Maximus leaves Gracianus in charge of Britain and heads off to Gaul. One of his first acts is to make Conanus Meridiadocus the founding ruler of Armorica and 'restock' the land with thousands of Britons. Meanwhile, in Britain, Gracianus fights off invasions by Picts and Huns led by Wanius and Malgo. Geoffrey follows a garbled version of Gildas, with the Romans returning and building the Wall. The enemy return, this time Norwegians and Danes, and seize territory up to the wall. The Britons appeal to Agicius and, having been rejected, decide to seek help from their cousins across the Channel.

The Britons send Guithelinus, the Archbishop of London, to King Aldoneus in Armorica. The king's brother, Constantine, comes to Britain with an army and accepts the crown. At first glance Geoffrey could be equating this Constantine with Constantine III (407–411). However, other than a son called Constans, they have nothing else in common. In fact, the later timeframe points to this Constantine arriving in the mid-fifth century, given he is grandfather to Arthur (Geoffrey dates Camlan to 542).

Constantine dies and his advisor Vortigern, leader of the Gewissei (we recall Bede's name for the West Saxons, *Gewisse*), conspires to place Constans on the throne only to poison him and seize power. Constantine's other sons, Ambrosius and Uther, still infants, are taken to Armorica to avoid their elder brother's fate. Shortly after, Hengist and Horsa arrive and are settled in Lindsey. Hengist builds a fortress and invites reinforcements and his daughter. It is from Geoffrey we learn her name, Renwein. She seduces the weak-willed Vortigern, and Hengist receives Kent in payment for his daughter's hand, removing the British earl Gorangonus.

St Germanus is mentioned briefly, calling in to question our timeline. Next, Octa and Ebissa arrive with 300 more ships and are allowed to settle in Northumberland. The Britons become restless and Vortigern is disposed. His son Vortimer is made king and fights four battles forcing the Saxons to leave. Renwein poisons Vortimer allowing Vortigern to take back the crown. Hengist returns with an unlikely 300,000 men.

The Britons again plot to overthrow Vortigern on account of the Saxon presence and so Hengist arranges a peace conference. But he treacherously arranges to have them all killed in what became known as 'The Night of the Long Knives'. On a pre-arranged signal, 300 British nobles are murdered with only one escaping. The Saxons capture Vortigern alive and force him to cede London, York, Winchester and Lincoln.

Vortigern flees to Wales and attempts to build a fortress. We then get a repetition of the tale of two dragons under the mountain from the HB. This time the boy is not Ambrosius Emrys but Merlin. Geoffrey seems to have combined two figures: Ambrosius Emrys from the HB; and Myrddin Wyllt (Mryddin the wild) mentioned in the AC and other Welsh legends. With Myrddin sounding a little too close to 'Merde' in Anglo-French, Geoffrey Latinised it to Merlinus.

Ambrosius and Uther come of age and return to Britain with an army. Pursuing Vortigern to the Castle of Genoreu in South Wales, the castle and its occupants are burned to the ground. Ambrosius is crowned king and his first act is to attack the Saxons who are defeated in two battles, Maisbeli and

Kaerconan. Hengist is executed and Octa and Eossa surrender. They are given Bernicia in Northumberland while Ambrosius rules from York.

Ambrosius determines to give the 300 nobles slain by Hengist a suitable memorial. Uther is sent to Ireland to steal the Giant's Ring and defeats an Irish king, Gillomanius. Merlin is called from the 'land of Geweissi' to magically transport the stones. Thus for Geoffrey's audience, Stonehenge is the resting place of the British nobles. Vortigern's son Paschent (Pascent is Vortigern's third son in the HB) allies with the Irish king Gillomanius and they seek revenge, invading Britain.

Uther sets out to confront them. The night before the battle 'a two-headed dragon' appears in the sky with a fiery tail. From this Uther obtains his famous epithet, Pendragon. Some scholars suggest this is a misunderstanding of the Welsh phrase 'chief of warriors'. An important point to remember when theorists attempt to link Arthur with actual dragon motifs. Interestingly there are two records of comets in the fifth century: The first in c.497 from a fourteenth-century text, *Flores Historiarum*; the second was seen from Brittany in c.457 and is recorded by a Conrad Wolffart in the sixteenth century. Alternatively, Halley's Comet passed over in c.451 and again c.526.

Uther prevails but his brother Ambrosius is poisoned by the Saxons and dies. Uther is crowned king and immediately has to confront the rebellious Octa and Eossa, who are quickly defeated and imprisoned. With Uther's position secure we then get the famous story of Arthur's conception. Merlin magically changes Uther's appearance so that he looks like Ygraine's husband, Gorlois. He gains access to Tintagel Castle and, with Ygraine believing it is Gorlois, Arthur is conceived. Gorlois is killed in battle and the apparently now happy couple marry. A sister, Anna, follows and she later marries King Loth.

Fifteen years pass and Uther is poisoned at St Albans while battling the Saxons. Arthur's reign begins, coincidentally at the same age as Clovis I, first king of the Franks. He is crowned by St Dubricius (traditionally dated to c.465–550). Arthur immediately goes on the offensive and defeats the Saxons, led now by Colgrin and Baldulf, at the River Douglas. Arthur pursues and besieges them at York but is forced to retreat to Lincoln. Once more the Bretons come to the rescue in the form of Hoel, a son of Arthur's sister and King Budicius. It is not clear if this is a different sister or a different husband of the same sister (or indeed a sister of Ambrosius and thus Arthur's aunt!). Later we are told Anna and Loth have two sons, Mordred and Gawain.

Arthur and Hoel go on the offensive and defeat the enemy at Kaerluideoit, Lincoln, and at Caledon Wood. The Saxons agree to leave but break their promise and sail to Devon. Hoel is left injured at Dumbarton and Arthur marches south. It is at this point Geoffrey places Badon at Bath. Colgrin and

Baldulf are joined by Cheldric (possibly Cerdic of the West Saxons) but the Saxons are soundly beaten. They are pursued to Thanet by Arthur's half-brother, Cador, Duke of Cornwall (recalling Vortimer's campaigns in the HB).

Arthur returns north and fights three battles against the Picts, another at Loch Lomond and one against a King Gilmarius of Ireland. He takes a break in the fighting to marry Ganhumara (Welsh Gwenhwyfar or our modern Guinevere) before conquering Ireland, the Orkneys and Gotland. No dates are given, but perhaps we can speculate a relatively short timeframe for these campaigns. Twelve years go by before Arthur begins his foreign campaigns, first invading Norway and Denmark. Next he marches on Paris, defeating the Tribune Frollo (who ruled in the name of the Emperor Leo) in single combat. The rest of Gaul is soon subdued.

The only Leo we could point to here is the Eastern Emperors Leo I (457–474), Leo II (474) or Pope Leo (440–461). We also have a Riothamus leading Britons in the Loire Valley c.465–72. But none of this ties in with the only date Geoffrey gives, which is for Arthur's defeat at Camlan in 542.

Arthur's reign throughout Britain and Gaul is secure and nine years pass in relative peace. This is broken when messengers arrive at Arthur's court at Caerleon-on-Usk. They bear a letter from the Roman Procurator, Lucius Hiberius, demanding tribute and submission. There is no record of a Lucius Hiberius, although a Western Emperor, Glycerus (473–4), was sometimes misspelled as Lucerius. Arthur's answer would have struck a cord with his Norman audience. Not only did Arthur refuse, but he pointed out Rome owed allegiance to him on the basis that his predecessors, Brennius and Constantine the Great, had defeated Rome. War looms and Arthur gathers his army and leaves Britain in the care of his nephew, Mordred.

Shortly after landing Arthur defeats a giant at Mont St Michel (another giant-killing act is related in the tale). Arthur marches across Gaul and there is a huge battle in the Saussy region between Langres and Autun near Dijon in Eastern France. The Romans are defeated and Lucius killed. Arthur prepares to invade Italy and capture Rome when he learns of the treachery of Mordred and Guinevere.

Allied with the Saxons under Chelric, Mordred had seized the throne and Arthur's wife. A furious Arthur races back to Britain, lands in east Kent and defeats his nephew at Richborough. Mordred flees west and is defeated again at Winchester before the final showdown at Camlan in Cornwall. A fatally wounded Arthur is taken to the Isle of Avalon so that 'his wounds might be attended to'. Although his death is not confirmed, he hands his crown to his cousin Constantine. Geoffrey dates to the year 542 which enables us to speculate the timeframe leading up to Camlan.

If Ambrosius and Uther were infants in the mid-fifth century this would allow an Ambrosius of fighting age 'in the time of Zeno' (474–491, from Bede). An Arthur born shortly after the comet of c.497 might be able to fight at Badon in 516 (from the AC). On the other hand, if we equate the Constantine in the HRB with Constantine III, then we must reject the 542 date and pull the entire timeframe back by several decades.

Geoffrey lists a number of kings after Arthur: Constantine; Aurelius Conanus; Vortiporus; Malgo and Keredic. These appear to be a direct copy of the five tyrant kings of Gildas, who in reality ruled simultaneously in different kingdoms. During the reign of Keredic, Britain is invaded by Gormund, King of the Africans, with an army of 160,000 aided by Isembard, nephew of Louis, King of the Franks. It is at this point that a considerable part of the island, Loegria, is handed over to the Saxons. The Britons sought refuge in the western parts of Wales and Cornwall. Geoffrey ends his tale with the death Cadwallader in 689, the seventh-century King of Gwynedd, the last Welsh King to claim lordship over Britain.

Discussion

The HRB delivers a number of messages to its intended audience. It provides the first attempt at a full historical narrative for Britain: a great and glorious past to rival that of the Romans. Three main characters stand out: Brutus, Brennius and Arthur. The proud history of both the Britons and Bretons is underlined, along with the hope, in the form of prophecies, that they will rise again if they avoid civil wars and discord.

The Saxons and Romans would have been viewed as a common enemy by the Welsh and Normans alike. It is perhaps telling that Arthur emerged as a popular character only after the Norman conquest.[10] Prior to that, Arthur is the more mystical and magical character of Welsh poems and legends.

Geoffrey was certainly an imaginative writer. He wove together known historical figures and events with mythical and legendary examples. Much of the narrative is fictional and likely invented by the author, yet 'history keeps peeping through'.[11] One example is when Geoffrey describes the Venedoti decapitating a whole Roman legion in London and then throwing their heads into a stream called Nantgallum or Galobroc in Saxon. In 1860 a large number of skulls were indeed found in the bed of the Walbrook in London.

Some contemporary writers accepted a historical Arthur: William of Malmesbury (*De Gestis Regum Anglorum*, c.1125) described how Ambrosius, 'the sole survivor of the Romans who became king after Vortigern', defeated the barbarians with 'the powerful aid of the warlike Arthur'. He continues:

'This is that Arthur of whom the trifling of the Britons talks such nonsense even today; a man clearly worthy not to be dreamed of in fallacious fables, but to be proclaimed in veracious histories, as one who long sustained his tottering country, and gave the shattered minds of his fellow citizens an edge for war.' Henry of Huntingdon (*Historia Anglorum*, c.1130) describes Arthur as 'the commander of the soldiers and kings of Britain' who fought twelve victorious battles against the invaders, the last at Mount Badon, where 440 of his men died. It is worth noting these both pre-date the HRB.

Others were not so generous: William of Newburgh, in *Historia rerum Anglicarum* ('History of English Affairs') c.1198, regarding Arthur accuses Geoffrey, who he claims: 'started up and invented the most ridiculous fictions', from 'the traditional fictions of the Britons, with additions of his own and endeavoured to dignify them with the name of authentic history'.

Ranulf Higden of Chester c.1352 remarked that if Geoffrey is accurate then it is, 'astonishing that the chronicles of Rome, of France, and of the Saxons should not have spoken of so noble a prince in their stories'. He found it equally surprising that there is no mention in chronicles of Frollo or Lucius Hiberius. In fact it is: 'to be marvelled why Geoffrey praises him so much, whom old authors, true and famous writers of stories, leave untouched'. Interesting that Ranulf accepts Geoffrey dates Arthur to the reign of Justinian (527–565).

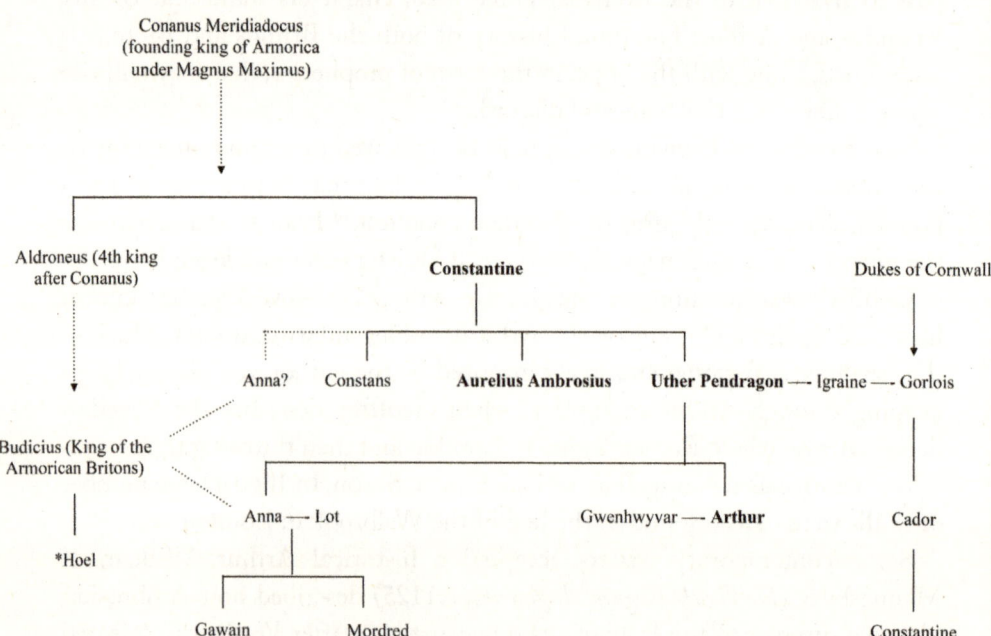

Figure 18: Arthur's family tree from HRB.

Geoffrey offers a slightly different family tree from the one in *Culhwch and Olwen*. Importantly he connects Arthur's family to the Armorican Britons through his paternal grandfather, Constantine. Time and again Geoffrey has the Bretons riding to the Britons' rescue. We will see later that Brittany and Cornwall share geographical and personal names, the latter in the genealogies. One important question here is this: has Geoffrey deliberately, or by mistake, switched Arthur's ancestry to Brittany? It is perhaps academic if his grandfather came from Kernev/Cornouaille in Armorica or Cornwall in Britain (Dumnonia is also found in both regions).

Gwalchmai is now Gawain but he remains Arthur's nephew, although with different parentage. Cador, son of Gorlois, is rendered in Welsh as Cadwr ap Gwrlais. Bartrum views this as a different figure from Cadwy ap Geraint. Yet both are associated with Devon and are of the same generation as Arthur. One point that is unclear is the connection with Budicius, King of the Bretons. In one section it is implied he is married to Anna, a sister of Ambrosius. In another to Arthur's sister of the same name. If the latter then we must assume she married twice as she was also marred to Loth.

Myrddin

The important thing to point out first is that the figure found in the ninth-century HB is not Merlin. Instead it is *Embreis Guletic*, 'Emrys the Overlord'. Naming himself Ambrosius, and son of a Roman consul, connects him clearly with the Ambrosius Aurelianus in Gildas and Bede. It is this figure, rather than Arthur, who these earlier and more reliable sources seem to connect to the victory at *mons Badonicus*. Admittedly it is not made clear if he was present, Nor would it negate a young Arthur accompanying Ambrosius. Geoffrey of Monmouth simply used the tale of the two dragons found in the HB and attached them to *Merlinus* in HRB.

As mentioned earlier, it is thought Geoffrey Latinised the Welsh form, Myrddin, as it sounded too similar to the Latin *merda* or French *merde*, meaning dung. One of the biggest problems with Geoffrey's Merlin is he spans several generations, from the time of Vortigern in the mid-fifth century to that of Rhydderch Hael in the late-sixth century.

Later writers saw these problems and this led to the suggestion there were two Myrddin's. Gerald of Wales writing c.1220 explains:[12] the first was called Ambrosius, who prophesied in the time of Vortigern; the second was born in Scotland and was named Celidonius. Clearly associated with the battle of Arfderydd, dated in AC to 573, 'in which Gwenddolau fell; Merlin went mad'. Gerald claimed it was this Merlin who lived in the time of Arthur. One triad references Three Skilled Bards, Taliesin, Myrddin Emrys and Myrddin ap Morfryn (also called Myrddin Caledonius or Silvester). It should be noted the earliest reference to the above battle in the AC spells it *bellum armterid* and makes no reference to Myrddin. The later manuscript inserts the reference to Merlinus. This Latinised form confirms the entry was post-Galfridian.

In the HRB Merlin is a very important figure. His timespan straddles several main characters and his prophecies are central to the story. But it is essentially an invention of Geoffrey of Monmouth.[13] It is often forgotten that Merlin disappears from the HRB after Arthur's conception at Tintagel. It is in his later work, *Vita Merlini*, 'The Life of Merlin', in c.1150, that Merlin's backstory is filled out. Merlinus was a king and prophet to the Demetae. This later work associates him more closely with the 'second' Merlin, but it is the image from the HRB which dominated medieval traditions. Subsequent French writers such as Robert de Boron and Chrétien de Troyes expanded on this.

The complex evolution of the literary character falls outside the scope of this book. What might be noteworthy is any historical basis to Myrddin. We can certainly dismiss Geoffrey's distortion of the figure from the HB, just as we can his assertion that Stonehenge was built by flying stones brought over from Ireland in the HRB.

The name Merlin is unknown before the twelfth century. Geoffrey of Monmouth introduced this form of the character in *Prophetiae Merlini*, 'The Prophecies of Merlin', in the early 1130s. His HRB Merlin is largely associated with the Emrys Ambrosius of the HB. It is the later work, *Vita Merlini*, which moves some of the events to the north. However, Welsh tradition associates Myrddin with South Wales as the legendary founder of Carmarthen (*Caerfryddin*, 'Myrddin's Fort').

In this text Geoffrey has Merlin serving the kings of Demetia (Dyfed). Later, he marches north with Peredur and his brothers to aid king Rodarch, who is married to Merlin's sister, Ganieda. The enemy is a King Guennolous. Overcome with grief after the battle, Merlin escapes to the forest where he lives in solitude. He is eventually reunited with his wife, Guendoloena, and his sister at Rodarch's court, but returns to the forest of Calidon. Later he meets Taliesin and in their conversation we learn that Arthur was sent to *Insula Pomorum* after the Battle of Camlan to be cared for by the healer Morgen, one of nine sisters who rule there.

Here Geoffrey is clearly connecting his Merlin, not with a figure dealing with a mid-fifth-century Vortigern, but one fighting alongside kings in a late sixth-century battle recorded in the AC for 573: 'The battle of Arfderydd between the sons of Eliffer and Gwenddolau son of Ceidio; in which Gwenddolau fell; Merlin went mad.'

As ever, a word of caution is necessary. There are three primary versions of the AC. The earliest (version A) is dated to the twelfth century but is thought to be based on a mid-tenth century original. This makes makes no mention of Myrddin, though it does mention the battle of Armterid (note the early spelling). Version B is dated to the late-thirteenth century and contains material drawn from HRB. This does reference Merlinus going insane after the battle. It is worth noting the Latinised spelling.

A line from *Y Gododdin* refers to Morien defending 'the fair song of Myrddin'. This could be taken to mean defending the culture or people (Britons), although again it may be a late addition. In the Welsh poem *Cyfoesi Myrddin a Gwenddydd ei Chwaer*, 'The Conversation of Myrddin and His Sister Gwenddydd' (Red Book of Hergest), Merlin's sister Gwenddydd refers to him as Llallogan ('Little Llallawg').[14] Here, then, we see an attempt to link an older, Welsh Myrddin, with a northern figure. Welsh tradition acknowledged these two separate figures, for example in the Triad, 'The Three Principal Bards of the Island of Britain': Myrddin, son of Morfryn, Myrddin Emrys and Taliesin.

Two Latin *vitae* of St Kentigern (Mungo) provides some clues – the first written c.1150, the second c.1180.[15] The second was commissioned by Jocelin, the Bishop of Glasgow, and was written by his namesake, a monk at Furness Abbey in north-west England. Jocelyn gave our saint royal parentage, none other than Owain, son of Urien and Teneu, daughter of Leudonus, (who some call Loth). Their son, Kentigern, becomes the bishop of Glasgow in the realm of King Rederech. This Rederech, or Rodarch in Geoffrey's *Vita Merlini*, can be identified as Rhydderch Hael of Alt Clud. This is the same figure mentioned in the HB as fighting the Angles of Bernicia alongside Urien. Among the kings retainers is a jester or fool called Laloecen.

A fifteenth-century text, *Vita Merlini Silvestris*, 'The Life of Merlin of the Forest', names the man Lailoken and records a meeting between him and St Kentigern. Here, too, the titular figure has fled to the forest due to a great slaughter at battle, which the author crucially places: the plain between Lidel and Carwannok. This has been located with some confidence at Arthuret, at the confluence of the Rivers Esk and Liddel.[16]

Notable features of this figure include: the ability of prophecy; the concept of a 'triple death' either for himself or another; a period spent in the wilderness; a great battle causing a madness. An Irish tale, *Buile Shuibbne*, 'The Frenzy of Shuibbne', presents a similar figure travelling to Britain and meeting a certain Alladhan, a 'deranged British wild man' known as 'The Man of the Wood'.[17] Wild men also feature in literature such as Enkidu, in the legend of Gilgamesh, of Nebuchadnezzar in the Old Testament. In the early centuries AD a number of Saints' Lives refer to hermits and other holy men seeking solitude in the wilderness. The *Buile Shuibbne* is dated to the late twelfth century and thus post-dates HRB and *Vita Merlini*.

Tolstoy, in *The Quest for Merlin*, found that Merlin was a historical, late sixth-century figure from the lowlands of Scotland.[18] Additionally much of the early Welsh poetry is based on authentic verse attributed to this figure. Tolstoy also locates the battle near Arthuret and Carwinley and claims to have discovered exactly where Myrddin fled to: Hart Fell mountain within the Forest of Celyddon in the kingdom of the Goddeu.[19] While this potentially historical figure was the basis of Geoffrey's Merlinus, it is suggested the figure attracted a mythical and magical tradition, specifically the Celtic deity, Lug or Lugh.

Tim Clarkson, *Scotland's Merlin, A Medieval Legend and its Dark Age Origins*, has analysed the legend and comes to a couple of conclusions:[20] Geoffrey's Merlin was based on a forest-dwelling Myrddin Wyllt, driven mad by a battle at Arfderydd; and this earlier figure was in turn adapted by a North British wild-man, Lailoken. It would thus appear the hagiographers of St Kentigern linked their saint to this northern figure, ignoring earlier associations with Myrddin. Likewise the Welsh tradition had no reason to attach 'their' Myrddin with a later northern saint.

Clarkson goes on to describe the evolution of the story, pulling in the different strands. A figure named Llallawg was born c.540 in northern Britain and grew to serve the local king based around the confluence of the Esk and Liddel. Geoffrey seems to have his combatants at Arfderydd mixed up. As we shall see Welsh tradition views Merlin as being on the side of Gwenddolau fighting against Rhydderch Hael. The details of the battle will be touched on later.

To summarise, we have a number of strands which come together to form this composite character. The first is the prophecies not of Myrddin, but Emrys Ambrosius, in the HB. The second is a tradition of a Myrddin connected with South Wales, as the legendary founder of Carmarthen. And third, the northern tradition of a wild-man, prophet and seer who fled to the woods after a disastrous battle. Geoffrey of Monmouth pulled these together to form his composite character and Latinise his name to *Merlinus*. Later hagiographers of St Kentigern appropriated this figure into their narrative.

If we take all this at face value, then we might have a historical figure contemporary with Taliesin and Urien whom Geoffrey used as one part of his composite character Merlin. It follows that all the later writers who based their Merlin on the one in the HRB are developing a literary invention and can offer no clues as to a potentially historical Arthur. One historian concludes that, 'almost everything we think we know about Myrddin was a reflection of Geoffrey's inventive habits and its legacy in Welsh literature'.[21] In particular the political content of the prophecies, at the time of writing, suggests they are fully the work of the author.[22]

Summary

A number of points need to be emphasised. First, an Arthurian tradition existed before Geoffrey of Monmouth put quill to parchment. If some of the Welsh tales and Saints' Lives hint at this, the carving at Modena Cathedral proves it. Second, Geoffrey was not writing history but it should be viewed in the historical context at the time of writing. There was already a literary tradition covering 'The Matter of France' or Carolingian Cycle particularly concerning Charlemagne and his knights. In addition 'The Matter of Rome' was a literary cycle concerning Greek and Roman mythology. The HRB was a central component of what became 'The Matter of Britain'. Geoffrey was able to kick-start a genre that rivalled any from the Continent.

Politically, Geoffrey lived in a time of great strife. The HRB was written just seventy years after William the Conqueror's victory at Hastings. Only a year after Stephen had snatched the throne from Matilda. No doubt swords were being sharpened between the rival supporters. He wrote just two years before open war broke out. A central message was the result of a disunited realm.

However it also provided the Normans with a narrative that allowed them to lay claim to Britain and indeed Europe. Had not Brutus ruled the whole of Ireland? Did Belinus and Brennius not conquer Rome? And of course Arthur conquered all, including the Roman emperor. Perhaps importantly, the Bretons played a prominent role. Not only were they originally Britons, but they rode to the rescue time after time. Just to make the connection even more secure, Arthur is descended on his father's side from Bretons. The same Bretons who composed a third of the conqueror's army in 1066.

It is possible Geoffrey 'was writing specifically, although not exclusively, for a Welsh audience'.[23]

However, it also delivered a powerful message to a Norman audience. Not only did it highlight the dangers of disunity, but also offered a model of, and legitimacy for, empire-building. This was surely music to the ears of his Norman and Breton readers. Not only did Arthur defeat the Anglo-Saxons, as William had done at Hastings, but he conquered the whole of Britain as subsequent Norman kings would attempt over the centuries. Even more impressive, Arthur gave legitimacy for claims further afield – from Ireland across to the European mainland.

While Geoffrey did include some historical figures (as well as many fictitious examples) he was happy to alter their story to suit his narrative; the very real Brennus of the Senones defeating the Romans and sacking Rome in 390 BC, for example. In the HRB Geoffrey names two brothers, Brennius and Belinus, Kings of Britain, who take the eternal city. Arthur in this context is another example of a king from Britain subduing Rome. The next chapter will begin investigating if the continental campaigns of Arthur had any historical basis.

Chapter Seven

The French Connection

The two earliest sources that link Arthur to the Continent are a Saint's Life and Geoffrey's HRB. The dating of the first is controversial. If the author, a Breton named William, Chaplain of the Bishop Eudo of Leon, wrote *Legenda Sancti Goeznovii* in c.1019, then this would predate the HRB by over a century. St Goeznovius, originally from Cornwall, became a bishop in Brittany and died c.675.

The author claimed the information in the preface came from an unknown source, *Ystoria Britanica*. It is possible this was a version of the *Historia Brittonum*, although that of course makes no mention of Gaul. William's preface describes how Vortigern invited the Saxons but: 'presently their pride was checked by Arthur, King of the Britons', and importantly, references his 'many victories which he won gloriously in Britain and in Gaul'.[1] It then describes a time of further incursions from Saxons and oppression of Britons and the church in particular. Many martyrs were made and some emigrated to Brittany. Ambrosius Aurelianus is ignored, and if the date is accurate this is the first reference of Arthur as a king. However, the possibility remains it is a later document and influenced by the HRB.

Geoffrey's epic pseudo-history has Arthur travelling across Gaul and battling the Romans. In his narrative, Arthur's adventures in Gaul occur after he has defeated the Saxons, Picts and Irish. Twelve years go by and he invades Norway and Denmark before marching on Paris and defeating Rollo. He then subdued the other provinces including Normandy, Anjou, Aquitania and Gascony. Nine more years go by before the Romans arrive demanding homage. Arthur's main Continental campaign is therefore shortly before he returns to Britain for his climatic battle at Camblan in 542. Thus Geoffrey is placing these battles firmly in the reigns of the sons of Clovis I.

The location of this campaign can be seen in figure 19. This clearly bears no resemblance to the political and military reality of fifth- or sixth-century Gaul. We can see the Loire Valley, village of Déols and town of Bourges where Gregory of Tours and Jordanes claim Britons were defeated by the Goths. One significant battle did occur near Autun in 532, but this was between the Merovingian kings, Childebert I and Clothar I against King Godomar of the Burgundians. It therefore appears to be an entirely fictitious campaign invented by Geoffrey.

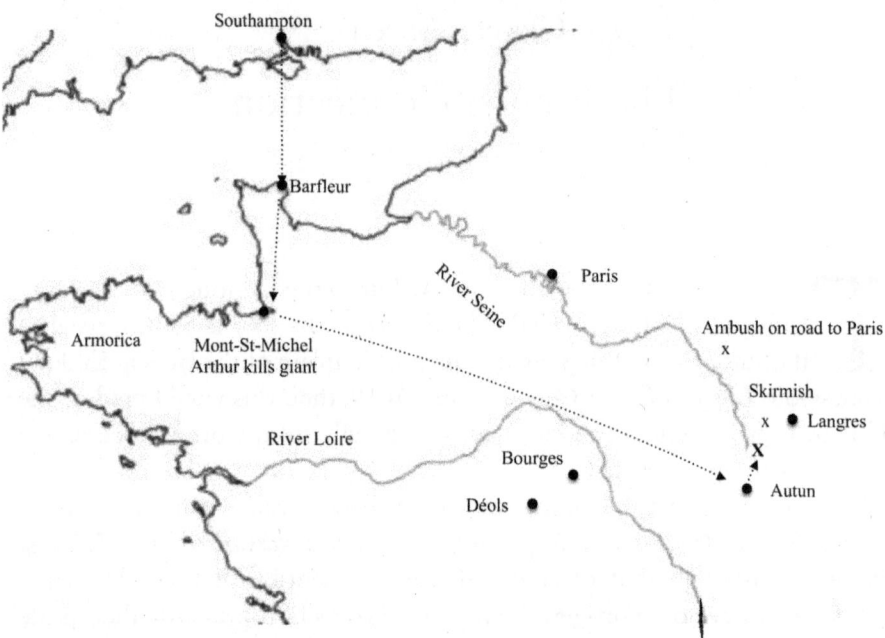

Figure 19: Arthur's war against the Romans in Gaul in HRB.

The figures Geoffrey chooses to name as Arthur's adversaries, the Emperor Leo and 'Procurator' Lucius Hiberius, have been linked to the fifth century. The former could be the eastern emperors Leo I (457–474) or Leo II (474) and the latter the western emperor Glycerius (473–474). Alternatively, there was a Pope Leo I (440–461). It is quite possible Geoffrey lifted and amended the career of one of the Roman emperors who did invade Gaul from Britain in the fourth and early fifth centuries. The table below shows the likely candidates. Although none of their campaigns resemble the one portrayed in HRB.

Table 7: Roman Emperors of Britain invading Gaul.

Year	Emperor	Comments
306	Constantine I	Declared Emperor at York. Reunited empire under one ruler. His mother Helen was dubiously linked to Coel Hen by late genealogies.
383–388	Magnus Maximus	Declared Emperor in Britain in 383 and crossed to Gaul. Killed the Western Emperor Gratian. Crossed the Alps in pursuit of co-emperor Valentinian. Executed by Eastern Emperor Theodosius outside Aquileia in north-east Italy in 388.
407–411	Constantine III	Invaded Gaul in 407 and was made co-Augustus with his son Constans up to the Alps by Western Emperor Honorius. Executed in 411. Aspects of his life possibly conflated in Geoffrey's HRB for Arthur's grandfather.

Alternatively, what we are looking for is a context in which a leader from Britain might fight on the Continent. We recall this campaign was preceded by a Roman embassy, which goaded Arthur into action. For examples of this we need to look at the history of fifth- and sixth-century Gaul.

Fifth and sixth century Gaul

After the death of Aetius in 454 the Western Empire experienced a succession of weak emperors, increasingly controlled by powerful Germanic generals up to the year 476 when Odoacer forced the last emperor, Romulus Augustus, to abdicate. A decade before, the fate of Roman Gaul still hung in the balance. The Romans vied for control with Franks, Visigoths and importantly, Britons.

Jordanes, writing nearly a century later, tells us that Eurich, king of the Visigoths, perceived the weakness and frequent change of emperors and vied for control of Gaul.[2] The western emperor Anthemius (467–72) requested aid from the *Brittones*. Their king, Riotimus, responded and came with 12,000 men 'into the state of the *Bituriges* by the way of Ocean'. The phrase 'by way of the ocean' has been used to claim he must have come from Britain. However, this could easily mean from Brittany, down the west coast and into the Loire. Indeed, the *Bituriges* are in the same area Geoffrey of Tours tells us the *Britanni* were expelled from. Jordanes leaves Riotimus having been defeated by Euric and losing 'a great part of his army'. He flees east to the Burgundians who at that time were allied with Rome. He seems to date this shortly before the death of Anthemius in 472.

Gregory of Tours gives a little more detail although does not mention Riotimus. We read that the Frankish king, Childeric, was fighting at Orleans while the Germanic general Odoacer came to another town on the Loire, Orleans, with the Saxons. Then the Roman *magister militum*, Aegidius, died, which allows us to date this to c.464. He had formed the breakaway kingdom of Soissons and was succeeded by his son, Syagrius. Sometime after this 'the *Britanni* were driven from Bourges by the Goths, and many were slain at the village of Déols'. This is just sixty miles from Orleans and very close to the Loire as it turns south. In a confusing passage, the Romans and Franks fight the Goths but then appear to turn on each other, before teaming up to drive the Saxons from the Loire valley: 'the Saxons fled and left many of their people to be slain, the Romans pursuing. Their islands were captured and ravaged by the Franks, and many were slain.' If this is the same event then we can place a large contingent of Britons fighting in the Loire between 464–472. Who were these Britons and what were they doing there?

The first attested strong evidence for British presence is the Council of Tours in 461 and the attendance of Bishop Mansuetus of the Britons. If there was an *episcopus Britannorum* in 461, then there must have been an established community there for some time for him to administer. In c.469 there is a letter by Sidonius Apollinaris on behalf of Prefect Arvandus from Lyon to Euric, King of the Goths, urging him to reject alliance with Anthemius and attack the Britons situated 'on the far side of the Loire'. A further letter from Sidonius to Riothamus appears to suggest he has some judicial power and so is based in the area. It is thus likely that Riothamus was based north of the Loire rather than Britain.[3]

Cunliffe in *Bretons and Britons*, states that into fifth-century Armorica a 'flood of British migrants arrived, coming mainly from the south-west peninsula and from southern Wales'.[4] This significant movement of people included clerics and stablished a tradition of links between the Britons of Wales and Cornwall and the Bretons of Brittany. Cunliffe places this movement beginning in the first decades of the fifth century.

The result of the war of the 460s seems to have been to confine the Bretons to north of the Loire and into the north-west peninsula. As the Western Roman Empire disintegrated it was the Franks who were feted to win the power struggle for Gaul. Clovis succeeded his father as king of the Salian Franks in 481 and proceeded to dominate the other Frankish tribes before defeating Syagrius and taking control of the Roman rump state of Soisson in northern Gaul in c.487. This is surely the last time a historical Arthur could have fought against, or with, anyone who'd identify as Roman – although there's nothing to suggest Britons were involved on either side. The Gallo-Roman border with the Bretons now became a Frankish-Breton one.

What we don't have is any evidence for any friction between the Franks and Britons or Bretons that might be the basis of an Arthurian campaign in Gaul. The relationship with the Franks was generally one of peace and there are indications of a treaty around 497.[5] Procopius, on the other hand, describes the Armoricans fighting off the Franks so that they were forced to make them 'their companions and relations by marriage'.[6] An Arthur fighting in this context would have been fighting small border wars against Franks rather than Romans.

Clovis turned his attention not to the Bretons, but the Burgundians and Visigoths, defeating the latter at the Battle of Vouille in 507. He was then granted the rather meaningless title of consul by the eastern emperor, Anastasius. Might an embassy from Anastasius, or even Clovis, have crossed the channel and reminded the Britons where they owed their allegiance?

Clovis died in 511 and his kingdom was split between his four sons. Gregory of Tours states that after his death the Breton rulers ceased to be called kings but were merely counts and subjects of the Franks. The sons of Clovis spent much of the next few decades expanding their kingdoms when they weren't fighting each other. There is no possibility an Arthurian army ravaged across sixth-century Frankish-Gaul and was missed by contemporary historians.

If we are to believe Procopius, the exercise of political influence was in the other direction. The Frankish embassy to Constantinople claimed: 'The king of the Franks actually sent some of his friends to the Emperor Justinian in Byzantium, and despatched with them the men of the Angles, claiming that this island [Britain], too, is ruled by him.'[7] The Salian law code under Clovis I (481–511) allowed for the Franks to seek the return of slaves in Britain. Theuderic I (511–534) recruited Saxons from Britain to fight against the Thuringians. It is precisely in this time period that Frankish luxury items appear in Kentish burials.[8] There then followed further expansion against the Thuringians in 531, Burgundians in 534, Provence region 537, the Visigoths in northern Spain in 542 and a Saxon war in 555–6. There was also a fair amount of internal rivalry, civil wars and assassinations.

There is a tantalising piece of evidence from the *Vita sancti Dalmatii*, written in c. 800, which records a *legio Bretonum* in Gaul in c. 530.[9] There is some dispute whether this force, if that is what it was, can be located north of the Loire or further east in northern Burgundy. It is likely the word 'legion' here simply means a body of troops rather than an actual late Roman legion. However, the implication is that these were recognised by St Dalmatius (bishop of Rodez c. 534–580) as Bretons or Britons. It is possible these troops were serving the Frankish king Theudebert at the time of the saint's journey, c. 534–41. We noted Theuderic recruited Saxons to fight against the Thuringians c. 530s and so it is quite possible Bretons or Britons were recruited as well. Additionally, Procopius's observation might apply to Britons as well as Saxons: 'So great apparently is the multitude of these peoples that every year in large groups they migrate from there [Britain] with their women and children and go to the Franks.'[10] Intriguingly, the Burgundians were finally overrun by the Franks in 534 after a major defeat at Autun in 532, very close to Saussy where Geoffrey of Monmouth claimed Arthur defeated the Romans.

While the Frankish kings were subduing what was to become of France, the eastern empire under Justinian was flexing its muscles. Here we get a curious incident at the siege of Rome in 538. The Ostrogothic army lead by Vitiges was besieging an Eastern Empire force led by Balisarius. During negotiations the Goths were made the following offer recorded by Procopius: 'And we on our side permit the Goths to have the whole of Britain, which is much larger than Sicily and was subject to the Romans in early times.'[11] Were the Romans simply offering up something over which they had no control? If we take Geoffrey of Monmouth's date for Camlan at face value, this is the only possible event that could have resulted in an embassy arriving from Rome at this time. One can only imagine what any Britons might have thought if a group of eastern Romans or Goths turned up and demanded authority over their island. But this is pure speculation and we have no evidence of any Continental involvement in Britain at this time.

After the mid-sixth century we have a couple of Frankish-Breton wars that could have created a pretext for the involvement of a warrior from Britain aiding the Bretons. The first comes after the death of Childebert I in 558. Another son of Clovis, Clothar I, briefly united the Franks once again. His son Chramus rebelled and fled to Chonoober, count of the Bretons. Clothar pursued his son into Brittany. The Bretons and Chramus were defeated and Chonoober was killed. Clothar died in c.561 so we can date this war to c.558–561.

This Breton ruler is of interest to us as he appears as Conomerus in Welsh tradition. He also appears in saints' hagiographies, including Gildas, and possibly the tale *Tristan*. Further wars erupted involving Waroch II and the Frankish Kings Chilperic in 578 and Guntram in 589, although these are likely too late for our timeframe. Still, it is perhaps telling that even at this late date Gregory portrays the Bretons as influential: Regalis the Bishop of Vannes pleads 'we have to do as the Bretons tell us'.

We thus have a number of events that could conceivably have resulted in either an embassy to Britain, or Britons fighting on the Continent:

1. 464–472 Britons fighting at Bourg-de-Deols and Riothamus defeated by Goths.
2. c.486 Frankish-Roman war results in defeat of last Roman enclave of Soissons.
3. 497 Treaty between Franks and Bretons.
4. 508 Clovis offered consulship by eastern emperor.
5. 530s Britons or Bretons fighting for Frankish kings.
6. 538 Romans offer Britain to the Goths.
7. 558–561 War between Clothar and Chonoober.

It is worth noting that no Continental source, including Procopius, Gregory of Tours or Jordanes, mentions Arthur or any other Arthurian-type figure. Nor do we have any historical gap where an army from Britain could have fought against a resurgent Rome. We are left with two likely scenarios: either

Geoffrey simply invented the whole thing to legitimise Anglo-Norman rule, or he exaggerated one of the events above. It is worth noting that no insular Welsh source places Arthur in Gaul.

Nevertheless, there was a common belief in Arthur as a historical figure in Brittany as well as Cornwall and Wales.[12] Brittany was maybe the main, if not only, route by which the legend entered the Continent.[13] In addition to the *Legenda Sancti Goeznovii*, another Saint's Life, St Efflam, connects King Arthur with Brittany. The tale can be traced back to Albert le Grand, monk of Morlaix, in the sixteenth century.

Efflam was an Irish prince who ran away from his new bride, Enora, on their wedding night to avoid breaking his vow of chastity. He sailed across the sea and landed at Lieu de Grève in the bay of Plestin-les-Grèves. Arthur had been staying with Hoel, Duke of Armorica, and assisting him in ridding the land of a dragon. For several days Arthur and his men tried to lure the beast from its cave to no avail.

Efflam and his small retinue were washed ashore in their wicker coracle and greeted by Arthur, who titles himself 'Arthur of Britain' and not, it is important to note, Armorica. As Efflam tells Arthur his tale, the dragon appears: one red eye in the centre of his forehead, shoulders covered with green scales like plates of mail, a powerful, long, black tail and a huge mouth with tusks like a wild boar. Arthur grabs his sword, Excalibur, and leads his knights into battle. For three days they fought and the dragon retreated to its lair as Arthur fell exhausted, craving water.

The saint produced clear water from a stone for Arthur to drink and marched up to the cave to renew the struggle on Arthur's behalf. All night he prayed and then at sunrise he commanded the dragon to depart. The beast roared out of the cave vomiting fire and blood, climbed a nearby rock and then crashed dead into the sea.

St Efflam settled in the region. His wife followed him to Brittany and was pursued by a local lord. This local lord was overcome by a miraculous paralysis and forced to repent by the saint. Efflam's death is dated to c.512 and thus his floruit is slightly earlier than the other Saints' Lives referencing Arthur. Evidence for medieval attitudes to Arthurian legend in the region is found in the writings of Adam of Tewksbury writing c.1170:[14] He stated that 'Arthur the Briton's' fate is considered unknown and if you were to travel to Armorica and claim he had died as other men die, you would likely be cursed or stoned. If you escaped unharmed you would discover that, 'Merlin the prophet spoke truly when he said that Arthur's departure would be obscured by doubt'.

French Romances

The reign of Henry II from 1153 was the catalyst for adapting the HRB to Anglo-Norman by Wace.[15] This in turn was an important step towards inspiring the courtly romances of Chrétien de Troyes. The French Romances were largely written between 1170–1280. The exploits of Arthur's knights described in Wace and some later tales take place in roughly the same time period:[16] The twelve years of peace the HRB claims Arthur enjoyed before the wars with the Romans.

The earliest surviving manuscripts of French Arthurian literature are from the last years of the twelfth century.[17] Our first example, Wace, was a Jersey-born cleric active in Caen. His *Roman de Brut*, c.1155. became *the* French version of Geoffrey's HRB and he was rewarded by Henry II of England. His most important addition was that of the Round Table, but in general Wace followed the the structure and sequence of events in HRB.

A decade-and-a-half later two other writers, Beroul and Thomas, allowed Arthur a small role in the story of *Tristan and Iseult*. Tristan being a Cornish knight involved in a love affair with an Irish princess and fiancée of King Mark of Cornwall. By the thirteenth century the story had become even more deeply embedded in an Arthurian world.

Robert de Boron's *Joseph d'Arimathie* (Joseph of Arimethea), was written in the late twelfth century. In the tale the narrator, a hermit living in the year 717, was given a divine book which he was commanded to translate. The following narrative can be divided into three sections. The first covers the burial of Jesus by Joseph of Arimathea, before which he collects drops of the Lord's blood in the Grail. Joseph and his son, Josephé, journey across several countries with the Grail, converting people along the way. After many adventures they come to Britain, bringing the Grail to the valley of Avaron (later translated as Avalon and associated with Glastonbury). It introduces many of the places and themes used in later tales.[18] Most notably the Rich Fisher King who is entrusted with the Grail. It is essentially a tale of conversion and the expansion of the Christian faith.[19] In Robert de Boron's *Merlin*, the author expands on the HRB while making Merlin's role more prominent. He introduces the sword in an anvil resting on a stone.

By the time Chrétien de Troyes began his work, in the last quarter of the twelfth century, there was already a rich Arthurian literary tradition in France. Yet his contribution is seen as 'highly original' and 'immense' in inventing a 'new fictional genre'.[20] He wrote five Arthurian romances: *Erec et Enide, Cligés, Lancelot* (or *Chevalier de la charrette*), *Yvain* (or *Chevalier au lion*) and *Perceval* (or *Conte de Graal*). His tales focused on quests of the Knights of the Round

Table. He is the first writer to introduce Lancelot, together with his affair with Guinevere. He also introduced the quest for the Holy Grail and the figure of The Fisher King.

This inspired unknown authors to write what became known as the Vulgate Cycle (*Lancelot-Grail* or *Prose Lancelot*) between 1210–1230. Galahad's quest for the Grail being one of the central themes: *Estoire del Saint Graal, Estoire de Merlin, Lancelot propre, Quest del Saint Graal, Mort Artu*.

Dated to a decade or more later, the Post-Vulgate Cycle significantly influenced Thomas Malory's work two centuries later. It includes similar works to those listed above. It introduces Arthur's incestuous affair which produces Mordred, links Tristan to the Grail Quest and has Arthur receiving Excalibur from the Lady in the Lake. To get a flavour of the Romances we will turn to perhaps the most famous of the French authors.

Chrétien de Troyes (c.1130–1191)

Erec et Enide

Arthur and his men are engaged in a stag hunt near Cardigan. Erec accompanies Guinevere but in the forest they are confronted by a strange knight, Yder, a maiden, and Yder's dwarf. The knight treats Guinevere's servant roughly and the queen orders Erec to follow him. In a far off town Erec defeats the knight, meets Enide and returns to Arthur's court with her.

They marry and are initially happy. But Erec overhears Enide crying over rumours that her husband neglects his knightly duties. He commands her to follow him in silence. They go through a number of adventures with Enide repeatedly breaking her promise, though remaining loyally by his side despite his harshness.

Giants, thieves and a villainous count are all despatched and there is a brief episode when they reunite with Arthur's men. Erec eventually forgives Enide for the perceived transgressions and they are reconciled. The tale ends with them being crowned king and queen at Nantes.

This is fundamentally the same story as Geraint and Enide from the Red Book of Hergest referred to earlier. However, it is thought the Welsh version derives from Chrétien rather than the other way round.

Cligés

The tale begins in Greece with the son of the Greek emperor Alexander travelling to Arthur's court in Britain. he becomes a knight and falls in love with Arthur's niece, Soredamors. They have a child, Cligés. Alexander returns to Greece to find his brother, Alis, has stolen the throne after their father's death. Alexander agrees to accept this on the condition that Alis remains unmarried and childless and Cligés is next in line.

Alexander dies and Alis breaks his promise and marries Fenice. Cligés and Fenice fall in love but Cligés follows in his father's footsteps and travels to Arthur's court where he is knighted. Returning home he and Fenice manage to escape together and but they are tracked down. He turns to Arthur for help, but while away Alis dies. Cligès and Fenice are free to marry, and Cligès becomes the emperor of Greece.

Lancelot (or Chevalier de la charrette)
Guinevere is abducted by Maleagant and Arthur sends Gawain in pursuit. He meets an unnamed knight who turns out to be Lancelot. The latter is forced to travel by cart, a dishonourable form of transport, which gives the story its title. Many trials and battles later, Lancelot finds Guinevere in Maleagant's castle at Gorre. Lancelot breaks into the tower and the pair share a passionate night together. He then challenges her captor to fight. An agreement is made to postpone the fight for a year.

Lancelot is tricked and taken prisoner while Guinevere is allowed home. A year passes and a disguised Lancelot is allowed out to fight in the tournament. At first he is victorious but Guinevere, suspecting it is Lancelot, sends her maid to command him to lose every bout, which he duly does. Convinced it is her lover, the next day she commands him to win, a tale copied in the 2001 film, *A Knight's Tale* starring Heath Ledger; Lancelot defeats all comers and then returns to captivity as promised. They agree another fight in a year's time but Maleagant conspires to have Lancelot locked away in an impregnable fortress. The following year Gawain is forced to fight in Lancelot's absence. Lancelot escapes and arrives just in time for the fight where he kills Maleagant. Being in public, the lovers tentatively embrace at the end.

Yvain (or Chevalier au lion)
Yvain seeks to avenge his cousin, Calogrenant, who was defeated by the knight Exclados in the forest of Brocéliande. Yvain is victorious and, with the help of the servant Lunete, marries his widow, Laudine. Gawain persuades Yvain to embark on a chivalric adventure and Laudine agrees when he promises to return within the year. Yvain forgets his promise and Laudine rejects him.

Yvain goes mad with grief. He is cured by a noble woman and tries to win back his wife. First he rescues a lion from a dragon and the beast proves a loyal companion on further quests, giving the story its title. Demons, three knights and a giant are defeated before he rescues Lunete from being burned at the stake. She helps Yvain win back his wife and he returns home with the lion at his side.

Perceval (or Conte de Graal)

Perceval was raised by his mother in Wales. One day he meets a group of knights and is so impressed he decides to travel to Arthur's court. Kay is rude to him but Perceval defeats a knight who has been troubling Arthur and sets out on an adventure. He rescues his love, Blanchefleur, and sends her captors to Arthur's court with his vow of revenge on Kay. On his adventures he encounters the Fisher King and sees a procession, part of which includes the *graal*.

Eventually Arthur and his knights catch up with Perceval and, after beating Kay and breaking his arm, Perceval agrees to return to Arthur's court. It is revealed the Grail contained a single host which sustained the wounded father of the Fisher King. The story turns to Gawain who liberates a castle containing he long-lost mother Morgause, and his grandmother Ygerne. The tale breaks off unfinished.

We can see in table 8 that the Vulgate and Post-Vulgate cycles were written a generation or two after Chrétien's work. In addition, we recall that three of his stories, *Erec et Enide*, *Yvain* and *Perceval* inspired three Welsh versions: *Geraint and Enid*; *Owain or Lady of the Fountain*; and *Peredur son of Efrawg*.

Table 8: The Vulgate and Post-Vulgate Cycles.

Cycle	Contents	Comments
Vulgate Cylcle or **Prose Lancelot** Unknown 1210–1230 French	Estoire del Saint Grail Estoire de Merlin Lancelot Propre Quest del Saint Graal Mort Artu	Introduced more Christian themes and Galahad's quest for the Grail.
Post-Vulgate Cycle Unknown 1230–1240 French	Estoire del Saint Grail Estoire de Merlin Quest del Saint Graal Mort Artu	Introduced Arthur's incestuous affair which produces Mordred. First to include receiving Excalibur from the Lady in the Lake. Links Tristan to the Grail Quest.

We will now turn to some of the themes that appear to have been introduced by French writers post-Galfridian.

The Round Table

First introduced by Wace in *Roman de Brut*, c.1155. It is not mentioned by Chrétien but does appear later in Robert de Boron's *Merlin*. Wace claimed it was created to prevent quarrels among Arthur's men. Layamon's *Brut*, c.1190, expanded on the tale adding it was made by a Cornish carpenter after violence at a Christmas feast. Traditional Welsh sources have no such tales but various Knights of the Round Table became central to many tales. Wace specifically cites the Bretons as telling many stories about the Round Table.[21] The implication is that the concept came from the Continent and was introduced into the tales by Bretons. Importantly none of these early tales describe the table. Later French Romances differ in the size and number of seats. The symbolism seems far more important than the physical characteristics.

A historical Round Table was made for Roger II of Sicily in c.1154.[22] It is also thought that Charlemagne (742–814) possessed a round table decorated with a map of Rome. References to this are found in two sources:[23] the contemporary Frankish scholar Einhard in *Vita Karoli Magni*, and a Benedictine monk, Notker the Stammerer, a few decades later in *De Carolo Magno*.

Its absence from Welsh tradition and the HRB raises some suspicion as to where Wace got the concept from. We have two sources confirming Charlemagne possessed such a table. There was a body of medieval literature concerned with the 'Matter of France' (also known as the Carolingian cycle). This focused on the exploits of Charlemagne and his knights. His Paladins, twelve legendary knights, performed similar chivalric and romantic exploits. The Arthurian legends cannot be seen in isolation from the rest of medieval literature. This seems a clear case of Wace lifting a concept from Charlemagne's life and using it in his tale of Arthur.

The Round Table hanging in The Great Hall at Winchester Castle has long been known to be a 'medieval fake', dated to the late thirteenth century and thus to the reign of Edward I.[24] The first record of it appears in 1464 by a John Hardyng. A century later John Leland viewed it as material proof of Arthur's historicity, noting that Edward, surnamed the *longe*, made much of the 'round order of the Knights'.[25]

Earlier we noted that Merlin was a creation of Geoffrey of Monmouth. A historical Arthur without Merlin might be difficult for some to accept. Here we have the first attested appearance of The Round Table decades after the HRB. If we take the evidence at face value, the most likely explanation is Wace used his imagination or knowledge of Charlemagne's table. There is certainly no mention of a round table in any of the early Welsh tales.

Arthur's sword

The earliest name is Caledfwlch in *Culhwch and Olwen*. This might be connected to the sword of Fergus mac Róich in Irish mythology, here called

Caladcolc or *Caladbolg*. The etymology of the name being 'hard-cleft'. Here though the sword can be monstrously large and chop off the tops of hills. In the HRB Geoffrey names the sword Caliburnus, and later French writers changed this to Calibor(e) or Escalibor(e). It is Malory we have to thank for the modern Excalibur. Robert de Boron first introduced the concept of the sword in an anvil upon a stone and Arthur being chosen as king. Later tales confuse the issue introducing two swords, Excalibur being received from the Lady in the Lake after the first sword broke. After Camlan, the French Romances have the knight Griflet return Excalibur to the lake; in Malory it is Bedivere.

A number of theories have been put forward for the source of this legend:

- A medieval sword of Saint Galgano (1148–1181) is embedded in rock in the Abbey of San Galgano in Italy and may have influenced Robert who was writing soon after.
- The 'London Stone' is a block of Limestone that was once a medieval landmark. Striking a stone with a sword was a popular medieval concept to signal authority. In John Cade's rebellion in 1450 he is said to have struck the stone with his sword and declared himself Lord Mayor.
- The use of a stone mould to cast metal would result in the sword being drawn from the stone once cooled (unlikely as swords of this period tended to be pattern-welded rather than cast in moulds).
- Possible confusion between Latin word for stone, *saxum* similar to *saxonum* for Saxon.

Of these, perhaps only the first is plausible as there is indeed an apparently twelfth-century sword embedded in rock which can still be seen today at the Rotunda at Montesiepi, near the ruins of the Abbey of San Galgano. Galgano died in c.1181 and it is likely Robert de Boron was aware of the legend.

Alternatively, in Norse legends Odin plunges the sword Gram into a tree, declaring whoever can pull it out can keep it a a gift. The hero, Sigmund, is the only one able to retrieve it and he uses it on many of his adventures. The Alans in the fourth century were reported to worship a sword 'fixed in the ground'.[26] However, there is no indication of anything resembling the themes in the Arthurian tales. Nor is there anything linking this practise with Sarmatians in the second century, a theory we will cover later.

Over 200 examples of named swords appear in several later Anglo-Saxon and Norse sagas and poems.[27] Although the earliest is dated to the tenth century. Welsh tradition also has named swords: *Dyrnwyn*, 'white-hilt', was owned by Rhydderch Hael, and was one of 'The Thirteen Treasures of Britain'.

Only a worthy man could draw it, at which point it came alight with fire. Inscriptions appear on hilts, scabbards and, less commonly, on blades. These often refer to the makers or owner:[28] 'Sigimer named the sword'; 'Audmundr made me, Asleikr owns me'; 'Biorhtelm made me, Sigeberiht owns me'; or simply 'Leofric made me'. While this practice may well go back to the fifth-century, we cannot tell if a Brythonic warrior of this period did the same.

I would suggest the simplest explanation is that early Welsh bards named Arthur's sword with a similar name to one found in Irish mythology. Later, Robert de Boron, hearing of the Legend of St Galgano, simply adapted and added it to the tale. Or, perhaps less likely, borrowed the pagan-Germanic tales of Odin thrusting *Gram* into the tree. Whatever the case, the important point is the concept of pulling a sword out of something to confer Arthur's kingship does not appear in the early traditional Welsh tales. Nor does it appear in HRB – and Geoffrey of Monmouth was not a man shy of playing fast and loose with history, nor averse to adding imaginative mythical elements. It might be worth noting Charlemagne also had a famous sword, *Joyeuse*, which today sits in the Louvre museum (although there are debates about this sword's actual date).

Arthur no doubt had a sword. A pattern welded *spathe*-type, hung from a strap across the shoulder.

Sidonius, in the fifth century, describes guests at a wedding of a Burgundian princess:[29] 'Green mantles ... with crimson borders. Baldrics supported swords hung from their shoulders.' A letter written by a secretary of Theodoric the Great (reigned 493–526) describes swords, 'capable even of cutting through armour, which I prize more for their iron than for the gold upon them'.[30] They were valuable items with a well-made sword taking seventy-four hours to manufacture, together with scabbards and fittings.[31] It has been estimated that a high status example might cost as much in modern terms as a quarter of a million pounds, or a Ferrari sports car.[32]

While the Romans did not generally name their swords, by the tenth century Welsh poems and tales were as keen to include named swords as Anglo-Saxon and Viking sagas. We have no way of knowing if sixth-century Britons named theirs. If it had a name it would be have been closer to Caledfwlch than a Latinised Caliburn. Certainly not Excalibur. Nor would he have received it from a maiden lying about in pools of water, any more than pulling it from a stone or anvil. Like the Round Table, it appears the 'Sword in a Stone' trope was created by French Romance writers, this time Robert de Boron. This will not be the last Arthurian theme to bite the dust.

Camelot

We recall an early Welsh Triad naming three of Arthur's courts: Pen Rhionydd in the north; Celliwig in Cornwall and Mynyw in Wales (St David's). It is Geoffrey in the HRB who places Arthur at Caerleon which is reflected in a later Triad replacing St David's with the former Roman legionary base. Chrétien de Troyes introduces Camelot for the first time but only mentions it in passing, placing it close to Caerleon. Later writers increased its importance and downplayed Caerleon.

Other tales name different sites: Quimper in Brittany in the Lancelot Romance; Carduel, Wales in Chretien's *The Knight and the Lion* (unidentified); Cardigan in Chrétien's *Erec and Enide*; and Stirling in Beroul's twelfth-century *Tristan*. But it is Camelot which has fired readers' imaginations from the late-twelfth century to the present. This has caused some to search for any place that might be connected to the name.

Perhaps the most obvious is Camelon, a Roman fort just north of the Antonine Wall. A similar idea links Camelot to the Roman name for Colchester, Camulodunum, with the Roman fort at Slack in Yorkshire being suggested for the same reason. Malory places it at Winchester, but Carlisle, Cadbury Castle and many others all have their proponents.

Rather than consider in depth the various theories and twisted etymologies put forward, this can be resolved fairly quickly. At the very start of *The Knight of the Cart*, Chrétien states that Arthur held court at Camelot, 'in the region near Caerleon' (with variant spellings across manuscripts: Chamalot; Camehelot; Chamaalot; and Camalot). Elsewhere Chrétien follows Geoffrey in regarding Caerleon as Arthur's principal court. In fact an early manuscript uses the Old French phrase *con lui plot*, 'as he pleased', instead of the name, *Chamalot*.

Chrétien's five Romances follow a similar pattern: a knight sets out from Arthur's court, has adventures, achieves some goal enabling him to return as a hero and receives the recognition he deserves. *Erec* begins at Cardigan, *Cliges* at Winchester, *Charette* at Camelot and *Yvain* and *Perceval* at Carduel. This last appears as a regular name for Carlisle in the middle ages, yet Chretien places it in Wales.[33] Although he may have viewed Cumbria as Welsh speaking. Only *Erec* ends at a named place, Tintagel. Thus Camelot as a place is not given any importance to the writer who first used the phrase.

The logical conclusion to this may feel like an anathema to die-hard Arthur enthusiasts. What is Arthur without Camelot? Yet it is very clear that no early source references Camelot at all. The earliest Welsh tradition places his court at Celliwig in Cornwall while the HRB moves it to Caerleon. The latter even Chrétien accepts as the location of Arthur's main court. Subsequent writers from c.1200 onwards took the name *Camelot* from Chrétien's passing comment in one story and ran with it. Hundreds of years later, scores of historians and amateurs have poured over manuscripts and maps in a vain attempt to find the source of a place invented by Chrétien de Troyes and mentioned only briefly.

Summary

The first point we can make is that Geoffrey seems, at the very least, to have exaggerated Arthur's foreign exploits. There is no evidence to support conquests of Denmark, Norway and Gaul by armies from Britain in the fifth or sixth centuries. Nor does his campaign resemble any of the candidates proposed, from Magnus Maximus to Riothamus. The most we can say is a historical Arthur *could* have travelled to Armorica, which would place him at odds with the Franks rather than the Romans. The only conclusion can be this is purely a literary device to please his Norman readers as was the continuous connection with Bretons.

This might also cause us to suspect the family tree proposed by Geoffrey. It is at least possible Arthur's grandfather was a Romano-Gaul who travelled to Britain. We have seen evidence that Britons in fifth-century Gaul which, along with place-name evidence, supports the literary tradition of a movement of Britons to north-west Gaul. Given the political situation as the Western Empire fragmented, there is no reason why some individuals did not travel the other way. We certainly have evidence, both archaeological and literary, of Germanic peoples doing just that.

However, it is worth noting that Welsh tradition presents an insular Arthur fighting across Britain and Ireland. The later French Romances derived much of their content from HRB. Some elements of pre-Galfridian Arthurian tradition may well have influenced it as well, although it is arguable the more significant influence was in the other direction, such as the Romance tales involving Owain, Peredur and Geraint. This strongly suggests that any original historical Arthur was wholly concerned with events in Britain.

So far we have met both a mythical and potentially historical figure in the HB. An Arthurian tradition must have developed between the ninth and eleventh centuries, although it was mainly a figure of magic and myth. Geoffrey of Monmouth drew on that to create his immensely influential pseudo-history. For the next 300 years other writers, most notably the French Romances, built on the legend. It acquired some important additions: the Round Table; the Sword in the Stone; and Camelot. At the same time, Welsh tradition maintained a slightly darker, mythical Arthur alongside stories derived from French writers such as Chrétien.

In the late-fifteenth century an unlikely figure attempted to pull together the various strands of the legend while sitting in a London prison. This man was Thomas Malory. His book, *Le Morte D'Arthur*, gave us what many would view as *the* story of Arthur today. It is on this text many a modern Arthurian film and book is based.

Before we turn to that famous book a point needs emphasising. Modern theorists that trawl through the French Romances or late Welsh tradition for evidence of the 'truth' behind the legend are making a fundamental error. All these sources are influenced by, and often derive from, Geoffrey of Monmouth's HRB. They are little more than fan-fiction, many containing transparent additions to, and distortions of, earlier versions. Theories that use Geoffrey's HRB are trusting a source which contains known errors and falsehoods. Trying to find a kernel of truth in his epic pseudo-history is to ignore the fact it is loosely based on a tradition that itself took six centuries to form.

Chapter Eight

Le Morte D'Arthur by Thomas Malory

The first edition of Thomas Malory's *Le Morte D'Arthur* was printed by William Caxton in 1485. That same year, on the field at Bosworth Richard III became the last English king to die in battle. The preface tells us that a *Thomas Malorye* translated certain French books into English. One particular manuscript gives us some clues as to the identity of the author:[1] he was a knight; he translated and wrote the book while in prison; it was completed between 4 March 1469 and 3 March 1470.

A number of candidates have been put forward for the identity of the author and three main ones stand out:[2] a Welshman from near the River Dee; a Thomas Malory from Papworth in Huntingdonshire near Cambridge; and Thomas Malory of Newbold Revel in Warwickshire. Of these, the academic consensus has leaned to the latter. If so, our author led an extremely interesting life.

It must be noted there is not a universal agreement. William Matthews in the *The Ill-Framed Knight* named a significant number of candidates and decided on a Yorkshireman. However, in a more recent book, *The Life and Times of Sir Thomas Malory*, P.C.J. Field falls decisively on the Warwickshire Thomas Malory after a thorough analysis of the evidence and arguments of Williams.[3] One point worth noting: Field suggests evidence for his birth points to c.1416 rather than twenty years earlier as some scholars previously argued.[4]

What is known about the life of this Thomas Malory is every bit as entertaining as an Arthurian tale. A brief look at his life will provide a vivid picture of the sort of man who created the basis of the modern legend. As with Geoffrey of Monmouth 300 years earlier, or indeed Nennius in the ninth century, the author is very much a man of his time. The book is thus a product of the period rather than an accurate portrayal of a historical figure. Written nearly a thousand years after the battle of Badon, and at a time when England had experienced the horror and upheavals of the Wars of the Roses.

Around 1439 Malory was still an esquire in his twenties, but sometime in the 1440s he acquired land and a knighthood.[5] By the end of that decade Malory would have been in his mid-thirties as civil war loomed in England. Malory was possibly living under the patronage of the Earl of Warwick and it is at this point he allegedly turned to a life of crime. The first charge names him, on 4 January 1450, laying in ambush with twenty-six other men in the woods of Combe Abbey, armed to the teeth with bows, crossbows, staves and various other weapons. Their target was the Duke of Buckingham, the arch enemy of Neville, the Earl of Warwick. Buckingham escaped but Malory remained at large with a band of about thirty men.

A few months later, with three other men, he allegedly broke into the house of a Hugh Smyth at Monks Kirby and 'carried off', or 'raped', Hugh's wife, Joan Smyth. Eight weeks later he was accused of the same crime against the same woman, this time at Coventry, taking goods and chattels worth £40 – a considerable sum. His next enterprise was extortion, first of 100 shillings then of 20. By 15 March 1451 the authorities had enough evidence to order his arrest along with nineteen others.

Malory evaded the law and turned to cattle rustling at Cosford, five miles from Newbold: seven cows, two calves, 335 sheep and a cart. This was followed up by another raid netting four oxen. By 31 July a royal commission directed the Earl of Warwick and the Duke of Buckingham to arrest him. But not before Malory managed to steal six does and damage £600 worth of goods at Caludon, a property owned jointly by the Dukes of Norfolk and Buckingham and the Archbishop of Canterbury. Thomas was finally arrested and imprisoned.

Two days later he made a dramatic escape, swam across the moat, and rejoined his band. What follows was perhaps his most audacious raid. He led a band of ten others to a monastery at Combe, stealing gold, silver and jewels belonging to the Abbot. He returned the next day with a force of a hundred men and did considerable damage before taking off with even more loot. He was still at large when charges were brought before the court at Nuneaton on 31 August 1451. By January 1452, two years after this recorded crime spree began, Malory was finally caught and imprisoned a second time at Marshalsea in Southwark, London.

Interestingly, he pleaded not guilty to this long-list of accusations and requested a trial by jury. Some have suggested Thomas may have been innocent and merely a pawn or victim in the machinations between Warwick and Buckingham.

It would appear he had managed to get out again, for in March 1453 came an order for his arrest once more. By the end of the year he was back in jail waiting for a jury to be called. In May 1454 he managed to get released, swearing good conduct and a promise he would return for trial on 29 October. Needless to say he did not attend. The prosecution demanded his guarantors be forced to pay the penalties laid down by the previous court. The guarantors informed the court Malory had a very good reason for not attending. He was already in jail in a different part of the country.

He had used his time on 'bail' to continue his criminal career, this time in Essex. Breaking and entering and burglary landed him in Colchester jail two weeks before his trial on 29 October. He escaped again, fighting his way out with presumably smuggled arms and outside help. Within the month he was back at Marshalsea awaiting trial. He was moved more than once over the next two years: Marshalsea, the Tower, Newgate and Ludgate.

It would appear he was bailed for a short time in 1457, but the last prison records place him at Newgate in 1460. He was thus in and out of jail for a decade while the Lancastrians held the throne. A year later, the Yorkist victory at Towton may have changed his fortunes. He appears to have been free by 1462 when Edward IV was on the throne and Neville of Warwick in the ascendency. A Thomas Malory is recorded as a soldier in a Yorkist force taking part in sieges in the north that year. It is important to note there is no record of him actually being tried, let alone found guilty which has caused some to argue that the author of our tale full of chivalry has been unfairly maligned.

A few years later the machinations of Neville of Warwick, 'The Kingmaker', may have left Malory without a friend in court. We recall *Le Morte D'Arthur* was completed between 4 March 1469 and 3 March 1470. There were already suspicions concerning Warwick's loyalty by the beginning of 1469 and he went into open rebellion in the July. Edward IV was imprisoned, but on his release two months later Warwick fled. It is suggested Thomas found himself back in prison around this time – only now under a Yorkist king. A year later Warwick returned with an army and it was Edward's turn to run. We can see how a knight loyal to Warwick might have to be kept under lock and key during this time. Warwick reinstalled Henry VI as king in October 1470 and it is perhaps at this point Malory was freed for the final time, the manuscript having been completed in prison while Warwick was in exile.

It is not possible to know where Malory's sympathies lay. However, his periods of imprisonment match Warwick's changing allegiances: incarcerated under the Lancastrians; let out after the Yorkist victory of 1461; back in prison when his patron switched sides and fled; finally released when Warwick returned and briefly reinstated Henry VI. Six months later, on 12 March 1471, Sir Thomas Malory died; a month later, the Earl of Warwick fell on the field at Barnet. By May the Lancastrians had been defeated at Tewkesbury and the Yorkists were back in control.

If Thomas Malory of Newbold Revel in Warwickshire was the author of *Le Morte D'Arthur*, then we have a man who might have felt very much at home in Arthur's warband. No stranger to warfare, he spent at least a decade of his life rustling, raiding, breaking out of prison and allegedly raping the same woman twice. If we are generous and point out that he was never convicted, we still have a man who seems to have been active during the wars in which his patron, Neville 'The Kingmaker', played such a central role.

The narrative

Malory gained much of his inspiration from the French Post-Vulgate Cycle of Romances and English translations available to him while in prison. It tells of the adventures of the King Arthur and the Knights of the Round Table. Raised by another family, Arthur miraculously pulls the sword, named Excalibur, from the stone and becomes king. Counselled by Merlin he rules wisely.

When he marries Guinevere her father gifts him the Round Table, around which 150 men can sit.

Knights such as Sir Gawain, his brother Sir Gareth, Sir Tor, and Sir Pellano play prominent parts. Yet, through his valour, it is Lancelot who proves to be the greatest knight.

The tale of Tristan and Isolde is incorporated into the narrative. As is Morgan le Fay as Arthur's sister who betrays him. Arthur is helped by the sorceress Nineve, who learned her magic powers from Merlin before killing him. As in the HRB, Arthur defeats Emperor Lucius of Rome.

Lancelot is in love with Guinevere but is tricked into sleeping with Elayne, daughter of King Pellas, and they have a son, Galahad. Guinevere banishes Lancelot from court and he wanders the land in grief. Elayne and her father cure Lancelot through the Holy Grail and he is welcomed back to Camelot and the Round Table. Galahad joins him and becomes a famous knight, drawing a sword from a floating stone.

Various knights set out on the Quest for the Holy Grail. Lancelot, Perceval and Bors experience deep religious conversion, although Ector and Gawain discover they are not pure enough to achieve it. Galahad, Perceval and Bors meet and continue the Grail Quest. Eventually, Galahad is identified as the knight who will achieve the Grail Quest.

Lancelot returns to court and becomes Guinevere's lover. Prompted by his incestuous son Mordred, Arthur sentences his wife to be burned at the stake. Lancelot rescues her and takes her to his castle of Joyous Gard. Gawain's brothers Gareth and Gaheris are killed and Gawain swears revenge. Lancelot returns Guinevere to Arthur but his supporters are banished. Gawain convinces Arthur to attack Lancelot. During this campaign, Mordred takes the throne and Guinevere for himself. In the subsequent battle Gawain is mortally wounded and Arthur and Mordred fall in battle. Soon after, Lancelot and Guinevere also die and the round table is dispersed.

Discussion

Thomas Malory's *Le Morte D'Arthur* is one of the greatest literary products of the middle-ages. It was hugely influential in the development of the legend and forms the basis of many a modern film and book. It draws upon the plethora of French, Welsh and other Arthurian tales that spread across Europe. Geoffrey's eleventh-century HRB was the catalyst for this explosion in interest. However a pre-Galfridian Arthurian tradition was popular, as evidenced by the Cathedral in Modena, the Life of Saint Cadoc and the earliest Welsh tales such as *Culhwch and Olwen*, *Pa Gur* and *Preiddeu Annwn*. It is impossible to tease out memories of threads of a historical figure from fan-fiction written centuries after equally dubious pseudo-histories, themselves written centuries after the alleged events.

We might find hints of a proto-Arthurian tradition in the earliest of sources. It is perhaps ironic and unfortunate that one of the results of Geoffrey of Monmouth's success is to doubt anything that comes after him. It is to just such evidence we will now turn. The genealogies pertaining to Arthur are all relatively late. It should be remembered that such genealogies were often constructed for contemporary political reasons. However, it is interesting that they maintain a similar tradition and it is one with an important distinction from that in the HRB. Could this be a half-remembered thread of a historical Arthur?

Chapter Nine

Genealogies

This is a difficult subject to get the grips with. The multitude of unfamiliar, and often similar, names can be very confusing. Compounded by the tendency of medieval scribes to adopt a variety of different spellings for the same name. This chapter will attempt to simplify this tricky subject. We must remember the genealogies that have survived are all late. None can be entirely trusted. Many were written centuries or a millennia after a potential historical Arthur.

We have already seen that some information concerning Arthur's family tree can be gleaned from *Culhwch and Olwen* and Geoffrey's HRB. The genealogies in this chapter are all post-Galfridian. However, there is an interesting consistency. Notably, they not only place Arthur within a list of kings of Britain, but show how he is connected to other figures who appear throughout the tradition. Importantly, none support any identification proposed by the myriad of modern theories. So while these genealogies are late and untrustworthy, they are important in demonstrating who writers in the middle-ages believed Arthur to be – and also reveal who they believed him not to be. Before turning to the lists of kings we must begin with his name: Arthur.

The name

The first point to emphasise is that a historical Arthur in the late fifth- or early sixth-century Britain would have been Christian. We get a hint of this in the imagery in the battle list of the HB and the entry for Badon in the AC. In both he is depicted as carrying Christian imagery. In the HB at the eighth battle at Guinnion Fort he carries the 'image of the holy Mary, the everlasting virgin, on his shoulders'. In the AC at Badon, Arthur 'carried the Cross of our Lord Jesus Christ for three days and three nights on his shoulders'. It is possible these Christian attributes were both late inventions and additions. However, we recall the evidence suggests indigenous paganism was in rapid decline by the end of the fourth century and was all but absent by the mid-fifth.[1]

Some Romans still clung to the old gods. A certain Volusianus, from a priestly family, blamed the sack of Rome in 410 on the neglect of Rome's traditional gods.[2] In contrast, Christianity had flourished by the time Constantine III took much of the remaining garrison to Gaul in 407, a generation after Theodosius the Great made Christianity the official state religion. Britain had a number of bishoprics, most urban centres had large churches and the population was 'mostly Christian'.[3] Twenty years later St Germanus travelled to Britain, not to combat paganism, but a heretical version of Christianity: Pelagiansim. Perhaps a century later, Gildas castigates the Britons in general and five tyrant kings in general. Though guilty of many sins, paganism isn't among them.

Concerning his name, the main debate lies in whether it is Latin or Brythonic. An etymology from the Latin name Artorius has been described as 'phonologically perfect'.[4] Indeed, the first attested reference, in the earliest manuscript of the HB, has *Arturus*. Arturus, or the more classical Arcturus, are both perfectly acceptable derivations from Artorius.[5] The only person Gildas names as leading the fight back is described as a Roman and has a very Roman sounding name, Ambrosius Aurelianus. It would be no surprise if civilian or military elites had Roman names whether they were Roman or Britons.

Breaking the name down, Griffin, in *Names from the Dawn of British Legend*, suggests it has an astrological connection[6] deriving from the 'guardian of the bear', referring to a well known star in the constellation of Bootes, next to the constellation of Ursa Major, The Great Bear. Thus the name could be taken to mean the brightest star in Bootes, the Guardian of the Bear.

The name was fairly common in Roman times. The gens Artoria was a minor plebeian family. However, the name Artorius is found in freedmen and senators alike. One Artorius appears later as one of the more imaginative candidates for Arthur. Lucius Artorius Castus served as a Praefectus of the Sixth Legion at York in the late second to early third century. We will come back to him in greater detail in the next chapter.

Thus is it perfectly plausible Arthur comes from the Latin. This doesn't mean he was a Roman of course. Simply that he bore a Roman name. Indeed many a Welsh king followed the same practise. Latin names such as Tacitus and Constantinus changed to Tegid and Custennin respectively. We also see the name Gaius in Arthur's favoured companion, Kai.

However not everyone in Roman Britain spoke Latin and there are many who support a Brythonic etymology. One of the earliest appearances may be in the Welsh poem *Y Gododdin*. The first part of the name, *Arth*, is commonly accepted as 'Bear' – a rough, unmannerly or fierce person.[7] Against this is the fact the ending, *-ur*, is not common in Bythronic languages. The ending 'ur' may have come from 'gwr' meaning man. However the -wr and -ur sounds are different and in Welsh poetry Arthur is always rhymed with -ur endings. Additionally, 'gwr' was earlier 'gur' and thus one might expect to see examples of figures named *Artgur* by the ninth century. However, no such examples exist.

This might lead us to suspect a Latin etymology is more likely. Yet we have seen how the earliest appearances of Arthur are attached to Irish dynasties: Arthur ap Pedr of Dyfed (late sixth century); Artuir mac Áedáin of the Gaelic kingdom Dalriada (late sixth century); Artur ap Bicuir (seventh century); and Artur, grandfather of Faradach (late seventh century).

Another suggestion is the name is a nickname, 'bear-man'. This conveniently allows theorists to propose anyone they like, however named. All that is required is some bear-like imagery or connection. One example comes from *De excidio* where Gildas calls Cuneglasus, 'bear ... driver of a chariot of the bear's stronghold'.[8] In the *Dialogue of Arthur and the Eagle* (fourteenth century but possibly as early as twelfth), Arthur is described as leading the 'battalions of Cornwall', 'bear of men' and 'bear of the host'.[9] A thirteenth-century copy of HB references Arthur as meaning 'horrible bear'.

However, in every story or poem our hero is called Arthur or some derivative. It is important to note that names such as Athrwys are not connected to Arthur. This name comes from a separate, and well documented, root as does the often misspelling, Arthwys.[10] Nor does Athrwys derive from the Latin, Artorius. We can therefore dismiss any name that is not etymologically similar.

Some have also attempted to connect his name to deities: *Artio* a Gaulish bear goddess from Switzerland; *Artaius*, another Gaulish god, linked to the Roman god Mercury but thought to derive from the Gaulish *artos*, meaning bear; and a Celtic god, *Matunus*, which derives from the Celtic *matu-*, also meaning bear. Despite the many mythological and magical elements in early Arthurian tales, there is no suggestion that he is some sort of god.

If we dismiss nicknames, gods and Arth-, or Ath-, type names, what are we left with? Importantly, we can conclude that the sources all regard Arthur as his personal name. Regardless of what it means or where it comes from, he is always referred to as Arthur. Whether it's the Arturus of the early HB, Artus in the doorway of Modena Cathedral or simply Arthur from many a Welsh tale.

There are still many who prefer a Brythonic derivation.[11] Others, however, view a Latin derivation from Artorius as more likely.[12] In many ways this is academic. The Western Roman Empire had fallen by the timeframe of a historical Arthur. Roman rule in Britain had ended decades before. Someone born in the late-fifth century might be able to ask his grandparents if they remember the visit of St Germanus or the reign of Vortigern; few alive would have experienced Britain under direct Roman rule.

The name was rare in medieval Wales with Arthur ap Pedr of Dyfed being the only pre-sixteenth-century example. No known examples exist in Wales until the mid-sixteenth century and then only on four occasions.[13] There is a distinction between the search of a historical figure of the fifth to sixth centuries and the academic study of Arthurian literature (usually between the twelfth and sixteenth centuries). Scott, *The Arthurian Place Names of Wales*, states there are two types of Arthurian place names: those that contain the name Arthur and those associated with him in folklore or literature.[14] Many of these names are first attested during the nineteenth century. Scott provides an invaluable Chronological list of all Arthurian place names in Wales with the earliest dated to c.1100.[15]

In summary, given the name's relative absence from Welsh genealogies, it is suggested a Latin origin is more likely. Gildas made some clear ethnic distinctions. The Britons were his 'fellow-citizens', tyrant kings as well. Ambrosius was almost 'the last of the Roman race'. Saxons were barbarians, 'hated by God and men'. Whether Arthur was a Roman, indigenous Brythonic warrior or Romano-Briton, the sources regard him as fighting alongside the 'Kings of the Britons'. Regardless of his exact ethnicity he was always referred to as Arthur. So it is Arthur we must search for in the genealogies.

The genealogies

We have seen how Arthurian traditions evolved over the centuries. The HRB may have popularised the legends and spawned a whole genre of writers who, in turn, produced distinctive French Romances. Yet an older Welsh tradition also survived which hints at a darker more mythical figure. These tales place

Table 9: Genealogies of Welsh kings and saints

Genealogy	Date	Kingdoms	Comment
Harleian	Compiled tenth century, earliest copy c.1100	Various Welsh kingdoms from fifth century, such as Gwynedd, Powys, Ceredigion	Descendants of Cunedda. Includes Welsh kings and saints. British library (MS 3859) also contains *Annales Cambriae* and *Historia Brittonum*.
Bonedd Gwyr y Gogledd (Descent of the Men of the North)	Earliest manuscript thirteenth century	Various northern Brittonic kingdoms from fifth century such as Rheged, Alt Clud, Elmet	Descendants of Coel Hen
Jesus College (MS 20)	Late fourteenth century	Various Welsh kingdoms from fifth century from South Wales	Various Welsh lineages

Arthur in the landscape of Britain in a large arc from Cornwall, through Wales to southern Scotland. They also point to the same relatively narrow timeframe of c.480–540. Such a man could fight at *mons Badonicus* c.500, interact with various saints and kings in the early sixth century and fight his final battle at Camlan in c.537/542.

Having covered *when* and *where*, it is now necessary to look at *who* Arthur may have been. The first point to note is that none of the earliest Welsh genealogies mention Arthur.[16] The later examples are even more suspect than the earliest king lists. The three main genealogies can be seen in table nine.

Ben Guy's 2020 book, *Medieval Welsh Genealogy, An Introduction and Textual Study*, is a must-have for modern Arthurian scholars. As can be seen in the table below, the manuscripts containing the relevant genealogies post-date the HRB.

Table 10: Manuscript dates.

	Date
Jesus 20 Genealogies	thirteenth to fifteenth century
Gwehelyth Morgannwg	seventeenth century
The Llywelyn ab Iorwerth genealogies	fourteenth century
The Llywelyn ab Iorwerth genealogies, Gutun Owain recension	Fifteenth to sixteenth century
Mostyn genealogies	fourteenth century
The Cwtta Cyfarwydd genealogies	fifteenth century

Some versions place Arthur not in relation to his ancestors, but rather in a list of 'High-Kings'. Jesus 20 Genealogies contains such a list of kings. The portion that concerns us is as follows:[17] Gwertheuyr Vendigeit (Vortigern), Emrys Wledic (Ambrosius Aurelianus), Vthur Pendreic (Uther), Arthur, Constantius, Aurelius, Iuor, Maelgvn Gvyned (Maelgwn), Caterius, Catwallavn, Catwaladyr Vendigeit.

This line of succession, Vortigern-Ambrosius-Uther-Arthur, appears to derive from the HRB. Here Arthur is followed by Gildas' five tyrant kings.

It must be noted there is no evidence the Britons had a concept of 'high kingship'. Yet we recall Gildas referring to a 'proud tyrant', leader of a council. It is just plausible such a position existed. Either evolving from the position of Roman *vicarius*, governor, or the 'unofficial' acknowledgement of the most powerful petty king. Again we recall Gildas' description of Maelgwn: 'mightier than many … higher than almost all the generals in Britain'.[18]

Other texts also mention Arthur:

> The Gwehelyth Morgannwg manuscript:[19] ...Dyfrig sant, archesgob pennaf Ynys Brydain a goronawdd Arthur (Dyfrig saint, the archbishop of the British Isles and the great Arthur);

> The Llywelyn ab Iorwerth genealogies:[20] (Yaen mab?) Kyduan mab Arthur; and also:[21] weithion y dywedwn vonedd wehelydion kymru y rei a wledychynt er yn oes Arthur hyt yn oes feibion Rodri Mawr (works that tell of the honour of the Welsh nobles who ruled since the time of Arthur until the time of the sons of Rodri Mawr).

If his place in a series of 'High-Kings' is consistent, what of Arthur's direct family tree. The Llywelyn ab Iorwerth genealogies, Gutun Owain recension, provide the missing figures between Geoffrey of Monmouth's Conanus Meriadocus and Aldroneus:[22] Arthur ap Vthur ap Kustenin (Constantine) ap Kadvor ap Tvdwal ap Morvawr (Meriadocus) ap Evdaf (Eudaf).

Arthur is named the son of Eigr, daughter of Amlawd Wledig. We also find Arthur's half-brother, Cador, as *Kadwr*: Kwstenin ap Kadwr ap Gwrlais iarll Kerniw (Constantine son of Cador son of Gorlois Earl of Cornwall).

Two other genealogies are similar:

> Mostyn genealogies:[23] Arthur map Vthyr map Kustenhin map Kynuavr map Tutwal map Moruavr map Eudaf...

> The Cwtta Cyfarwydd genealogies:[24] Arthur vab Vther vab Kustennin Venigeit v Kynor v Tutwal v Turmvr Moruavr V Karadoc

We can see these three sources in figure 20. The figure of Moruavr is the same Conanus Meriadocus from the HRB which places him four generations before Aldroneus, King of Armorica. It is Arthur's paternal grandfather, Constantine, the brother of Aldroneus, who comes to the aid of the Britons and is crowned king. Figure 20 shows the Welsh versions of his name: Kustenhin, Kustennin Vendigeit, or Kustenin.

This mass of different names and variant spellings might cause the reader to shrug and wonder why this matters. Those above don't contradict the HRB. However, other genealogies referencing the same figures clearly point not to Armorica, but Devon and Cornwall. We recall the similarity in place names between the two regions and the apparent movement of people in the fifth century.

Genealogies

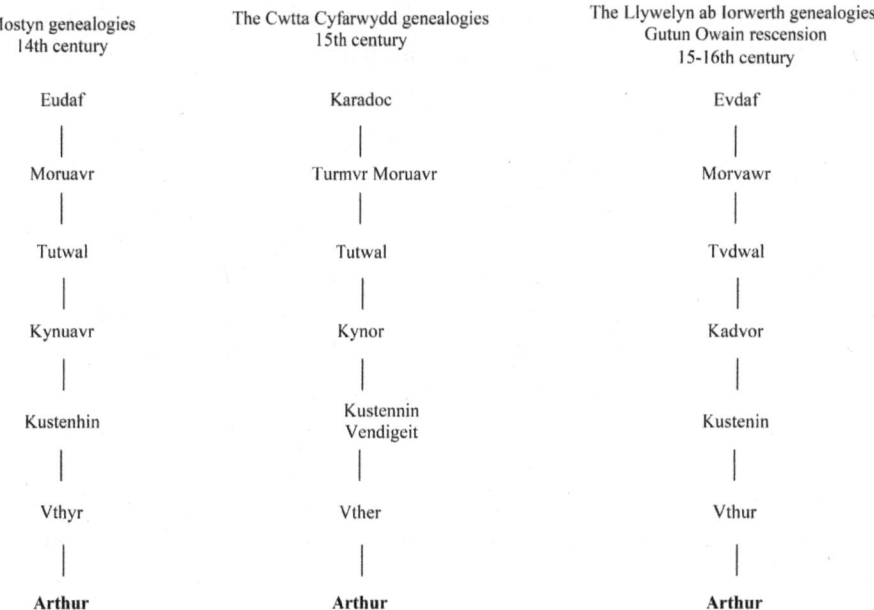

Figure 20: Genealogies showing Arthur's paternal family tree.

The Jesus 20 Genealogies provides the ancestry of Geraint:[25] Geraint map Erbin map Kynvavr map Tudwavl map Gvrwavr. We recall from *Geraint and Enid*, Geraint's father, Erbin son of Custennin, rules in Cornwall. Here, then, Erbin is brother of Uther and thus Geraint is Arthur's cousin. In *Brut y Brenhinedd* Constantine's name is Custennin Fendigaid rather than Kustennin Vendigeit (from the Cwtta Cyfarwydd genealogies). Another version can be found in *Bonedd y Saint*, which importantly names Erbin's father as Custennin Goreu. His cognomen clearly points to the West Country as it derives from *Gornou*, 'of Cornwall'.

This enables us to construct a family tree for Arthur's paternal line, with the only difference being (aside from spellings) the relationship of Erbin and Geraint to Arthur. Some historians, such as Chadwick, have found 'no valid reason for doubting the authenticity of the genealogy

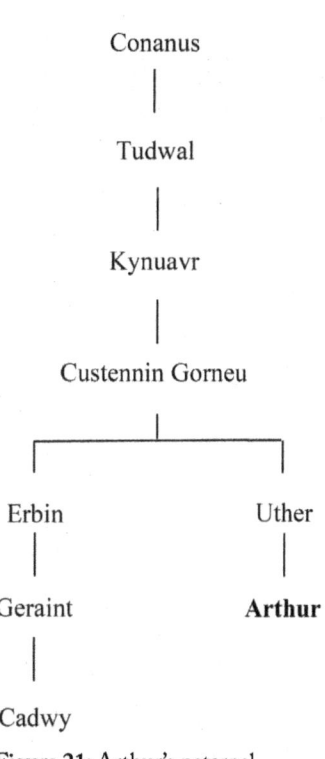

Figure 21: Arthur's paternal Dumnonian family tree.

recorded in the *Bonedd y Saint*, which I have recreated in figure 21.[26] Bartrum is equally certain that Arthur's grandfather is identified as Custennin, reflected in the various versions of his name above and in the HRB as Constantius.[27]

In some ways, whether Arthur's grandfather was from Armorica or Cornwall is rather academic. He still has a West Country connection through his mother. However, it does help to increase the suspicion that links to the Continent, and Armorica in particular, were an invention of Geoffrey of Monmouth. Let us now look at his maternal family tree.

Arthur's mother Eigr is a granddaughter of Cunedda, who we will come to shortly. Cunedda's line is allegedly connected with the other great house, the Coelings, through marriage to a daughter of Coel Hen. We will meet some of the latter's descendants at the Battle of Arfderydd. Thus Arthur is connected to the sons and grandsons of Cunedda via his maternal grandmother, Gwen. His grandfather, Amlawdd Wledig, feature in various tales; In the *Life of St Illtud* he is the saint's maternal grandfather; in *Culhwch and Olwen* he is Culhwch's maternal grandfather. Another sister, Gwyar, supposedly marries Geraint, who we recall elsewhere is Arthur's first cousin (but from his father's side in some sources). Amlawdd Wledig is given a pedigree which would make him a first cousin to Custennin Fendigaid/Gorneu.

If we leave aside this confusing web of often contradictory genealogies, we can make the following observation. Arthur's mother, Eigr, is connected to the southwest via her first husband, Gorlois. In *Culhwch and Olwen*, Arthur's stepbrother is Gormant, son of Ricca, 'the chief-elder of Cornwall'. In the HRB, it is Cador not Gormant. In the Llywelyn ab Iorwerth genealogy above, we see his name as *Kadwr*: Kwstenin ap Kadwr ap Gwrlais iarll Kerniw (Constantine son of Cador son of Gorlois Earl of Cornwall). In the *Life of Saint Carannog*

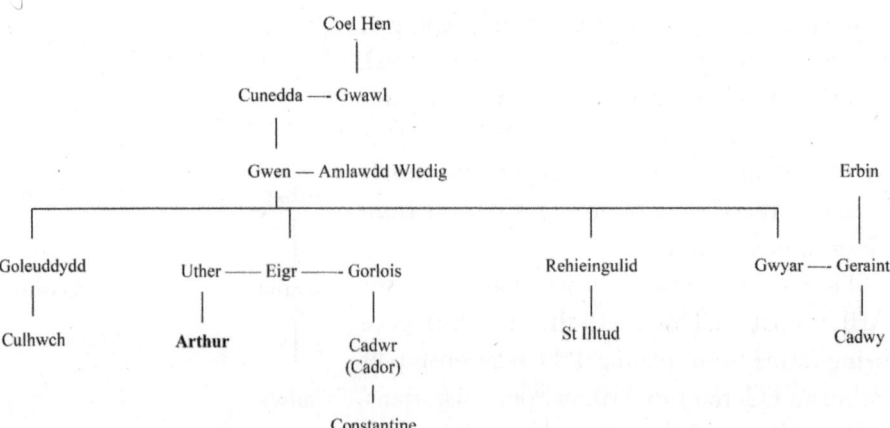

Figure 22: Arthur's maternal family tree.

the saint traversed the Severn estuary from South Wales to where Cadwy and Arthur reigned. We also recall Geraint's son being called Cadwy.

While the two figures Cador (Cadwr in Welsh) and Cadwy are independent they are both connected to the southwest.[28] Cadwr ap Gwrlais is Cador, son of Gorlois. One would expect him to inherit his father's title as Earl of Cornwall and this is exactly what we see in the sources. His son, Constantine, is the man to whom Arthur entrusts the kingdom after Camlan in HRB. This figure may well be one of Gildas' five tyrant kings:[29] 'Constantine, tyrant whelp of the filthy lioness of Dumnonia'.

Cadwy ap Geraint appears in *Rhonabwy's Dream* and as one of Arthur's knights in *Culhwch and Olwen*. It is Cadwy's realm to which Carannog travels and we have seen how both Geraint and Erbin are regarded as ruling in Cornwall.

Dumnonia

What conclusions can we come to regarding Arthur's direct family tree? First, he is connected to the southwest through various sources, many of which place one of his courts at Celliwig in Cornwall. One tradition connects him via his mother and her first husband ruling in Cornwall. Importantly, it is his half-brother and his progeny who inherit that power. If we accept Geoffrey's account in the HRB, Arthur's paternal grandfather is from Armorica. However, the Welsh sources maintained a tradition connecting this line with Cornwall. It may be that Geoffrey did have good reasons to place Arthur's conception in Cornwall other than the fact his patron Prince Robert, Earl of Gloucester, was the brother of the Earl of Cornwall.

It is important to remember these genealogies reflect what writers thought many centuries later. At best they are an attempt at an accurate portrayal of Arthur's family tree; at worst they have been deliberately constructed for political purposes. Nevertheless, there are some consistencies. Arthur's father was Uther, son of a prince from Armorica or Dumnonia. His mother was Eigr, whose first husband also ruled in Dumnonia. Now let us look at how Arthur is connected to the other king-lists and family trees. Remembering that many candidates proposed by theorists exist in these very genealogies.

Cunedda

We first meet Cunedda in the ninth-century HB which, referring to Maelgwn reigning in Gwynedd, states Cunedda (his great-grandfather in the genealogies) had come to that country with his eight sons. It goes on to explain he came from *Manaw Gododdin* in the north. This area is traditionally placed in West Lothian between the kingdoms of Alt Clud and Gododdin. Outside the HB and Harleian genealogies we don't find the place-names Manaw (or Manau) and Gododdin together. The Latin name for Gwynedd, Venedotia, is thought by some to derive from an Irish group, the Fenni. Alternatively, the name Gwynedd might derive from the Venicones (mentioned once by Ptolemy in the second century and placed north of the Firth of Forth) rather than the Votodini (Gododdin).

The text helpfully provides a timeframe: he arrived '146 years before Maelgwn reigned', expelling the Irish from the area 'with immense slaughter'. A very rough calculation might place Maelgwn c.500–550, his father 475–525, grandfather 450–500 and thus Cunedda 425–475, not the 146 years claimed in the HB. Yet Bartrum dates him to 370, which would make his movement to North Wales a possibly redeployment while Britain was still under Roman authority.[30] Cunedda's paternal ancestry suggest a Roman connection: Cunedda ap Edern (Aeturnus) ap Padarn Beisrudd (Paternus of the Red Tunic) ap Tegid (Tacitus).

His eldest son, Tybion, died in Manaw Gododdin before he came south. Some of the remaining eight sons became the founding fathers of a number of kingdoms in North Wales: Ysfael; Rhufon; Dunod; Ceredig; Afloeg; Einion Yrth; Dogfael; and Edern. Two daughters are recorded: Tegid and Gwen, the latter Arthur's grandmother. These children of Cunedda went on to have children of their own. However, it is the next generation that concern us. This generation, Cunedda's great-grandchildren, includes a number of figures that feature in the various Arthurian traditions as well as Arthur himself.

I have constructed a family tree for Cunedda showing the relevant descendants. Not only does this show Arthur's familial relationship with these figures, it also demonstrates how scribes, albeit centuries later, regarded Arthur. It is difficult for modern theorists to propose characters such as Cynlas (possibly Gildas' Cuneglasus), or his father Owain, or even Maelgwn as the

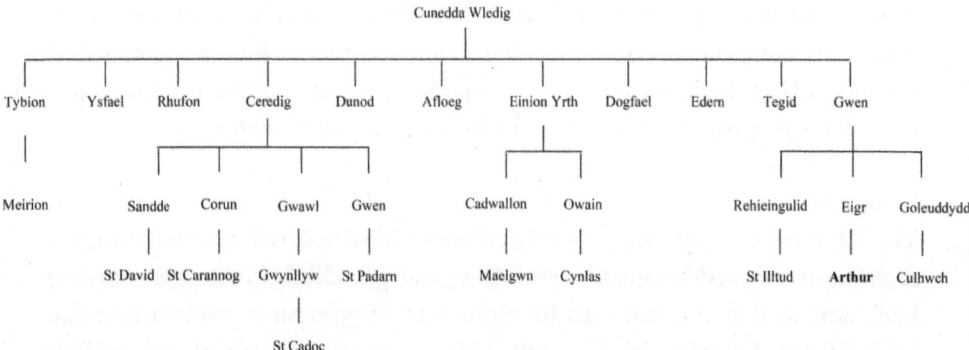

Figure 23: The descendants of Cunedda.

original Arthur. The Welsh scribes clearly saw Arthur as a separate figure. They may well have been wrong. They might even have deliberately added Arthur for political purposes. All we can do is accurately say what these copyists wrote, centuries after a historical Arthur might have lived.

Many of the earlier kingdoms take their names from Cunedda's sons: Rhufoniog, Ceredigion, Merionydd, Dunoding, Dogfeiling, Edeirnion. Some soon disappeared as they were absorbed by larger neighbours. Perhaps the most important ones to remember are Gwynedd, Ceredigion, Rhos and Glywysing.

Coel Hen

The descendants of Coel Hen can be found in *Bonedd Gwŷr y Gogledd* ('The Descent of the Men of the North'). The earliest manuscript dates to the late thirteenth century, but it could be a century earlier. Figure 23 shows the main figures. Other than Urien (*Vryen*) I have used the spellings in Ben Guy's book and added Arthur's maternal lineage.[31] It is worth noting Arthwys map Mar, who is suggested as a possible candidate for Arthur. However, there is nothing to support this other than his name and the fact he was around the correct timeframe.

Jesus College genealogies offer a possible link to the kings of Elmet: Gwallavc m Llyennavc m Mar m Coel Hen (missing out Keneu).

The Harleian genealogies have: Guallauc map Laenauc map Masguic Clop map Ceneu map Coyl Hen.[32]

The same genealogies also give the kings of Alt Clud: Ryderch Hall m Tutwal m Kedic m Dyuynwal Hen m Idnyuet m Maxen Wledig.

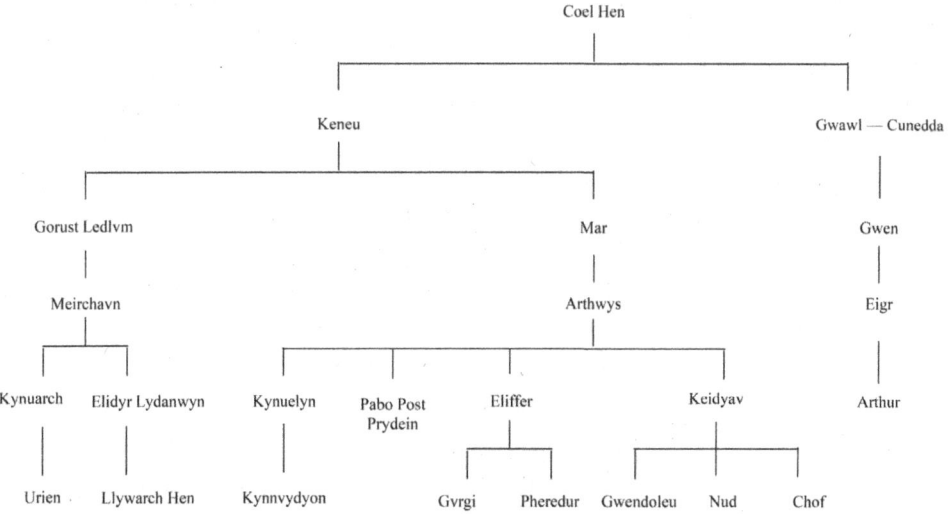

Figure 24: The descendants of Coel Hen.

A couple of points are worth noting here. In the *Bonedd Gwŷr y Gogledd* Rhydderch is the same generation as a number of figures claimed to have been combatants at Arfderydd, namely Gwenddolau and the sons of Eliffer, Gwrgi and Peredur. Rhydderch's ancestor, Maxen Wledig, is none other than Magnus Maximus, the usurping Roman emperor who died in 388. This makes Coel Hen of the same generation. It places Cunedda at the same time, or perhaps a generation later, marrying Coel's daughter.

This makes it difficult to date accurately and with confidence. There are six generations between Coel Hen and the figures who fought at Arfderydd. If one allows a fifty-year lifespan and twenty-five years for each generation, one finds oneself about two generations short. We get a similar problem when addressing Cunedda's 146 years before the reign of Maelgwn. However, figures such as Urien and Rhydderch are considered historical and can be firmly placed at the end of the sixth century. It is possible Cunedda and Coel Hen are both better placed in the early to mid-fifth century rather than the late fourth. It's equally possible a generation or two has been missed.

The safest thing to do is accept these were all constructed centuries after the figures are claimed to have lived and thus the whole thing is suspect. We must therefore exercise great caution when making claims based on these tables. Yet it does fall in line with a number of other sources that place Urien and Rhydderch in the late sixth century and a battle in the north, c.573, between descendants of Coel Hen. Taking the genealogies as a whole, it suggests a historical Arthur a generation before these events, which places him firmly in the early to mid-sixth century, rather than the late fifth.

Battle of Arfderydd

The earliest form of the name for the location of the battle is *Armterid*. This version of the word suggests the copyist got his information from an earlier source rather than poems concerning Myrddin. It is dated to 573 in the AC: 'The battle of Arfderydd between the sons of Eliffer and Gwenddolau son of Ceidio; in which Gwenddolau fell; Merlin went mad.' It is worth noting that until the time of Geoffrey of Monmouth, this battle only appears in the AC. The HB and other early sources ignore it.

An analysis of the various later sources reveals the following details of the conflict:[33] on one side was Gwenddolau, son of Ceidio. On the other were the sons of Eliffer, among them Gwrgi and Peredur (later Welsh traditions add another son (and possible Arthurian candidate), Arthur *Penuchel*, 'High-Head'). In the genealogies Ceidio and Eliffer are sons of Arthwys, a great-grandson of Coel Hen. This is, therefore, another 'cousins-war', like so many dynastic struggles down the centuries. Myrddin fought alongside Gwenddolau and saw his lord fall in battle.

Four Triads mention the battle. The warband of Gwenddoleu, one of the 'Three loyal War-bands', kept fighting 'forty-six days after their lord was slain'. Another refers to the 'battle-fog of Gwenddoleu'. A third praises the 'Retinue of Dreon the Brave at the Dyke of Arfderydd'. Lastly, the battle itself was one of the 'Three Futile Battles', supposedly because it was fought over a lark's nest.

The site of the battle is later said to be, 'in the plain between Lidel and Carwanolow'. One popular candidate is near Arthuret, close to where the Liddel and Esk meet. Earlier forms for the nearby village of Carwinley include *Karwindelhou* and *Carwendelowe*, which may represent the *caer*, or fort, of Gwenddolau. A half day's march from Carlisle and Hadrian's Wall to the south. Both Clarkson and Tolstoy accept a site near the confluence of the Rivers Esk and Liddel. A sixteenth-century source states there are two forests called *Calidon*. Importantly, it places the source of the Clyde in the mountains *in* the forest of this southern *Calidon*.[34] It would not have to stretch too far further south to be within a day's ride of a battle near Arthuret to the south-east.

In summary, we have a battle fought among kings associated with the north of Britain. It is remembered in Welsh tradition as one of the Three Futile Battles. An unnecessary and disastrous conflict. The earliest manuscript dates this battle to 573 and places it at Armterid, making no mention of Myrddin. A later version, post-dating Geoffrey of Monmouth by over a century, connects Merlinus to the battle. The Latin spelling suggests it was a late addition by a reader of Geoffrey's *Vita Merlini*. Its location is unknown, but modern writers have suggested it was near the village of Arthuret close to the modern England-Scotland border.

Other kingdoms

King lists survive for other kingdoms. Powys, for example, has a number of variations. In the HB we recall the tale of St Germanus deposing the tyrant Benlli and placing Cadell Ddyrnllug on the throne, and from his descendants 'the whole country of Powys is ruled, even to this day'.[35] Yet a separate tradition associates Vortigern with Powys. The Pillar of Eliseg is a ninth-century stone in Denbighshire, Wales, commemorating the Kings of Powys. It reads: 'Britu son of Vortigern, whom Germanus blessed and whom Sevira bore to him, daughter of Maximus the king who killed the king of the Romans.' The HB names four sons of Vortigern: Vortimer, Cateyrn, Pascent and Faustus. There is no mention of a Britu. Pascent is said to have ruled in Builth and Gwerthrynion. Later genealogies (Jesus College and Harleian) do indeed place Pascen or Pasgen as a son of Vortigern. While there is a hint of two competing traditions for Powys, and regarding the nature of Vortigern, there is no connection with Arthur.

In Dyfed, however, we do get an Arthur. Four different genealogies place Arthur (or in one case Arthan) as son of Pedr or Petr. This Arthur is a grandson of Gourtepir who, it has been suggested, is another of Gildas' five kings: 'Vortipor, tyrant of the Demetae'. This Arthur had a son called Noe, and Bartrum dates him from c.560.[36] Nothing more is known and there is no Arthurian connection. A memorial stone found in Castell Dwyran, Carmarthenshire, Wales, has been dated to the fifth to sixth century. It bears an inscription in both Ogham and Latin that might refer to Vortipor: *Memoria Voteporigis protictoris*. The word, *protictoris*, might reflect a late-Roman title: Protector. The Ogham script is also suggestive of an Irish connection. The *civitas* of the Demetae appears to have fractured into three: it's core, Dyfed; in the east, Brycheiniog; and Ceredigion to the north.[37] The first two have significant Irish settlement and early genealogies appear linked to the Deisi from Ireland. The Deisi, 'vassals', were immigrants from south-east Ireland, Counties Waterford and Tipperary, who settled in south-west Wales.[38] We find a stone at Viroconium, Wroxeter, dated to the late fifth century, with similar Irish links: *Cunorix* son of *Maqui Coline*.

Another Irish Arthur is Artúr mac Áedán from Dál Riada. Dál Riada, Dál Riata or Dalriada was a Gaelic kingdom spanning western Scotland and north-east Ireland. Artúr or Artuir is mentioned in Adomnan's *Life of St Columba*. Here Columba predicts Áedán will be succeeded by his youngest son, Eochaid Buide and that his brothers, Artúr among them, will die in battle.

Artúr dies fighting the Miathi who have been associated with the Maeatae, a tribe around the Clyde-Forth Isthmus. The Annals of Ulster dates the battle to 595, the Annals of Tigernach dates both Artúr's death and the battle to 594. His name is recorded in a tenth-century copy of a possibly seventh-century text: *Senchus Fer n'Alban*, 'The History of the Men of Scotland'. As with Arthur ap Pedr, little is known. There is no hint of an Arthurian connection.

The *civitas* of the Silures in South Wales appears to have also split. The Roman name of Caerwent, *Venta Silurum*, giving us Gwent with Glywysing, in the south, having a tribal origin.[39] Here we find one popular candidate for our hero, Athrwys ap Meurig. A line of kings includes the following: Athrwys ap Meurig ap Tewdrig. There is some confusion as to the dating of this figure, or even whether there were two individuals of the same name (which would require the same parental and grandparent name). Certainly one figure, found in the Book of Llandaff and genealogies, can be dated to the seventh century.[40] Living at the time of St Oudoceus (a seventh-century saint), his sons included

Morgan, Ithel and Gwaidnerth, his wife Cenedlon, daughter of Briafel Frydig. So again, no Arthurian connection. He is never mentioned as king himself and appears to have died while his father, Meurig, still lived.

A possible second Athrwys ap Meurig is referenced in a deed of the Book of Llandaff: *Athruis rex Guenti regionis pro anima patris sui Mourici*.[41] Here he is associated with disciples of St Dubricius, which would place him in the sixth century. However, he is not found anywhere else and may simply be a misplaced duplicate or error. The name Athrwys was misspelt in a translation by Iolo Morganwg in the eighteenth century, causing later writers to change it to Arthur.[42] Spelling is important here as Arthur does not derive from Athrwys. In fact early manuscripts use variations such as Adroes or Atroys. We will cover this figure and the veracity of the Book of Llandaff in a little more depth later.

There are many other Arth- type names in the genealogies such as Arthfael, Arthmail, Arthen, Arthal, Arthafad, Arthgal and others.[43] In fact it seems that people will jump on any name beginning with A, as the media excitement around the Artognou stone found at Tintagel showed (again, more on this later). Just for completeness, let as look at the lists for the Anglo-Saxon kings.

Anglo-Saxon kings
These too were written centuries after the founding kings. We find these in the HB (early ninth century), the ASC (late ninth century) and The Anglian collection (late eighth century) as well as from Bede (early eighth century). We don't, of course, find any Arth- type names, but we might find clues as to his enemies, where they are named.

The first attested kings are in bold towards the bottom of figure 25. Most kingdoms trace their line back to Woden and thus include those who were king before they arrived in Britain. It is a little difficult to accept the earliest kings descending from the Germanic god. Yet if we take it at face value we have a number of kings dated to the late fifth to early sixth centuries, when a historical Arthur might have lived.

We recall in the HB that Arthur's battles come after Hengest's death, and his son Octa came down from the north to Kent. In the HRB the Saxon kings at Badon were Balduf, Colgrin and Cheldric. Only Cerdic of the West Saxons could be associated with any of these names. He is recorded in the ASC as arriving in 495 (although scholars believe a date of 532 is more likely). Also in the HRB, Octa and Eosa were killed by Uther. If we look at the table we see Octa, the son of Hengest and Oesa and grandfather of Ida. In the *Dream of Rhonabwy*, Osla 'big-knife' is the opponent at Badon and Osla Gyllellvawr is one of Arthur's men in *Culhwch and Olwen*.

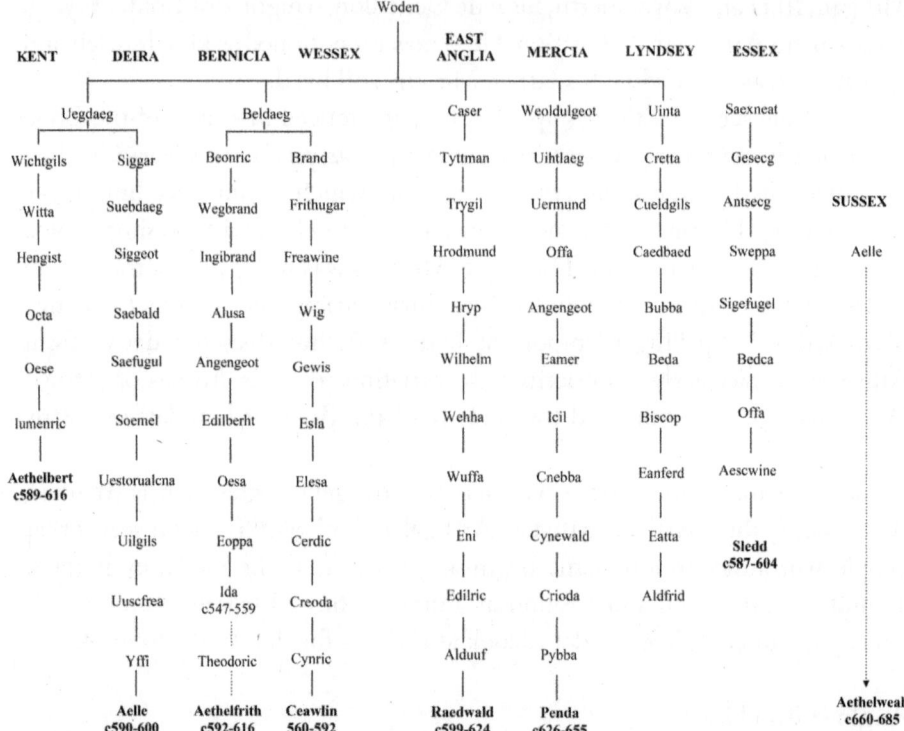

Figure 25: Genealogies of the Anglo-Saxons.

The HB tells us that Hengest's son Octha and his cousin Ebissa campaigned against the Picts and were given land '*near the wall*'. We see Octha represented as Octa in figure 25, and from him 'sprung the kings of the Kentishmen. Then Arthur fought against them....' No more is heard of Ebissa. However, let us look at the Bernician kings, specifically Oesa, grandfather of Ida. A surviving French document from c.850 states that Oesa and Eosa were the first Bernician royal dynasty to arrive.[44] With Ida reigning from c.547, this would date Oesa to around 500.[45] Oesa's son, and Ida's father, is Eoppa.

A corruption of *Ebissa* to *Eoppa* in the Vespasian genealogy list would not be difficult and from that to *Eobba* a simple step.[46]

Anglian Collection, eighth century: Oesa, Eoppa, Ida.
Historia Brittonum, early ninth century: Ossa, Eobba, Ida.
Anglo-Saxon Chronicle, late ninth century: Esa, Eoppa, Ida.

In summary, the HB claims Arthur fights against the Saxons between Hengest's death and Ida's reign. The HRB has Octha and Eosa (Ebissa?

Eoppa?) killed by Uther, and Arthur fighting Cheldric (Cerdic, 495–530s?). In Welsh tradition Osla is either one of Arthur's men or his opponent at Badon. Here we have few options: Oesa, Ida's Grandfather, in Bernicia; Oese in Kent; or Offa in Essex. There the clues end.

Searching for evidence of possibly fictitious figures from Arthurian tales in equally suspect genealogies might seem a fool's errand, but it is perhaps a useful exercise. The HB claims Arthur fought between the floruits of two figures, Hengest and Ida. Later genealogies list kings reigning at the time. Arthurian legends name a number of enemies. Unfortunately, none of the names match and people are left, as so often in Arthurian studies, to twist etymologies and timeframes to fit their theories.

Consistencies and inconsistencies

There are a number of important consistencies (and inconsistencies) concerning Arthur's family.[47] Looking at the entirety of the genealogical and literary record, his mother, when named, is always Eigr, Igraine or some variation. His father is Uther, Uthr, Uthyr, again with variations. Uther often comes with the epithet Bendragon or Pendragon. Arthur's wife is Gwenhwyfar or, as we know her today, Guinevere. Three half-brothers are named: Madog ab Uthr; Cadwr ap Gwrlais; and Gormant ap Ricca. His sisters are Anna, Elen, Gwyar and Morgen. Out of these, Morgen seems the most obvious late addition by French Romance writers. Sons include: Amhar, Gwydre, Llacheu, Cydfan and Smerbe (from a late Scottish tradition[48]). One daughter, Archfedd, is named as marrying a Llawfrodedd Farfog in *Bonedd y Saint*.

While Uther is known to Welsh traditions pre-Galfridian, it is the HRB that confirms him as Arthur's father. There are references in possible earlier sources to Madog ap Uthr and Eliwlod ap Madog ap Uthr, giving us another of Arthur's nephews.[49] Two manuscripts of the HB, from twelfth to thirteenth century, contains a gloss after the words concerning Arthur's role as leader: *ipse dux erat Bellorum*. It says:[50] In British *Mab Uter*, that is in Latin 'terrible son', because from his youth he was cruel.' As this addition post-dates the HRB it may well be a pun on his father's name, *Uthr*.

According to the HRB, Uther acquired the epithet 'Pendragon' when a comet appeared on the eve of his victory: a star 'of great magnitude and brilliance' with a single beam, shining from its tail. At the head was a ball of fire shaped like a dragon. From the dragon's mouth 'stretched forth two rays of light'. In fact, Pendragon just as likely means 'chief warrior' as 'head dragon'. Yet this has been used to associate Arthur with dragons for evermore. Thus the prophecy of Emrys in HB, or Merlin in HRB, involving a red and white dragon is roped in. They are originally described as *vermes*, 'worms', wrapped in a cloth in a vessel. Later, Emrys explains they represent a *draco*, dragon. It is true that in the tales of Saint Efflam and Carannog Arthur battles a dragon and a serpent, but in general the links between Arthur and dragons are tenuous. The late Roman battle standard, the *draco*, was ubiquitous on the battlefields of north-west Europe and has no particular significance.

We have seen how Geraint is sometimes married to a sister of Arthur and in other sources an aunt, making his son Cadwy a nephew or cousin. Gwalchmai is the son of either Anna or Gwyar, with the latter sometimes made the daughter of Eigr and her first husband. All this might be understandable confusion after many centuries with conflicting accounts and errors being passed down. The evolution of Morgen, on the other hand, seems more deliberate. We meet Morgain la Fey as one of the nine sisters ruling in *Insula Pomorum* in Geoffrey's *Vita Merlini*. She later becomes a sister or half-sister to Arthur and changes from a healer to a wicked sorceress.

Concerning Avalon, this is first mentioned by Geoffrey of Monmouth when Arthur is taken there to be healed by Morgan Le Fay after Camlan. *Insula Avallonis* means isle of fruit (or apple) trees. Later Welsh texts use the name *Ynys Afallon* or *Afallach* which could be linked to *Emain Abhlach*, a mythical island paradise possibly identified with the Isle of Man or Arran. In Geoffrey's *Vita Merlini* a sea voyage is taken to the 'Isle of Apples'.

Morgan and her sisters reminds us of the nine women in other tales. In *Preiddeu Annwfn* the cauldron is 'warmed by the breath of nine maidens'. Arthur kills the nine sorceresses of Gloucester in *Peredur son of Efrawg*. The final quest of *Culhwch and Olwen* has Arthur killing the witch Orddu. In *Pa gur yv y porthaur?* Cai kills nine witches in the uplands of Ystafnwn.

French Romances later identified Avalon with Glastonbury. Interestingly, there is an Avallon in Burgundy in the direction that Riothamus travelled following his defeat. More popular candidates include Aballava or Avallana, a Roman fort at the western end of Hadrian's Wall. This is not far from one of the candidates for Camlan, the Roman fort *Camboglanna*. Interestingly, in the year AD 45 the Roman geographer Pomponius Mela gave an account of an island off Brittany, home to nine priestesses.

Accounts of Mordred are also not always consistent. Spellings include Medrod, Modred, Medraut or Medrawt (AC), and Modredus (HRB). Mordred was not always considered a villain.[51] In the early twelfth-century the poet Meilyr Brydydd praises a king of Gwynedd of possessing 'the nature of Medrawd'. In the same century, Gwalchmai ap Meilyr praises a king of Powys for 'Arthur's strength, the good nature of Medrawd'. Early bardic references portray a man of high valour and courtesy, one of the 'Three Royal Knights of Arthur's Court'.[52] The reference to Camlan in the AC is ambiguous, telling us only that Arthur and Medraut fell together, not whether they were adversaries. The HRB effectively portrayed him as a villain and the French Romances carried that forward. He begins there as the son of Anna and Loth making him Arthur's nephew. Later, he is the illegitimate and incestuous son of Arthur and his sister Morgause.

Summary

Arthur is portrayed as the son of Uthr and Eigr and the husband of Gwenhwyfar. Other familial relationships are not so consistent. However, Kai and Bedwyr are his companions in a number of tales and are never portrayed as being related to him. Cousins include Gwalchmai (Gawain), Culhwch and Geraint. The earliest genealogies do not mention Arthur at all. Of all the lists of kings for the many petty kingdoms of Britain not one makes Arthur a king of that region. Instead, when he does appear in genealogies from the thirteenth century, he is linked to the rulers of Dumnonia or Cornwall via his mother's first husband. On his father's side we have two options. If we accept the HRB, his grandfather came from Armorica. However, the Welsh maintained a tradition that his grandfather was associated with Cornwall.

When later genealogists constructed their lists and tables, Arthur was connected to the House of Cunedda via his maternal grandmother. As Cunedda himself was married to a daughter of Coel Hen, Arthur is indirectly connected to the Men of the North. We can doubt the veracity of these sources but we should not forget what they say. Many a book will trawl through these tables and pluck a figure on which to hang a theory. This inevitably means ignoring or explaining why their man isn't actually called Arthur. Or perhaps hasn't got parents called Eigr and Uthr.

When sources do place kingship upon Arthur it is as some sort of High-King of Britain. Invariably this follows the same pattern as in the HRB: Vortigern, Ambrosius Aurelianus, Uther, Arthur, Constantine. While it is possible some sort of unofficial position was maintained, there is no evidence. Bede describes seven Anglo-Saxon kings as holding *imperium* south of the Humber. It is plausible Ælle of the South Saxons had some influence over the various Germanic peoples as did Ceawlin of Wessex and Æthelberht of Kent. Perhaps Ambrosius Aurelianus held a surviving Roman title: *vicarius*, governor, *comes* or *dux*. Later copyists might translate this position as king. Holders of these titles might call themselves king.

However, again we have no evidence Arthur held such a title. Early Welsh tales portray a warband leader or petty king, one among many. He may hold a court at Celliwig, but it is his half-brother or cousin that rules in Dumnonia.

In the HB he is not a king but a 'leader in battle'. He lived in a world full of kings and warlords. Gildas lists five of the former and they are not the chivalrous kings of the French Romances.

While we cannot prove Arthur was not a figure of myth we have so far shown two important things. First, some people in the middle ages viewed him as historical. Second, the compilers of genealogies had a fairly consistent opinion of who he was, and perhaps as importantly, who he was not. They attached him to two distinct groups of kings and saints: the descendants of Cunedda in northern Wales, and those of Coel Hen in northern Britain. One wonders how some modern theorists are able to ignore that and come up with the proposals they do.

Chapter Ten

Alleged Forgeries, Burials, Crosses and Stones

We now have a clearer picture of who medieval copiers of genealogies believed Arthur to be. Equally important is who they believed him not to be. There are no glosses in the margins of medieval manuscripts explaining that a particular Welsh or northern king was the Arthur of legend. Before we turn to some of the more common modern theories it is useful to give some examples of suspect evidence that have appeared over the centuries. We will begin with a medieval land dispute. This was no mere fence dispute between suburban neighbours; the subsequent row reached the Pope in Rome. From one side of this dispute we get a document that is often used by modern theorists to bolster the case for their particular Arthur.

The Llandaff Charters

The *Liber Landavensis*, The Book of Llandaff, is believed to have been written between 1120 and 1140 and contains 159 charters across 128 vellum pages claiming to date from the fifth to the eleventh centuries. A recent study found it is rightly notorious for its bogus documents.[1] It was adapted and improved to favour Urban, the bishop of Llandaff, in a land dispute against the bishops of St Davids and Hereford. It is neither an accurate copy of contemporary pre-twelfth century records nor genuine, but instead should be viewed as one Bishop's legal case against his rivals. It is impossible to identify reliable entries from the text before 1050.[2] One of Urban's helpers may have been Caradog of Llancarfan and it has been suggested he was the author of the book.[3] We recall two Saints' Lives derived from Llancarfan, one of which was authored by possibly the same man.

Nevertheless some of the charters are considered genuine. Wendy Davies viewed some at least as deriving from an early source.[4] Indeed, a very recent study, by Patrick Sims-Williams, accepts there must have been some history and tradition at Llandaff for Urban to use.[5] While Davies dates some of the charters to the mid-fifth-century, Sims-Williams finds the earliest goes back to the seventh century.[6] The book includes the lives of three saints: St Dyfrig (Dubricius, c.465–521), Teilo (c.500–560) and Euddogwy (Oudoceus c.530–620) and also references a number of figures from the genealogies including, importantly for our study, a certain prince of Glamorgan, Athrwys ap Meurig.

At first glance this looks rather hopeful for our quest, as the book of Llandaff does indeed name an Arthur as the king of Gwent: *Athruis rex Guenti regionis pro anima parts sui Mourici.*[7]

Unfortunately this is one of the later charters chronologically and thus may have been a late addition.[8] This figure granted a number of churches in Ergyng which was witnessed by disciples of St Dubricius. Additional charters seem to date this figure too late, in the time of St Oudoceus, the seventh century. They allow us to identify some immediate family members: Morgan his son, Meurig his father, and his grandfather Tewdrig. None of these subsequent charters name him as a king, suggesting he may have died before his father. Elsewhere his name is spelled as Athwrys, a name not synonymous with Arthur. None of his relatives' names match those from Arthurian tradition. So we have the wrong name, at the wrong time and no evidence of anything remotely Arthurian. Just to emphasise the point, a number of later genealogies also record his name and it is worth noting the various alternative spellings (and missing family members).

The genealogies give us the following:

The Harleian genealogies:[9] Morcant map **Atroys** map Teutubric
Jesus college:[10] Morgant m **Adroes** m Meuric m Theudric
Gwehelyth Morgannwg:[11] Morgan ap **Adroes** ap Meyrig ap Twedrig
The Llywelyn ab Iorwerth genealogies:[12] Morgant ap **Athwrys** ap Meuric ap Teuderic

Other spellings include Athrues, Athues, Athraws, Athyrwys, Arthrnes. None of these, or those in the genealogies above, can be can be equated with Arthur. The reader should beware of theories presenting this figure as Arthur, dating him to their preferred timeframe and then attributing all number of events and deeds to his name – alongside twisted etymologies that attempt to turn his father into Uther. Dubious etymologies aside, the names Athwrys or Adroes are never connected to Arthur's genealogies and we must assume medieval Welsh copyists were well aware he was considered a different person.

In summary, we have a twelfth-century source considered suspect by historians, containing additions, amendments and forgeries. Yet some of the charters may reflect an accurate record back to the seventh century or possibly earlier. The one figure that might be relevant appears to be in the wrong timeframe, with the wrong name, the wrong family connections and no evidence of anything remotely Arthurian connected to him.

The Glastonbury burial

The HRB was completed shortly after the death of Henry I. It was clearly intended for an 'elite, court consumption'.[13] It was dedicated to Henry's eldest legitimate son, Robert, the influential Count Waleran and, in one instance, King Stephen himself. Henry II began his reign in 1154 and took a keen interest in Arthurian literature. In his formative years he was raised by his uncle Robert of Gloucester, the very man Geoffrey dedicated the HRB to. Henry II also patronised the Norman cleric Wace and a copy of *Roman de Brut* was presented to his wife, Eleanor of Aquitaine. Towards the end of Henry's reign Layamon wrote the first version of the *Brut* in English. The Arthurian legends offered Henry, ruling lands from the Pyrenees to Scotland, as an alternative to the tales of Charlemagne.

Arthur had already been associated with Glastonbury by Caradoc of Llancarfen (a contemporary and friend of Geoffrey of Monmouth).[14] Fire ravaged much of the monastery in 1184 and the following events have thus been labelled a money-making exercise to boost tourism and grants. Allegedly, a Welsh bard told the king himself where Arthur was buried and the excavation was duly ordered.[15] Henry died in 1189 but support continued under Richard I. The discovery finally took place in 1191.

Gerald of Wales, writing in c.1216, gives a detailed account of the events.[16] He begins with the claim that Arthur was himself a patron of the abbey at Glastonbury and was highly praised in their records. The mystery surrounding his death is noted, along with the legends of his survival in some otherworldly place. Then he recounts how Arthur's grave was discovered in the author's own lifetime.

The body was in a 'hollowed-out-oak-bole' buried deep in the earth, between two stone pyramids. There was a stone slab, underside of which was a leaden cross which Gerald claimed to have seen himself. The words facing towards the stone: HERE IN THE ISLE OF AVALON LIES BURIED THE RENOWNED KING ARTHUR, WITH GUINEVERE, HIS SECOND WIFE.

Arthur's bones took up two thirds of the coffin with Guinevere's at his feet. A lock of blond hair, 'still fresh and bright in colour', crumbled to dust when a monk touched it. Abbey records pointed to its location, as did 'visions and revelations'. In addition, Gerald claimed an 'old British soothsayer' informed Henry II the exact whereabouts of the grave, 16ft under the ground. The remains were carried into the church and buried in a marble tomb.

A number of of writers confirm the story, although there are slight variations of the inscription.[17] Ralph of Coggeshall, writing in 1221, gives a slightly different account. The grave was found while monks were digging a grave for a fellow-monk who wished to be buried at that spot. This time the cross was placed upon the 'coffin'. The inscription is also different: *Hic iacet inclitus rex Arturius in insula Avallonis sepultus* ('Here lies the famous king Arthur, in the isle of Avalon buried').[18]

An unknown source from Magram Abbey claimed the body of Arthur was placed in a marble tomb in the Abbey church, but adds Mordred's remains for good measure. Nearly a century later, in 1278, Adam of Damerham tells of the visit by Edward I and his queen, Eleanor. The tomb was reopened and the bones of both Arthur ('of great size') and Guinevere were placed in their own caskets and the tomb placed in front of the high altar.

Historians assume this was a medieval hoax.[19] The style of lettering dated between tenth to twelfth centuries rather than the sixth. An excavation of the site in the late twentieth century found slab-lined graves dating to the tenth century just below material dumped in the same century. The suggestion is that Henry attempted to kill two birds with one stone; first, to kill off the idea of a returning Arthur leading a Welsh revival, and second, to appropriate the ruler of all Britain and conqueror of Rome to rival Charlemagne.

The tomb and Arthur's remains were sadly lost shortly after the monastery fell in 1539 as part of Henry's Dissolution of the Monasteries. But the cross survived. John Leland, Henry VIII's antiquarian, claimed to have seen the cross (described as a foot in length) in 1542.

HIC IACET SEPVLTVS INCLYTVS REX ARTVRIVS IN INSVLA AVALONIA
('Here lies buried the famous king Arthur in the isle of Avalon').

In 1590 William Camden recorded the inscription on the cross in five lines in *Britannia*.[20] HIC IACET SEPVLTVS INCLITVS REX ARTVRIVS IN INSVLA AVALONIA. This can be translated as: 'Here lies buried the famous king, Arthur, in the Avalonian isle'. In a 1607 edition of Camden, a sketch of the cross (approximately six inches) displayed a different arrangement. We can see the two layouts in figure 26.

Neither Leland nor Camden mention Guinevere, suggesting Ralph of Coggeshall's account is more accurate and Gerald invented or imagined the reference to Arthur's wife. The shape of the cross points to a date between the seventh and eleventh century. It is perhaps too early to be a twelfth-century fake, but too late to be a genuine sixth-century object. The last known location of the cross was Wells in Somerset in the eighteenth century, after which it

Inscription from c. 1590

HIC IACET SEP
VLTVS INCLITVS
REX ARTVRIVS IN
INSVLA AVALO
NIA

Inscription from c. 1607

HIC IA
CET S
EPV
LTVS INCL
ITVS REX
ARTU
RIV
S IN
INSV
LA A
VALO
NI
A

Translation: 'Here lies buried the famous king, Arthur, in the Avalonian isle'

Figure 26: The Glastonbury Cross inscription.

seems lost.[21] It was in the possession of one William Hughes, an official of Wells Cathedral.

This is not the last we hear of the cross. In November 1981 a man allegedly found a small lead cross in the mud excavated from a lake in the grounds of Forty Hall, Enfield, in Essex. Enfield council sought to retrieve the item found on their land. Details of the story was taken up in 2012 in *History Matters*, by the barrister for the London Borough of Enfield, Richard Mawrey.[22] The man, Derek Mahoney, claimed to have discovered the cross using a metal detector in the sludge of the recently drained lake at Forty Hall. Mr Mahoney had taken the cross to the British Museum in December 1981. The Keeper of Medieval and Later Antiquities examined it briefly and estimated it to be roughly the same size as the one claimed to have been discovered in 1191. They were interested in investigating further but Mr Mahoney refused to leave the cross in their care.

Enfield Council became aware of the issue and instructed Mr Mawrey to retrieve the cross. A court injunction was duly served but Mr Mahoney point-blank refused to reveal the whereabouts of the item and was duly committed to prison – although he would be released as soon as he gave up the cross. This he refused to do, claiming it was well-buried in a waterproof container. The successful prosecution and subsequent prison sentence for contempt of court was reported in *The Enfield Advertiser*.[23]

Mr Mawrey describes a 'disturbed individual' who even argued against his own release at a later hearing. An appeal by the Official Solicitor did eventual result in the early release of the protesting Mr Mahoney. The article pointedly remarks Mahoney was a member of the local archaeological society and had worked for a nearby manufacturer of lead toys. Sadly, it is believed that Mr Mahoney passed away and the cross was never recovered. Was this a hoax within a hoax? We may never know.

Despite the general belief that the whole episode was a twelfth-century scam, Leslie Alcock in *Arthur's Britain* provides a counter argument.[24] The inscription is indeed more likely dated to the tenth than the sixth century. But that requires a twelfth-century monk to forge a tenth-century-looking inscription, believing it was sixth century. Instead, the argument is made that known renovation works by St Dunstan in the mid-tenth century removed or disturbed the tomb, and a stone bearing a dedication to Arthur was removed. By this time Arthur may have been connected with kingship, Avalon and Glastonbury. Wishing to mark the spot, a tenth-century inscription with added references to 'illustrious king' and 'Avalon' was placed with the coffin. It is an imaginative argument and one wonders why the tradition developed that Arthur's grave could not be found. And why did a tenth century English king (at the time Edmund or Eadred) not trumpet the discovery? Without tangible evidence we must leave this intriguing story to one side and reluctantly accept the scepticism of academics.

Iolo Morganwg
Iolo Morganwg was born Edward Williams in 1747 and became a well-known Welsh antiquarian, poet and collector. His 'bardic-name' means Iolo of Glamorgan. After his death it was claimed he had forged several manuscripts. Mary-Ann Constantine's book, *The Truth Against the World: Iolo Morganwg and Romantic Forgery: Iolo Morganwg and the Romantic Tradition in Wales*, investigates the 'hidden influences behind Britain's most successful (and hence, perhaps, least visible) Romantic forger'. Another, more recent, book states he, 'shaped, moulded and distorted historical and literary evidence'.[25]

We will begin with one of his more famous claims. In *De Bello Gallico*, Julius Caesar reported that the druids of Britain and Gaul did not generally use writing in their teaching, preferring to train their disciples over many years to commit their knowledge and verses to memory. However, this is not to say they did not teach writing at all, as Caesar went on to explain that in other contexts they used 'Greek letters'. The debate over what he meant precisely has been considerable. It is with this snippet in mind that Iolo claimed to have discovered an authentic British version, the bardic *Colbren*, a primitive alphabet made up of notices on a stick, initially consisting of ten letters. Iolo went on to carve his own *peithynen*, a kind of abacus, used to form sequences of words in Coelbren script.[26] Constantine states: 'His bardic alphabet brought him closer than any of his creations to being openly denounced as a forger, and should by rights have sparked off the 'Iolo controversy' which in fact took another century to materialise.'[27] Not everyone was convinced of its authenticity at the time and one of his friends, Walter Davies, even wrote to him asking him directly if he was in fact the author.[28]

In addition, Iolo's 'Triads of Britain' were 'manufactured by the score' and were a 'spider's web of pseudo-history'.[29] Examples of these forgeries can be found in Rachel Bromwich's *The Triads of the Island of Britain*.[30] I will spare the reader from the complex web of accusations and evidence. His ultimate denouncement and motivations can be found in Constantine's final chapter.[31] A discussion of Iolo's forgeries can also be found in Knight and Long's *Fakes and Forgeries*.[32] Lastly, Scott Lloyd states Iolo Morganwg,'created his Romantic view of the Welsh past by forging documents and inventing a bardic tradition complete with its own alphabet'.[33]

This is not to say we must dismiss everything Iolo Morganwg wrote. There are some that argue he was a flawed genius who produced some work of value at least. The important point for this book is that Iolo Morganwg is regarded as controversial and unreliable. A theory that relies upon evidence from the pen of this late eighteenth-century writer is equally suspect. We will see in the next chapter that some modern theorists accept 'evidence' from this source, neglecting to warn the reader of the serious questions surrounding his work.

The Artognou stone

Richard, Earl of Cornwall, brother to Henry III, built a castle on the site Geoffrey named as the place of Arthur's conception. Evidence for as many as a hundred buildings have been found at post-Roman Tintagel, which would make it one of the largest settlements in Britain with trade links across the Mediterranean.[34] In July 1998 archaeologists working at Tintagel discovered a broken slate measuring 35cm by 20cm used as a drain cover in the east side of the headland. The layer in which it was found dated to the sixth century.

In the magazine *Archaeology*, the article 'A Dark Age Beacon' by Jason Urbanus makes a number of observations.[35] The engraving consists of seven lines with a few words or letters per line. The stone was not meant for display but seems to have been used for practice. The opening line contains the Latin name Tito ('for or by Titus'). It also includes Brittonic names: Budic and Tud (or Tuda) along with phrases *viri duo*, 'two men', and *fili*, 'sons'. The inclusion of Greek letters and ornate style suggests the scribe was aware of Christian manuscripts. Further down we get the important phrase: PATER COLI AVI FICIT ARTOGNOU COL[I] FICIT ('Artognou, father of a descendant of Coll, has had this made'). The inscription has been dated to the late seventh to early eighth century. Experts have dismissed any connection between the name Artognou and Arthur.

None of this prevented newspapers at the time, and since, claiming this evidence supported the existence of a historical Arthur at Tintagel. They even named this the 'Arthur stone'. Before we dismiss this out of hand it is worth making the following point: even if the stone clearly said Arthur, this still would not support a historical Arthur. Given that theorists claim our hero was rather popular in the early middle ages, one would expect a number of different Arthurs all scratching their names on stones and slabs all over Britain. Even if the stone clearly referenced *the* Arthur, this still would not prove a historical rather than mythical figure. The fact is, here we have a stone with a number of different names, none of which are Arthur. Artognou is not Arthur. Attempts to translate this as 'bear-knowing' and link it to Arthur are, at best, hugely speculative.

Summary

I could have started this chapter further back in time. The Saints' Lives are a good example of medieval writers prioritising the message over historical accuracy. We have noted academics are suspicious of certain texts such as the HB and HRB, with one scholar describing Geoffrey of Monmouth as 'an extremely skilful forger'.[36] Many modern theories about Arthur use the HRB and later French Romances as part of the foundation. Any theory using these sources as its foundation is building on sand.

What the Book of Llandaff shows is both how and why some medieval documents were constructed. And constructed they were, and for a specific purpose. This doesn't necessarily mean everything in it is untrue. It does, however, mean we must treat it with caution. It also demonstrates the importance of checking the source material for original or variant spellings.

The doubts surrounding the grave found at Glastonbury shows people were as keen to use the legend for their own ends as they are today. We see this with the modern media reaction to a stone found at Tintagel, which has little to connect it to Arthur.

We will now turn to some of the modern theories to see if any hold water. Readers are now armed with a healthy level of scepticism as well as a good idea of the evolution of the legend. Hopefully it is clear that theories based on fifteenth-century texts alone are no more valid than one based on a twentieth-century film. We also have a brief summary of the relevant genealogies, making it easier to spot tenuous links and questionable etymologies.

Chapter Eleven
Theories

There are far too many theories about Arthur to cover in one book, let alone one chapter. As pointed out in the introduction: while they can't all be right, it is possible they are all entirely wrong. This chapter will look at some of the most common theories and their flaws.

Modern authors have put forward a whole plethora of different theories. Unfortunately many depend on substantial leaps of logic, convoluted etymologies and a loose reading of genealogies – aside from the uncomfortable fact that none of the sources or genealogies are contemporary or can be relied upon. Higham, in *King Arthur The Making of the Legend*, lists just a few of the best-known theories and the areas to which they are attached:[1]

- Scotland and the north: Carroll, Ardrey, Stirling, Breeze, Moffatt, Goodrich, Johnson,
- The North: Keegan, Field, Bromwich.
- North Wales: Blake and Lloyd.
- South Wales: Blackett & Wilson, Gilbert, Barber.
- Shropshire: Phillips and Keatman.
- West country: Alcock
- Devon and Cornwall: Dunning, Castledon.
- Lincolnshire: Green, Leahy
- Essex, Middlesex, East Anglia: Storr, Morris, Laycock.

His final analysis of the legend dismisses these various theories to conclude: 'we can now agree to discount King Arthur as a "real" figure of the past, leaving him and his deeds to the "smoke" and "highland mist" of make-believe and wishful thinking: it is there that he properly belongs'.[2]

Mike Ashley, in *The Mammoth Book of King Arthur*, lists over twenty potential claimants (see table 11).[3] However none are particularly convincing with many having no Arthurian link at all. The more speculative examples will be left to one side and focus on the more likely candidates.

Table 11: List of potential candidates for King Arthur.

Candidate		
Ambrosius Aurelianus c. 450–500	Owain Danwyn fifth century	Cadell fifth century
Riothamus c. 430–470s	Saint Arthmael c. 482–552	Riocatus fifth century
Artúr mac Áedán died c. 594	Lucius Artorius Castus c. 150–250	Brychan c. 430–500
Arthwys ap Mar fifth century	Pascent fifth century	Dyfnwal c. 455–525
Arthur ap Pedr 550–620	Vortipor c. 470–540	Cerdic c. 480–550
Athrwys ap Meurig c. 610–680	Agricola c. 440–510	Caradog 445–515
Cynlas c. 480–550	Arthfael ap Einudd c. 480–550	Urien of Rheged c. 535–590s

To demonstrate how these theories stand up to scrutiny the next section will analyse in depth one of the more well known the 'Sarmatian Connection' and theories concerning the Roman Officer, Lucius Artorius Castus. Harry Sidebottom, a well-known historian and author, reviewing a recent book on this (*Artorius, The Real King Arthur* by Linda A Malcor and John Matthews) concluded: 'if this is an accurate snapshot of non-academic Arthurian studies, to borrow the phrase of Walter Kerr, Me No Leica'. While this chapter may go some way to supporting his point, I hope the remainder will offer an antidote to this rather bleak view.

The 'Sarmatian connection' and Lucius Artorius Castus theories

The theory connecting a rather obscure second- to third-century Roman Officer to Arthurian tradition has gained some ground over recent years. Not least because of the 2004 film *King Arthur*, starring Clive Owen and Keira Knightley. This placed Arthur in the the early fifth century, shortly after the Roman withdrawal. In the film he leads a unit of Sarmatian 'knights' fighting against the 'Woads' (supposedly indigenous fifth-century Britons led by Merlin) and an incursion of Saxons. The film uses the names of the West Saxon leaders from the ASC, Cerdic and Cynric (actually dated to 495), but inexplicably has them invade from north of Hadrian's Wall. The climatic battle of Badon is placed by the Wall.

One of the themes of the film is that Sarmatian knights had been sent to Britain and then replaced as sons followed their fathers over several centuries, bringing their stories with them. Another is that the leader of these knights was traditionally called Artorius, and his exploits were remembered down the centuries. All good fun to watch – but as usual with Hollywood films, not exactly historically accurate.

The first suggestion that Lucius Artorius Castus might be connected to King Arthur was made in 1924 by Kemp Malone, a professor of English literature, largely on the likely etymology of the name Arthur, from the Latin Artorius. The theory was revived by Helmut Nickel in the 1975, who linked Artorius with Sarmatian cavalry posted to Britain. These 'knights', it was claimed, formed the basis of legends of the round table. The carrying of red dragon banners influenced the name Pendragon.

Covington Scott Littleton, an American anthropologist, developed a similar 'Sarmatian connection' theory with Anne Thomas in the 1970s. Littleton co-authored a book with Linda Malcor, *From Scythia to Camelot*, which linked Arthurian legend with Caucasian mythology, most notably the Nart sagas. These tales were written down in the nineteenth century, but may date back to medieval times.

There are a number of facts that are used to weave together this theory. First, there was indeed a Lucius Artorius Castus posted to Britain, specifically as *praefectus* of the Sixth Legion, which was based at York. His memorial stone with his career was found in Croatia in the nineteenth century and has been dated roughly within the Antonine and Severan period, c.160–240. Second, 5,500 Sarmatians were sent to Britain after their defeat by the Romans in 175. According to a fourth-century source, the Alans (another Scythian tribe) worshipped a sword stuck in the ground. One group of Alans settled in the Caucasus region, from which the later Nart Saga tales derived.

A recent evolution of this theory was published in a 2019 journal article by Malcor, Trinchese and Alessandro in the Journal of Indo-European Studies, *Missing Pieces: A New Reading of the Main Lucius Artorius Castus Inscription*. Subsequently, this has been expanded on in the 2022 book, *The Real King Arthur*, by Matthews and Malcor.

In order for the theory to work a number of assertions have to be made, among which are the following: Artorius can be dated accurately and fitted to the period when the Sarmatians were in Britain; he can be linked to these Sarmatians; he fought a number of battles in northern Britain; the missing letters on the stone inscription, *adversus arm-*, can be expanded to *adversus armatos* (against armed men); the use of the word *dux* in the inscription can be used to prove Artorius was a governor of Britain. These need to be looked at in turn. First we must turn to the surviving inscriptions.

Figure 27: Drawing of stone inscription by Charles Evans-Gunther.

One noted academic expands the damaged sections to reveal the following (missing letters and expanded abbreviations in brackets):[4]

> L(ucius) Artori[us Ca]stus centurioni leg(ionis)
> III Gallicae item [centurioni le]g(ionis) VI Ferra-
> -tae item centurioni leg(ionis) II Adi[ut(ricis)] (P{iae} F{idelis}) i]tem
> centurioni leg(ionis) V M[a]-
> -c(edonicae) item p(rimo) p(ilo) eiusdem [leg(ionis)] praeposito
> classis Misenatium [pr]aef{f}(ecto) leg(ionis) VI
> Victricis duci legg(ionum) [triu]m Britan(n)ici-
> -{an}arum adversus Arm[enio]s proc(uratori) cente-
> -nario provinciae Li[burniae iure] gladi(i) vi-
> -vus ipse sibi et suis [... ex te]st[amento]

One possible translation of the sarcophagus is as follows:[5]

> To the divine shades, Lucius Artorius Castus, centurion of the Third Legion Gallica, also centurion of the Sixth Legion Ferrata, also centurion of the Second Legion Adiutrix, also centurion of the Fifth Legion Macedonica, also chief centurion of the same legion, in charge of (Praepositus) the Misenum fleet, prefect of the Sixth Legion Victrix, commander of three British legions against the Armenians, centenary procurator of Liburnia with the power of the sword. He himself (set this up) for himself and his family in his lifetime.

There is some debate as to the date for the stone. Some scholars place it in the Antonine period (c.160–190).[6] Others place it in the early third century.[7] In short, the style of the stone points to the second-half of the second century, while the lettering and words suggest early third century. There is almost universal acceptance that the crucial missing letters can be reconstructed to give us *adversus Armenios*. To support this, the original reading of the inscription by the archaeologist Francesco Carrara in AD 1850 recorded the now weathered stone as ADVERSUS ARME- with a ligatured ME.

We do indeed have three Roman campaigns in, and against, Armenia: 163, 215 and 233. The campaigns of 163 and 233 were part of wider Parthian war, although the Armenian campaigns were separate and distinct. Perhaps importantly, in 163 the Roman Governor of Britain, Statius Priscus, was sent east to prepare to lead the attack on the Armenian capital at Artaxata. This has caused some academics to favour this timeframe.[8]

Caracalla's Armenian War of c.215 was fought the year before his Parthian campaign and is the one I tentatively put forward in my own book, *The Roman King Arthur? Lucius Artorius Castus*. Intriguingly we have a reference to a '*dux Armeniae erat et item legatus Asiae atque Arabiae*' under Emperor Macrinus in c.217.[9] There was certainly a successful campaign in c. 215–6 as the Romans granted their client king Tiridates II the Armenian crown in AD 217. Caracalla was also in Britain when his father, Septimius Severus, died at York in 211. It is thus likely he was familiar with officers of the Sixth in the Caledonian campaign of 208–11.

But what of the suggestion *Armatos*: armed-men? Roman memorial stones commemorating a career and campaign were rather specific in naming the enemy. Internal enemies were labelled rebels, public enemies or deserters (e.g. *adversus rebelles, hostes publicos*). External enemies were also routinely named – Parthians, Germans or even barbarians. There is no example of a vague term such as 'armed men' being used on such stones. The word *Armatos* is found in literary sources (where one would expect to see Latin words) and a law code (the *Lex Ursonensis*, the foundation charter of the Caesarean *colonia Iulia Genetiva* at Urso near Osuna in the province of Seville, Andalusia, southern Spain). This latter written on a number of bronze tablets. None of these examples are the same context as a memorial stone.

Let us now turn to the word *dux* and leading three British Legions. The missing letters in the sixth line could give *trium, duarum, alarum* or *num* (short for numerus). It cannot be assumed he led all three entire legions. Generally, this would mean vexillations of those legions. The absence of the letters VEX for vexillations is not considered a problem by experts. Their interpretation of the word *dux* is more damning. In the second century, *dux* simply meant a temporary ad hoc command. Various examples exist from the first century onwards. Dux began to evolve as an official post in the early third century. Crucially, then it meant over a geographical area and not a body of troops as in the inscription. It was not an official post in Britain until the fourth century, after the reforms of Diocletian or, more likely, Constantine I.

Nor could Artorius have been a governor of Britain, even if he did temporarily command all three legions. There were two types of Roman provinces: imperial, where the governor reported to the emperor; and senatorial, where the governor reported to the senate. With the exception of Egypt and some minor provinces, they were all administered by someone of senatorial rank in this period. Castus was most definitely an equestrian as his last post was as a civilian procurator. Every single attested governor of Britain for this period was of senatorial rank, *legatus augusti pro praetore*.

A *praefectus legionis* for this period was a camp prefect, *praefectus castrorum*. In earlier decades this would be signified by the letters by CASTR, but this was dropped towards the end of the second century. In fact we have an example of a similar inscription dated to 198–209 for a certain Publius Saliienus Thalamus of the Second Legion at Caerleon (RIB 326): praef(ectus) leg(ionis) II Aug(ustae). It was not until the reforms of Emperor Gallienus after the mid-third century that equestrians routinely commanded legions and were titled *praefectus legionis*. There are some minor exceptions to this, for example under Septimius Severus, but not, crucially, in Britain.

So in brief, Castus was a camp prefect of the Sixth legion at York and was likely given a temporary command over two or three vexillations of the legions in Britain. Unless we find an enemy with the letters ARM....S, the most likely candidates were Armenians, therefore pointing to the campaigns of 163, 215 or 233.

Another important point concerns military structure. The legionary command structure was separate from the auxiliary units. They were led by senatorial legates. Auxiliary units had their own command structures and were led by an equestrian *praefectus* (or *tribunus*). The latter reported direct to the governor. They would only come under the command of a legionary legate when on a specific campaign. A legionary camp prefect was therefore within the legionary command structure and would not normally command auxiliary units. The inscription makes no reference to such a command. Which brings us to the Sarmatians.

First, it is worth noting there is no hint from the stone inscription that Artorius Castus had any contact with any auxiliary groups, let alone specifically Sarmatians. There is also no evidence he fought a single battle. At this stage in his career he would have been in his fifties and more likely dealing with logistics and maintenance of the camp, which for the Sixth was at York.

The Scythians were a nomadic people of Eurasia who covered a wide area north of the Black and Caspian seas from around 800 BC. By the end of the millennium various independent tribes had emerged, including the Sarmatians and Alani. The Greek historian Hippocrates describe the Sarmatians in the fourth century BC. By the time of Marcus Aurelius one particular group, the Sarmatian Iazyges, were settled north of the Danube. As they left no written records, there is no way of knowing if they had similar traditions as the Alans in the fourth century let alone Nart Sagas of the nineteenth.

Now we come to a crucial piece of evidence. In 175 the Sarmatians surrendered to the Romans and as part of the settlement, the defeated Iazyges 'furnished as their contribution to the alliance eight thousand cavalry, fifty-five hundred of whom he sent to Britain'.[10] Cassius Dio makes no further comment. We don't know how many (if any) arrived, or what they did when they got there.[11]

It is likely one unit at least did. Two undated inscriptions (RIB 594 and 595) from Ribchester refer to a Sarmatian cavalry unit, *alae*. Two further inscriptions can be dated, one to 225–35 (RIB 587) and the other to 241 (RIB 583). These inscriptions refer to a *numeri* suggesting the unit had been reduced in size. Ribchester was large enough for a unit of 500. They also refer to a legionary centurion from the Sixth Legion, presumably being promoted to temporary commander of this auxiliary unit. None of this supports the claim a legionary camp commander led 5,500 Sarmatians.

Let us assume some of the 5,500 arrived. Auxiliary units tended to be of 500 or 1,000. Each would have had its own equestrian *praefectus* commander. This commander would have been following the *tres militiae* career path which did not include a *praefectus legionis*. The Sarmatians themselves would have served twenty-five years and then gained Roman citizenship. The unit name may have continued but this would not necessarily be an indication of ethnicity. If some survived up to c.200, they may well have settled in the *vicus* around Ribchester.

In the second century, Ribchester was likely within the hinterland of the legionary fort at Chester where Legio XX Valeria Victrix was stationed. It was only after the first division of Britain under Caracalla that Ribchester found itself in the same northern province as York, the headquarters of Legio VI Victrix. Hence why we start to see centurions from the Sixth legion taking temporary positions there in the second quarter of the third century (while noting a *praefectus legionis* would remain at York within the legionary command structure).

If auxiliaries married local women their children may well have joined up. After Caracalla extended Roman citizenship in 212 the distinction between auxiliary units (usually non-citizens) and legions (made up of citizens) became less important. But there was no arrangement, as in the film, where sons followed their fathers from the steppes to Britain over many centuries.

With no connection between Artorius and Sarmatians, we are left with dragon banners, swords and folklore. Draco banners were used extensively in the Roman army. The link with Arthur is rather tenuous. The title Pendragon was added by in the HRB to Uther not Arthur. This is likely a misunderstanding of the Welsh phrase 'chief-warrior', which Geoffrey mistranslated. Nor can we link the Alan practice of worshipping a sword in the earth. In Arthurian legend the sword is not worshipped and was first in an anvil upon a stone, later placed in the stone itself.

Lastly we have the alleged similarity of the Nart Sagas to the Arthurian tales. The Narts were not written down until the nineteenth century and thus could have been influenced by Arthurian tales moving east from the twelfth century.[12] Colarusso and Salbiev's book, *Tales of the Narts*, contains eighty-nine tales spread over 425 pages.[13] The consensus seems to be that the core of the content is no later than AD 500–700.[14] Thus it post-dates by many centuries contact between Sarmatian Iazyges and Alans. In all these many tales, there are just two concepts that are noted by Istvanovits and Kulcsar as parallels:[15] The sword and a magical cup.

I can only urge the reader to compare the two traditions. I did just that in my 2022 book, *The Roman King Arthur? Lucius Artorius Castus*. I found no similarity between the stories. A magical god-like Batraz figure battling gods and spirits eventually dies. Only in a much later version is a sword involved (along with gunpowder and canons, conveniently ignored) and, other than being tossed into the sea, has nothing in common with Excalibur. The second concept involves the bowl Wasamonga. This magical, moving bowl contains various spirits who attack Batraz's father who luckily had 'whiskers as sharp as steel'. Somehow this bowl is equated with the cauldron in various Arthurian tales, such as the cauldron of Diwrnach in Ireland in *Culhwch and Olwen*.

The entire theory rests on several layers of connected assumptions. The fall of any one of which causes the entire edifice to fail. My own research found no support for any of the claims. What of the wider academic community? Guy Halsall in his 2013 book, *Worlds of Arthur, Facts and Fictions of the Dark Ages*, dismissed the theory entirely.[16] Istvanovits and Kulcsar describe the Artorius-Arthur theory and connection with Sarmatians as 'imaginative and controversial'.[17] They conclude they are 'not wholly convinced by the arguments that challenge King Arthur's indigenous Celtic roots'. Nicholas Higham's

2018 book, *King Arthur, The Making of the Legend*, devotes three chapters to Lucius Artorius Castus, the Sarmatian connection and a comparison with the Ossetian Narts. He found the theory 'entirely unconvincing', and one that should be dismissed.

Anthony Birley, an expert in Roman Britain, simply remarks about the idea: 'It must now lapse.'[18] Tomlin, one of the leading experts in Roman epigraphy, found the prospect of Priscus being accompanied in 163 by one of his own senior officers in Britain, Artorius Castus, leading detachments to Armenia: 'a brighter suggestion than to invoke the Celtic shades of Arthurian legend'.[19] Ken Dark points out that the theory requires a memory to be preserved across several centuries with no trace in between. There is great doubt that a middle-ranking Roman officer would be the basis of much later Arthurian legends.[20] Concerning the Sarmatians, one scholar found 'a mixture of sound scholarship on the early Steppe nomads with inaccuracies and flights of historical and etymological fancy'.[21]

A 2020 article by Bradley Skeen analysed the claims made in the 2019 article, *Missing Pieces*.[22] He found the explanation concerning Latin dative and nominative case confused, leaving the interpretation 'without parallel in Latin epigraphy'. The position on the terms *praepositus* and *dux* were 'entirely unsupported' and suggested a 'misunderstanding about the term'. The proposed precise date for his floruit had 'very little foundation'. The proposed translation was 'simply without precedent' and 'impossible to accept', and the word *Armatos* had 'little justification'. He noted the initial excavation report by F. Carrara (1851/52) which showed that the M before the break is in ligature with an E making ARME[NIO]S was dismissed without explanation but remains the most likely reading.

The Artorius' cursus lacked any reference to Sarmatians and 'there is no other evidence for any part of that assertion'. The wider theory involving LAC leading Sarmatian warriors is 'entirely unsupported since there is no evidence of any such campaign'. Thus the connection between LAC and Sarmatians 'can only be asserted without evidence'. Even more damning for their interpretation was the absence of reference to *dux* in the shorter, second inscription on the sarcophagus. Which strongly suggests the proposed interpretation of the larger inscription and his career is untenable. Finally, he concludes the contention that the genesis of Arthurian mythology was the repurposing of national Sarmatian mythology (cognate with the Nart sagas) as praise of Castus is 'no more convincing than it ever was'.

Despite a lack of current academic support a new book, *Artorius, The Real King Arthur* by Linda A. Malcor and John Matthews appeared in 2022. We will finish this topic where we began, with Harry Sidebottom's review in the *Telegraph*, 17 December 2022, in which he found the work suffered from 'out-of-date scholarship and wishful thinking', 'improbable assumptions' and a 'cavalier approach to evidence'. Parts he labelled simply as 'fiction' and 'completely unconvincing'. No doubt the authors, and other proponents of the theory, will continue to robustly argue their case.

My own opinion is that it is one of the weakest of all the theories about King Arthur. There is no link between a second- or third-century Roman officer and Sarmatians. No link between either of these and later Arthurian legends. Nothing to suggest later legends look back to Roman times. The theory stands upon a number of hugely speculative proposals, along with a unique interpretation of the inscription and some spectacular leaps of logic. With all this removed (and the theory requires many of the claims to be true at the same time) one is left with simply a name and the assertion, without evidence, that this must be the original Arthur.

Arthur of southern Wales

The theory that Arthur was a prince of the Silures can be traced back to a sixteenth-century error.[23] After the rediscovery of the Book of Llandaff, a John Prise, c.1545, noted a land grant to Noe ap Arthur ap Pedr of Dyfed. The Latin text also refers to an *Athruis fili Mourici* on twelve occasions, one of which titles him *Rex Athruis*, as noted earlier. The Welsh equivalent is *Athrwys*. The following century, Francis Godwin, a Bishop of Llandaff, misspelt the name as *Arthruis* and this seems to have been copied by subsequent antiquarians. This additional 'r' has been used by a number of modern theorists, but the name appears to have been originally *Athruis* – which leads to *Athrwys*, and not *Arthruis*, *Arthrwys* or Arthur.

It is worth repeating the genealogies:

The Harleian genealogies[24] Morcant map **Atroys** map Teutubric
Jesus college:[25] Morgant m **Adroes** m Meuric m Theudric
Gwehelyth Morgannwg:[26] Morgan ap **Adroes** ap Meyrig ap Twedrig
The Llywelyn ab Iorwerth genealogies:[27] Morgant ap **Athwrys** ap Meuric ap Teuderic

We can see none spell the name as Arthrwys, Arthwyr. The closest is Athwrys. As noted earlier, other spellings include Athrues, Athues, Athraws, Athyrwys, Arthrnes. None of these, or those in the genealogies above, can be equated with Arthur. We have already seen Arthur has a separate and distinctive pedigree. He is never portrayed as connected with this particular line of kings.

Bartrum looks in detail at potentially two figures named Athwrys ap Meurig. One he dates firmly to the seventh century, born in c. 620. An alleged earlier figure may be a duplication of the same person. However, even if there was a second Athwrys ap Meurig the charters and people he is associated with are also dated to the early seventh century.[28] Wendy Davies correctly spells his name Athrwys and dates him to 625–655.[29]

Aside from having the wrong name and living at the wrong time, I could find nothing to support any significant Arthurian connection. Nevertheless, a number of theorists have maintained this belief. Scott Lloyd in *The Arthurian Place Names of Wales* provides an excellent analysis of the evolution of the legend and covers a number of different theories. A number of these look to an Arthur in southern Wales.

One prominent example is the works of Wilson and Blackett. Lloyd notes they place 'a strong emphasis on the works of Iolo Morganwg and make frequent use of inaccurate Victorian editions of medieval Welsh texts, while ignoring most modern editions and discussions'.[30] He notes they 'have been largely ignored by the scholarly community'.

The central claim in their book *Artorius Rex Discovered*, is that Arthur is a composite of two figures. The later figure is Athwrys ap Meuric discussed above. Here he is dated to c. 503 to c. 579 and his name spelled *Arthrwys*.[31] Other names are linked to this figure: Arthwyr, Arthmail, Arthmael, Arthfael and Arthwys.[32]

A persistent theme is notable: English 'academic paranoia' causes Welsh historical sources to be 'consistently and completely ignored'.[33] The English Establishment 'dare not admit' that King Arthur was the king of Glamorgan and Gwent.[34] There are 'no lengths to which they will not go to conceal the truths'.[35] Archaeologists are damned as 'Roman mad'.[36] Leslie Alcock in particular (author of *Arthur's Britain*) comes in for specific criticism: 'being an Englishman he fails to comprehend the true nature of the Welsh nation and its states'.[37]

A number of claims stood out: the Romans allegedly did not achieve a conquest of Britain, but rather got footholds and held some areas in south-eastern Britain;[38] several Roman Emperors are equated with British kings from Welsh Genealogies;[39] King Arthur visited Florida in the year 555 and Prince Madoc ap Owen of Gwynedd followed his example in 1070;[40] and the legendary King Brutus landed on Aberavon beach around 500 BC with 6,000 warriors and families (although the authors accept they don't have 'the so dearly loved evidence of conventional historians').[41]

The first 'Arthur' is claimed to be a son of Magnus Maximus, the usurping Emperor 383–8.[42] The known son of Maximus, Victor, is equated with Uther, allegedly titled 'Pendragon of Cardiff' and 'Augustus of Gaul'. Alternative variations of his name are claimed to be Arthun, Anhunn and Andragathius (Andragathius was in fact the *magister equitum* of Magnus Maximus. Rather than dying in battle Andragathius, 'who was then cruising in the Ionian Sea … threw himself into the sea' after his master's defeat[43]). This first Arthur they describe as 'king of Greece' and 'Conqueror of Europe'.

It was a difficult book to assess as there were no footnotes, endnotes or references in the 1986 copy I reviewed, just a list of reference manuscripts and books at the back. Weight is given to the twelfth-century Llandaff Charters and the work of Edward Williams (Iolo Morganwg), both of which have been covered previously. A vigorous defence is made concerning Iolo Morganwg, who they argue has been unfairly maligned as a fraudster, and thus the Coelbren alphabet is claimed to be a genuine form of lettering which predates the Roman alphabet and was the original script in which Khymric was written.[44] Further books include *The Discovery of the Ark of the Covenant* (in southern Wales), *Where Jesus is Buried* and *Moses In The Hieroglyphs*. I remain unconvinced.

A second book featuring the theories of the authors above was written by Adrien Gilbert *The Holy Kingdom: Quest for the Real King Arthur*. This received an unfortunate 'unreadable nonsense' by one reviewer.[45] I will leave the debate about an alleged cross and Tombstone of Arthur to experts in Latin epigraphy, along with the claim a cave in West Wales contains the true cross of Jesus.[46] Here I will focus on the claim concerning 'the first Arthur'. In Gilbert's book Arthur I's pedigree is given thus:[47]

> Eidinet ap **Arthun** ap Maxim Gulc tic qui occidit Gratian cum regum Romanorum.

Yet in the actual genealogies (which must be noted are all from many centuries after) the name is **Anthun**:

> **Anthun** map Maxim Guletic qui occidit Gratianum regem Romanorum.[48]

In addition, the Brecon manuscripts – commonly known as the Brychan MSS – give the following spellings: Annhun and Annwn. I could find no genealogies that use the spelling Arthun. In addition, the Anthun, or derivatives such as Annun, derives from the Latin Antonius and not from Arthur at all. A discussion about Annun ap Macsen Wledig (Magnus Maximus) and Annun Ddu (an ancestor of the legendary Brychen) can be found in Bartrum.[49] Along with a possible explanation as to why later sources recorded an Antonius as *rex Grecorum*. Another curious theory that is sometimes found in this area is the claim the Welsh, or Britons, were a lost tribe of Israel. I found nothing to support this either, but no doubt developments in genetics will deal with this one way or the other.

Chris Barber in *King Arthur*, also proposed Athrwys ap Meurig of Gwent, but claims Athrwys abdicated and retired to Brittany as St Arthmael (St Armel). I can find no support for this in Bartrum, Ben Guy, or anywhere else. The earliest source for the saint dates to the thirteenth century and provides an unrelated pedigree to him. As with so many theories, we hit another dead-end with little more than speculation.

There is nothing particularly implausible about Arthur being associated with Glamorgan or Gwent (or any other part of Wales). However, in conclusion I found little to support the theory of either **Athwrys** ap Meuric or an unverified son of Magnus Maximus as the basis for King Arthur.

Arthur of Rhos or Powys

One pair of candidates for Arthur derives from the comment by Gildas when referring to Cuneglasus: 'thou bear ... driver of a chariot of the bear's stronghold'.[50] It is admittedly quite interesting that Gildas uses the word 'bear', but as we have seen, he uses similar animal imagery for his other kings: Constantine is the 'whelp of the filthy lioness of Dumnonia'; Aurelius Caninus is a 'lion-whelp'; Vortipor, like a 'leopard in your behaviour, spotted with wickedness'; and Maelgwn, 'dragon of the island'.

A common possible identification of Cuneglasus is Cynlas Goch ap Owain. In this Bartrum finds there is 'little doubt' and places him in the genealogy of the kings of Rhos, Gwynedd.[51] Unfortunately we have little further we can say even if the identification is sound.

We noted earlier that the Welsh soldier and writer Elis Gruffydd, in the sixteenth century, records a tradition associating Arthur with northern Wales. Another area of interest is the Roman town of Viroconium in Shropshire just thirteen miles from the Welsh border and forty miles south east of Ruthin, where traditions claim Huail, elder brother of Gildas, was executed by Arthur. Here we find evidence for a continuation of town life, possibly a bishopric and a surviving centre of power.

An alternative suggestion for the reference to 'bear' in Gildas is the father of Cynlas, Owain Danwyn. Bartrum also records him as a king of Rhos and his nephew, Maelgwn, as king of Gwynedd.[52] Cynlas and Maelgwn were cousins, great-grandsons of Cunedda and thus according to later genealogies, second cousins to Arthur.

Graham Phillips, in his 2016 book *The Lost Tomb of King Arthur*, proposed that Owain Ddantgwyn was actually king of Powys ruling from Viroconium.[53] The association seems to rely on Owain possessing a bear-type nickname. In addition, we read the banner of the Earls of Warwick included a bear emblem, and a fifteenth-century writer claimed they descended from a warrior called Arthgallus.[54] To top it off, he declared the grave of King Arthur had been found in Shropshire.[55] Situated on private land, it requires permission from the landowners and the relevant Secretary of State to investigate further. Metal detecting and digging being illegal without permission.

There is nothing implausible about an Arthur using Viroconium as a power base. From there a leader could exert power into many areas mentioned: southern Wales; Dumnonia; the Wessex area; east towards Lindsey; and north, where many of the proposed battle sites lay. It's proximity to Baschurch is also noteworthy.

However, apart from a possible, tenuous, connection with bear imagery through Gildas, there is nothing substantial to go on. The suggestion that Maelgwn, in this theory supposedly playing the part of Mordred, killed his uncle Owain Ddantgwyn doesn't stand up. Owain was Maelgwn's paternal uncle and Gildas very specifically tells us Maglocunnus killed his *maternal* uncle. So even if Maelgwn was Maglocunnus, he killed the wrong uncle. An uncle who was not called Arthur, but whom we are urged to believe had a bear-type nickname. In addition, we note tradition has Mordred dying alongside Arthur at Camlann. In this theory, Maelgwn supposedly kills Owain and rules in Gwynedd, while Cynlas rules in Powys. So even if Maelgwn and Cynlas can be equated with two of Gildas' tyrant kings, the details don't appear to match. Aside from the fact Bartrum places Owain and Cynlas in nearby Rhos and not Powys, which has a distinct an very different set of genealogies.

Phillips has a number of other titles: *Atlantis and the Ten Plagues of Egypt*; *Merlin and the Discovery of Avalon in the New World*; *The Search for the Grail*; and *The Templars and the Ark of the Covenant*. I haven't read these and so cannot comment as to their content. However, I remain sceptical about claims regarding the Holy Grail, Ark of the Covenant, Merlin or Dark Age journeys by King Arthur across the Atlantic.

In summary, I find associations with Powys, Viroconium and Baschurch interesting. However, I found the theory to be constructed with a large number of tenuous links. We have nothing linking Owain with Arthur, or Arthur to Owain (or indeed Cynlas). Additionally, this identification is at odds with what Welsh genealogists claimed about both figures. The theories require us to ignore the fact that they appear as separate people with a different pedigree entirely.

The Pennine Dragon, Arthwys ap Mar

Simon Keegan, in *Pennine Dragon, The Real King Arthur of the North*, suggests Arthwys ap Mar is Arthur. Here at least we have a name that is, at face value, similar to Arthur, although in later manuscripts his name is always spelled Athrwys.[56] Nothing else is known about him. While it looks similar however, this name has a different and well-documented root.[57] Nevertheless, he is around the correct time period, although a generation earlier than where scribes have placed Arthur. Two genealogies list Arthwys. The first lists: Athrwys ap Mar ap Kenav ap Koel Godebog.[58] The *Bonedd Gwyr y Gogledd* also has the following: Arthwys ap Mar ap Keneu ap Coel.[59]

This places him a generation before Arthur appears in the genealogies and a grandfather to the men that fought at Arfderydd. As with Owain Ddantgwyn we have nothing to say about this figure other than he appears in the lists of kings. At least here we have someone who had an Arth-type name, even if it is one with a different etymology.

The proposed family tree does not appear to be supported by the genealogies listed previously.[60] It is also claimed that Arthwys ap Mar was known as Arthur Penuchel.[61] However, Arthur Penuchel is listed as a brother to Gwrgi and Peredur (the princes who fought at Arfderydd) and thus a grandson of Arthwys.[62] In order to make this work we read that his father, Mar, was associated with York, which in turn became mistranslated as Iubhar.[63] Yet York has a well-attested etymology Similarly Pendragon Castle in Westmorland can't be used to support this theory as it was built in the early twelfth century and there is no evidence of pre-Norman occupation of the site.

Again there is no reason why a historical Arthur could not be located in this region and timeframe. The problem is that, as with so many theories, it appears to disintegrate when exposed to scrutiny. There is little to support it other than an Arth-type name and being roughly the right timeframe. Bartrum declares he appears in the genealogies only as a link and 'nothing is known' about him.[64] Some later sources spell his name *Athrwys* but more importantly the genealogies don't even hint at a connection with Arthur.

Artuir mac Áedáin

The name *Artuir* does indeed derive from the Brittonic name *Arthur*. It is also true that his father, Áedán mac Gabráin, had a number of Brittonic familial links. Áedán ruled in Dál Riada, Dál Riata or Dalriada, a Gaelic kingdom spanning Western Scotland and north-east Ireland. His reign was c. 574–609. We have already noted how limited references to Artuir in the sources are:

Adomnan's *Life of St Columba*; the Annals of Ulster; the Annals of Tigernach; and the tenth-century text *Senchus Fer n'Alban*, 'The History of the Men of Scotland'.

Artuir appears to have died fighting the Miathi (a tribe around the Clyde-Forth Isthmus) in c. 594–5. It thus seems likely he was born in the second half of the sixth century. Little more can be said and aside from the name I could find no Arthurian connection. Keith Coleman, in *Áedán of the Gaels, King of the Scots*, also found no link between Artuir mac Áedáin and Arthurian legends.[65]

Adam Ardrey, in *Finding Arthur: The True Origins of the Once and Future King*, uses a number of later sources to argue for Arthur's identification as Artuir: For example John Fordun's *Chronica Gentis Scotorum*, Chronicles of the Scottish People.[66] Fourteenth- and fifteenth-century sources are relied on to place The Round Table at Stirling.[67] Arthur's battles are placed in the north, with Artuir naturally leading his father's forces to victory. Gwenddolau is proposed as Uther Pendragon, Badon dated to 588 at Badden, Argyll and Bute in Western Scotland and Camlan is placed at Camelon, Falkirk, with Avalon in Iona. Adomnan's omission about Camlan, and presumably Artuir's identification as Arthur, is put down to 'ignorance, laziness or cynicism'.[68]

One proposed battle site, Trimontium, is described as the 'Roman capital of Scotland ... remembered as the City of the Legion.'[69] However, the fort was an auxiliary cavalry fort, not a legionary fortress, with a maximum garrison of 1,000. It is also thought to have been abandoned c.180s. This is likely to have been a casualty of the raid during the reign of Commodus, referenced by Cassius Dio.[70] In c.182–4, tribes 'crossing the wall that separated them from the Roman legions, proceeded to do much mischief and cut down a general together with his troops'. More importantly, the fort was never referred to as 'City of the Legion'.

Another example can be found in an attempt to associate Áedáin's wife, the 'Lady of Strathclyde', with Arthur's mother.[71] I found the explanation tenuous and filled with serval 'ifs', none of which convinced.

Medieval Scottish writers did begin to take note of Arthurian tradition and incorporate into their texts. However, this was many centuries after even the HRB, itself 600 years after Arthur's alleged timeframe. In fact Scottish writers, such as John of Fordun, emphasised that Arthur was an illegitimate king, having been born out of wedlock. The true heir, they claim, was in fact Mordred, born to Arthur's sister Anna and the Scottish noble, Loth.

In conclusion, I could find no evidence for Artuir being Arthur, aside from his name. He appears too late and has no apparent Arthurian connection.

Arthur ap Pedr

Here at least we have a candidate called Arthur, although perhaps a little too late. Bartrum dates him from c.560.[72] The genealogies place him in Dyfed as a grandson of Gourtepir (possibly 'Vortipor, tyrant of the Demetae' from Gildas). The link to Irish settlement is interesting in light of the existence of other Arthurs with Irish ancestry. The presence of the Ogham and Latin inscription there, *Memoria Voteporigis protictoris*, suggests Irish mercenaries may have been hired and their rulers given the Roman title *protictoris*, Protector.

Other than the name, there is nothing to link him to Arthur or to link later traditions back to him. Given the survival of Dyfed one might expect the genealogists and copyists to highlight the connection. Yet we get nothing. Once again, later genealogies present them as separate individuals.

Riothamus

Championed by Geoffrey Ashe, in *The Discovery of King Arthur*, it is claimed the name doubles as a title, *Rigotamos*, 'great-king' or 'over-king'. Unfortunately, it seems certain that this was a personal name as evidenced by a surviving letter from Sidonius Apollinaris. We have already noted he may well have been located north of the Loire rather than Britain, and in any case we know nothing else about him. The one battle we know about was a defeat. The suggestion he was heading towards Avalon after his defeat has equally little merit. The legendary place only appeared in the legend in the twelfth century (Geoffrey's HRB). While Riothamus allegedly fled east towards the Burgundians, the town of Avallon is 200 km away from Bourg-de Deols, and at the time was known as Abalo.[73] Given that battle was dated to c. 471, it seems unlikely he would survive to fight at Badon in 490s or 516.

Ambrosius Aurelianus

This is in my opinion the best candidate, but it relies on one of his names being forgotten or left out by Gildas. Alternatively we would have to fall back on a bear-type nickname. Should we find a ring or stone bearing the inscription, *Ambrosius Artorius Aurelianus*, even the most sceptical historian would be forced to at least raise an eyebrow in interest. However, aside from his likely association with Badon (implied by Gildas) there is nothing else we can say about him. Nor do any later traditions hint at this identification (or indeed any of the previous suggestions).

The earliest Arthurian source, HB, makes clear Ambrosius and Arthur are two separate figures. The first is the boy prophet Emrys who explains to Vortigern why his castle walls keep collapsing (the tale of the red and white 'worms' or dragons). The second is the warrior Arthur, leading the kings of the

Britons in battle. Later tradition, such as the HRB, make Ambrosius brother to Uther and thus Arthur's uncle.

It is worth noting that Arthur is rarely associated with Badon in the earliest Welsh tradition and Gildas could be interpreted differently. One could argue both Ambrosius and Arthur fought at Badon, either one, or neither.

Constructing an Arthurian theory

Above is just a short collection of the many theories that cry out from the shelves of bookshops. I found none particularly convincing and a modicum of scrutiny leaves one with a handful of speculations and leaps of faith. Just to prove how easy it is to construct a theory out of not very much I will now present the following: Arthur, King in the North.

Easy to begin, as I can claim our first attested source is *Y Gododdin*. The throwaway line, 'he was no Arthur', can be accepted as part of a genuine sixth-century oral poem from the very area of Britain to which our theory points. Next we turn to the HB. While only the Harleian recension has all seven sections the Chartres manuscript is the earliest copy dated to c.900, a century after it is thought to have been written.[74] This version has Rhun, son of Urien, as the author (I may neglect to mention it doesn't actually contain the battle list). This allows me to suggest a much earlier date for its construction, as the HB claims Rhun baptised Edwin of Northumbria in 627. Dating it to less than a century after Camlan. In fact, if I claim Rhun wrote it c.600, I could argue he might have had spoken to elderly first-hand witnesses now in their eighties.

It has also been suggested by some scholars that the AC derived some of its information from a lost northern source. Thus Badon and Camlan were entered by a northern copyist. All that is left is to explain why northern versions of the HB and AC appeared in Wales centuries later. Not a difficult problem, with the enduring links between the regions. The battles from the HB also present no problem. The first eleven can all be associated with northern locations and I can gloss over any uncertainty.

1. River Glein: River Glen in Northumberland.
2–5. River Duglas in the *regione linnuis*: Lindsey.
6. Bassas: Baschurch, Shropshire.
7. Silua celidonis, cat coit celidon: Caledonian forest north near the River Liddel and the village of Carwinley.

8. Castellum Guinnion: Vonovium, the Roman fort at Binchester near Durham.

9. Urbe Legionis, cair lion: Chester.

10. Traht treuroit: in the north near locations mentioned in Pa Gur, such as Din Eidyn.

11. Monte breguoin, bregion: Bremenium, the Roman fort at High Rochester.

All these sites are on the borders of the former northern province of Britannia Secunda. It is therefore possible to argue Arthur inherited the role of the Roman *Dux Britanniarum*. The reference to *Dux Bellorum* in the HB can be used to support this.

What of Badon? There's no particular issue with having a northern Arthur heading south to aid the southern kings. Alternatively, it can be argued that Arthur was erroneously attached to the battle, as the earliest Welsh tradition makes little of his connection. However, a number of northern locations are equally possible. First, there is Buxton in Derbyshire, named *Aqua Armemetiae* by the Romans, and the only other spa town in Roman Britain after Bath. Perhaps the author of the HB knew the battle was 'near the baths' and made a mistake, which Geoffrey of Monmouth copied. Buxton has the advantage of being surrounded by hills. Additionally, the Roman road heading north-east to Doncaster is still called Batham Gate today. Linguistically, Badon to Batham is as acceptable as Bath.

Second, there is a village called Wall a couple of miles north of Hexham. We recall Octha was given land 'in the north about the Wall that is called Guaul'. Hexham was once called Hagustealde, meaning 'young warriors enclosure'. If Octha came down from the north and 'then Arthur fought against them', it is reasonable to suggest he attacked the mercenaries left behind. Ten miles further west is Bardon Mill, which could easily have derived from Badon with a long 'a' sound such as in 'father'.

Other options for Badon are available, notably Bowden hillfort in the Scottish Borders and Badden in Argyll. Camlan can be located at Camelon, Camboglanna or Cambuslang. With all our battles now firmly in the north, what to do about Celliwig in Cornwall? This association with Cornwall only occurred after Geoffrey of Monmouth in the early twelfth century. However, it is possible the word Cernyw was mistranslated.

Instead, Cernyw may have derived from Cernywys, itself coming from the Cornovii, the tribal area that evolved into Powys. Place names such as Llangernyw in Denbighshire and Lann Cernyw, recorded in the charters of the *Book of Llandaff* suggest the Cornovii may have been pushed westwards by the Mercians (many thanks to Charles Evans-Gunther for this intriguing suggestion). An Arthur from North Wales, thirty miles west of Chester, might be a reasonable choice for *Dux Bellorum* for northern kings. The pedigrees of Uther and Eigr can now also be moved from Cornwall to Powys.

The Welsh poem *Canu Heledd* tells of the destruction of Pengwern. It refers to *Eglwyssau Bassa* (Churches of Bassa) and the same name appears in the nearby village of Baschurch, which appears in the Domesday Book of 1086 as *Bascherche*. Within the collection is the death-song to her brother, Cynddylan, *Marwnad Cynddylan*. One suggested translation of a single line is: 'the young whelps of great Arthur, the mighty fortress'.

Pengwern is sometimes mistakenly referred to as a seventh-century sub-kingdom of Powys in modern Shropshire. However, there is no evidence that such a sub-kingdom existed and it was instead a place-name. Gerald of Wales explains that the name means the 'head of the alder-grove' and is in fact the town of Shrewsbury.[75] It is just possible this is the Penrhyn Rhionydd in the North, recorded as one of Arthur's Three Principal Courts in Triad 85.

Powys evolved from the Roman *civitas* of the Cornovii centred on Viroconium, Wroxeter.[76] We see evidence here of a British controlled area into the sixth century, a century before Mercia penetrated that far west.[77] The evidence points to a continuation of occupation and land use with the rebuilding of the basilica in timber rather than stone. Thus regarding deurbanisation in the fifth century, Wroxeter maybe the 'exception that proves the rule'.[78] Many fifth-century towns in Gaul became fortified centres for bishoprics and maintained some urban functions.[79]

A tombstone dated to the late fifth century suggests the presence of an Irish chieftain named Cunorix. The presence of Irish mercenaries can be used to explain why the name Arthur was popular with Irish dynasties such as in Arthur ap Pedr in Dyfed and Artuir mac Áedáin in Dalriada (I would have to ignore the obvious question of why it is not seen in Welsh pedigrees).

Our next task is to trawl through the later French and Welsh tales to find examples connecting him to the area. Not too difficult. The Dream of Rhonabwy places events at Rhyd-y-Groes on the Shropshire-Welsh border. The poem *Pa gur yv y porthaur?* mentions Din Eidyn twice. Kai battles the *chinbin* ('dogheads' possibly led by Gwrgi Garwlwyd, 'rough-grey man-hound') on the mountain at Edinburgh. The French Romance *Perceval* begins at Carduel, a regular name for Carlisle in the middle ages (although placed in Wales by Chrétien). Geoffrey of Monmouth has Arthur fighting beyond the former Antonine Wall. All that is required is to emphasise every event in the North and minimise those in the South.

We now have a coherent scenario, a contracting former northern Roman province fighting battles on its borders against enemies from the north and south and the emerging Anglo-Saxon kingdoms of Bernicia and Deira on the east coast of Yorkshire and Northumbria. With Arthur, hailing from north-eastern Wales, and Shropshire appointed as *dux bellorum* by the kings of the emerging kingdoms. The descendants of these kings fighting at Cattraeth and Arfderydd.

Lastly, we need a candidate. Here I present Cuneglasus, one of the five tyrants Gildas castigates: 'thou bear ... driver of a chariot of the bear's stronghold'. Thus Arthur can be explained away as a nickname, bear-man. To add another layer of evidence I can identify this figure as Cynlas Goch the son of Owain Danwyn, who ruled in Rhos, a sub-kingdom of Gwynedd. Alternatively, I could use Arthwys ap Mar from *Bonedd Gwyr y Gogledd*. Or his supposed grandson, Arthur Penuchel. Whichever I chose, I would need to explain the absence of Eigr and Uther from his genealogies.

Now we have a working theory from which to construct a book. In my opinion, it would actually be far stronger than any of the others previously covered. Unfortunately, each layer disintegrates on close inspection. The sources *might* derive from a northern source and the battles *could* be located in the same region. The rest is largely speculation mixed together with highly selective passages from late medieval fan-fiction.

A chapter providing a brief summary of the legend, a chapter on the historical background and then into our northern interpretation of the HB. A further chapter explaining why all the battles must be in the North and we are half-way to finishing an average sized book. Perhaps a little padding out with selected excerpts from Arthurian tales and we have a best-seller.

I have no doubt that such a book, carefully packaged and marketed, especially if written by someone with access to the media, would do far better than a more sober, yet historically grounded investigation of the legend. Now that you have seen how the sausage is made can you resist the urge to buy? Can I resist the urge to write it?

Summary

These are not the only theories. Dozens more appear in any search for Arthurian books. Scott Lloyd summarises a number of examples, including many of the above, and finds they 'suffer from a number of basic deficiencies':[80] They lack a proper understanding of the reliable source material; they assume Ordnance Survey maps can be used to reconstruct places from over a millennia ago; and they lack knowledge of academic literature.

A quick look at Bartrum's *A Welsh Classical Dictionary* of figures in Welsh history and legend reveal two dozen Arth- or Athr- type names. As we have seen, Arthur is always referred to as Arthur. This wont prevent more books supporting any of the figures above, or coming up new ingenious theories based on not very much. We can conclude this chapter with a number of facts:

- Despite scholars looking over the various sources over many centuries there has been no consensus as to Arthur's identity.
- Every single theory to date has failed to provide sufficient evidence and most, if not all, fall apart upon investigation.
- None of the genealogies, or indeed any of the poems or tales, support any of the theories as none link any of the proposed individuals to Arthur.
- The genealogies that do reference Arthur, while late and unreliable, are fairly consistent as to his name, his immediate family tree and how he is connected to other Brythonic pedigrees.

In *Worlds of Arthur* Guy Halsall, a leading authority on the early medieval period, is unequivocal: 'The claim of any book that purports to present such a history should be rejected immediately and out of hand. Such attempts represent fiction, no more no less.'[81] He concludes '[the] … quest for King Arthur is fruitless'. More damning still, he writes that to pretend to have provided the answers sought by that romantic quest from the surviving written sources is 'downright dishonest'.[82]

All this might cause us to despair of ever uncovering the truth. I would argue this is unduly pessimistic. We have already seen that the sources are fairly consistent as to a rough timeframe. In terms of geography the likely battle sites and locations mentioned in poems and tales associate him with a wide geographical area. Having determined *when*, with a rough idea of *where*, he can be placed in a more accurate historical context. On the cusp between a fragmenting, or fragmented, provincial structure and the emergence of petty kingdoms. In addition we see a new post-Roman Brythonic cultural identity in contrast to one influenced heavily by an in-coming Germanic material culture. This just leaves *who* Arthur was. I will argue in the last chapter that this question is not as problematic as it seems. I will not claim to reveal the truth. Instead I offer something more nuanced. That is, *if* Arthur was historical, this is the most likely explanation based on the sources.

Chapter Twelve

Conclusions

As one Arthurian scholar puts it: 'Arthur is either a historical figure, who, in Britain at some time about AD 500, quickly attracted many mythological attributes, or a mythological figure who in the same period quickly attracted many historical attributes.'[1]

The evolution of the tradition can be summarised as follows:[2] the earliest securely dated reference is in the HB in c.830. The battle list of the HB and two battle entries in AC are arguably the most important examples for a historical Arthur. The *Mirabilia* in the Harleian manuscript is the earliest source associating Arthur with a topographical feature. The Latin *vitae* of Welsh saints, from c.1090, provide the first reference to Arthur as a king. Arthur's popularity derived from Geoffrey of Monmouth's HRB from c.1138. No Welsh texts can be shown to definitively predate HRB. Arthurian tradition only had a visible impact on Welsh literature after the HRB was translated into Welsh in the early thirteenth century *Brut y Brenhinedd*. Despite the 'explosion' of Continental and English material from the late twelfth century in Welsh poetry, he is 'notable only by his absence'. It is only when Geoffrey's HRB began to be called into doubt in the sixteenth century that Welsh authors started to take an interest, perhaps inspired by a growth in nationalism under the Tudors. Increasing numbers of Arthurian place names are first attested only in the seventeenth century.

By the late eighteenth century Arthur can be described as a 'minor literary character ... ignored by Welsh antiquarians and ... little more than a footnote in history books'.[3] Interest in the legend was revived in the nineteenth century after the publication of new editions of Malory and Charlotte Guest's *Mabinogion*. The origin of the legend can be traced back only to ninth-century northern Wales with the composition of the HB. It is perhaps significant that Elis Gruffydd's story of Huail continues a theme found in three separate twelfth-century sources and he places Huail's execution in the same place the HB was written.

Figure 28 provides a timeline of events between the end of Roman authority and the arrival of St Augustine in 597. The next figure shows how the legend evolved across the centuries. The key dates being as follows:

Conclusions

- c.480–540 A potential historical Arthur.
- c.830 First attested reference to a historical figure in the *Historia Brittonum*.
- Ninth–tenth century: possible origin of earliest Welsh tradition.
- 1138 Geoffrey of Monmouth's HRB published.
- Late twelfth to thirteenth century: French Romances written.
- From mid-thirteenth century: earliest manuscripts of Welsh tales.
- 1485 Thomas Malory's *Le Morte D'Arthur* published.

The final figure shows when the specific texts appeared, along with the introduction of the main themes to the story.

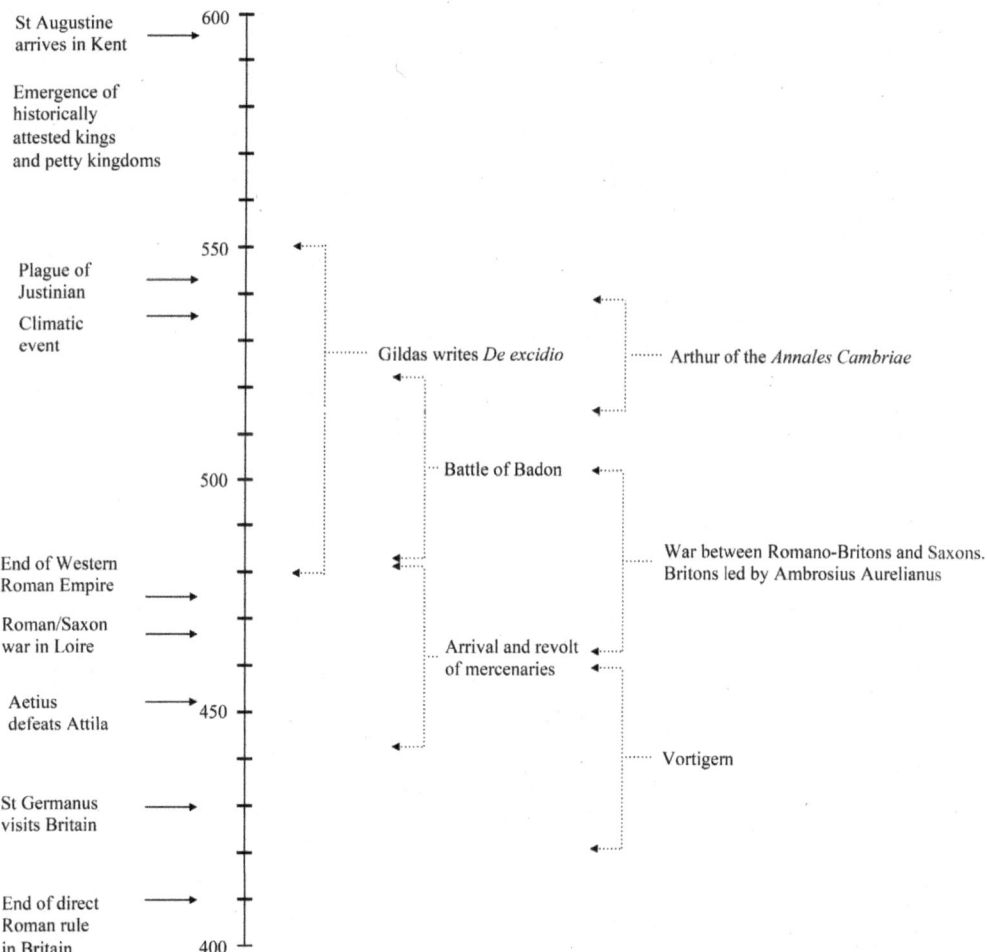

Figure 28: Timeline 400–600.

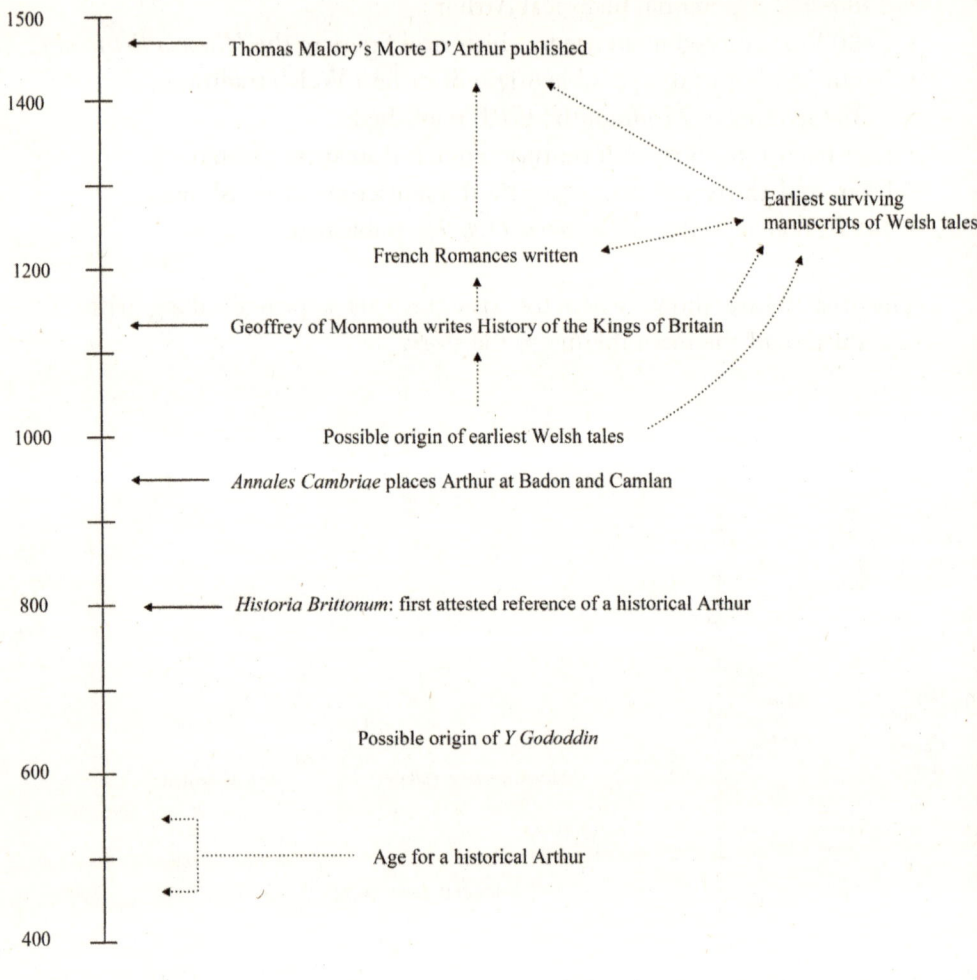

Figure 29: Evolution of Arthurian tradition up to c.1485.

The case for a mythical Arthur

It is a relatively easy task to make a case that Arthur was not a historical figure. Not a single contemporary source even hints at his existence. He does not appear in any literary source for 300 years. When he does there is no reason to place the battle list over and above the two magical topographical features in the 'Wonders of Britain'. The battle list is as likely to be an invention of the HB's author or Welsh bard as a genuine battle-poem of a real figure.

Arthur is notably absent from prophetic poetry and as a long-awaited leader.[4] In the middle ages Owen Glyndwr and Owain Lawgoch were added

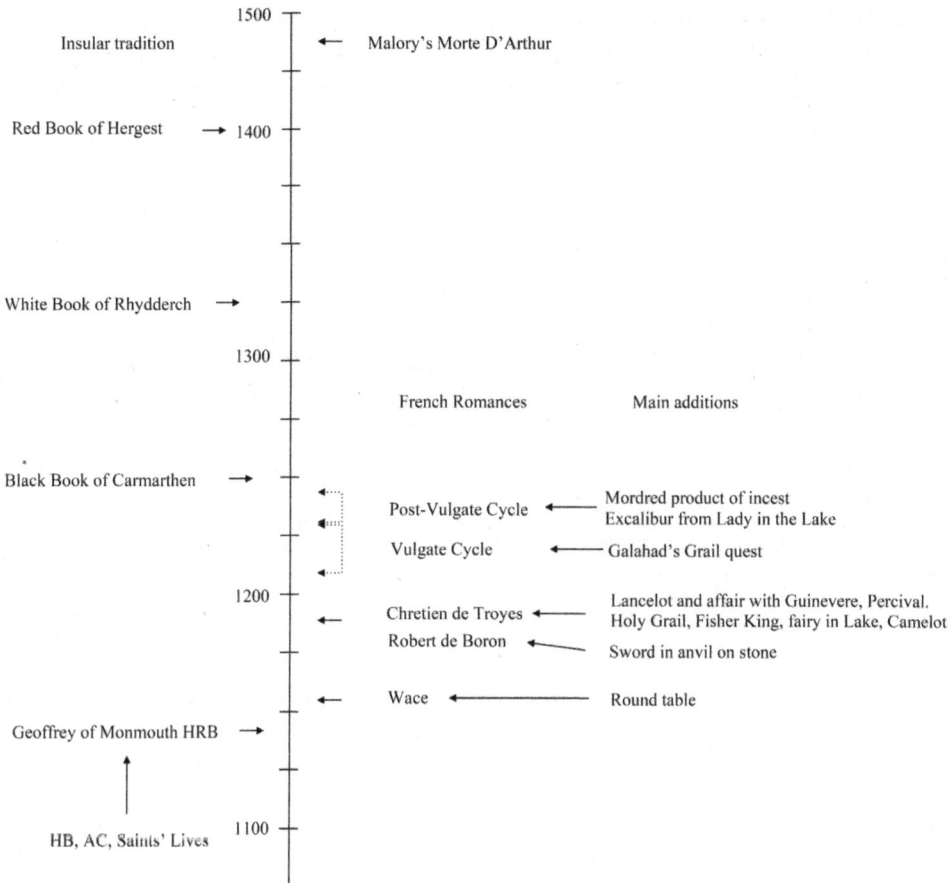

Figure 30: Insular and continental sources.

to Cynan and Cadwaladwr, but not Arthur. Whatever tradition had developed by the time of Geoffrey's HRB, the Arthur of legend and magic was the dominant one until the twelfth century.[5]

Arthur's nearest equivalent in Irish myth is Fionn. His band of warriors, *fian*, are very similar to the exploits of Arthur's men in the earlier tales such as *Culhwch and Olwen* and *Pa Gur*: 'A roving band of men whose principal occupation were hunting and war.'[6] Arthur is often a humorous or petty figure, such as in the *Life of St Padarn* where he is buried up to his chin as punishment for trying to steal the saint's cloak. In *Pa Gur* he has to argue with a mere gate-keeper, and impress him with his exploits before he is allowed in.

Medieval belief in a historical Arthur was 'neither total nor naive'.[7] Contemporary historians were divided over Geoffrey's HRB. William of Malmesbury (c.1125) dismissed Geoffrey as a liar and William of Newburgh (c.1198) accused Geoffrey of inventing the whole thing. Ranulf Higden (c.1352) noted the absence of evidence from contemporary literary sources. Gerald of Wales (1146–1243) gives the example of a man possessed by demons who recovers when the Bible is placed upon him. However, when a copy of HRB is placed upon him the demons return.[8] He goes on to describe the tales about Arthur at the time of writing as 'nonsense' and 'fallacious fables', although he accepted Arthur as a historical figure worthy of being 'proclaimed in veracious histories'.

Geoffrey's book was accepted by some as there was no authoritative alternative version. Arthur was broadly accepted because there was nothing to fill the gap between the end of Roman Britain and the arrival of St Augustine. His popularity in the courts of Europe was secured by the subsequent evolution of the legend into a variety of different tales and languages, such as the French Romances.

Later English kings, such as Henry II with the monks at Glastonbury, were only too happy to exploit the tradition. Soon after his father's death in 1189, Richard I named his nephew, Arthur, heir. Curiously, there is a record of the king gifting 'Caliburn' the sword of King Arthur, to King Tancred of Sicily. It is worth noting the spelling in the HRB is used. The general consensus is this sword was a fake.[9]

A century later Edward I wrote to the Pope claiming authority over Scotland on the basis of Arthur's conquest.[10] In 1284, Edward I held a Round Table tournament at Nefyn on the Llyn peninsula in north-west Wales. On returning to London he placed the *talaith* (crown) of Llywelyn to the shrine of Edward the Confessor at Westminster Abbey. Some later English sources refer to this *talaith* as the 'Crown of Arthur', yet no Welsh source refers to a crown of Arthur.[11] Both Edward IV and Henry VII claimed descent from Arthur. It was noted that The Round Table hanging in The Great Hall at Winchester Castle has been dated to the reign of Edward I.[12] Edward also arranged a tournament which is thought to have been based on Arthurian themes in 1290 at Winchester.[13] He took on the role of Arthur, and his queen, Eleanor of Castile, that of Guinevere. Some scholars argue that The Round Table at Winchester was built precisely for this tournament.[14]

This association with Winchester may have come about due to early thirteenth-century French tale *Mortu Artu*. While it places Arthur's court at Camelot, it includes a tournament arranged at Winchester. Here we have a reason for Edward I to locate his tournament in the same town. Only natural then to hang the very table constructed for the event in Winchester Castle. Malory's placement of Camelot at Winchester 200 years later may well be the product solely of Edward I's enthusiasm for Arthurian themes rather than any literary or oral tradition. In 1278 Edward I and Queen Eleanor visited Arthur's grave at Glastonbury. The bones were ceremoniously moved to a new resting place. A black marble tomb in front of the high altar in the Cathedral, two lions guarding each end. Seven decades on Edward III established the Order of the Garter, an order of chivalry 'almost certainly inspired by Arthurian legends'.[15]

Yet for a long time Arthur was largely ignored by Welsh bards and writers. The earliest manuscripts written in Welsh only appear after the publication of the HRB. Even then Arthur was at times a peripheral figure, who only came to the fore with the revival of Welsh nationalism in Tudor times and later in the nineteenth century.

In summary, it can be argued the mythical Arthur found in the 'Wonders of Britain' within the HB was the foundation of the earliest tradition. The version of Arthur in *Culhwch and Olwen*, *Pa Gur* and *Preiddeu Annwn* is one operating in a mystical 'otherworld' full of magic and monsters. A favourite among generations of bards and their audiences, the stories evolved over several centuries before Geoffrey of Monmouth's pseudo-history historicised Arthur and made him famous. This spurred a plethora of 'fan-fiction' across Europe, most notably among French Romance writers alongside later Welsh and English versions. This culminated in Malory's *Le Morte D'Arthur*, leaving us with the legend we know today.

The enormous interest in Arthur has fuelled a huge amount of time and effort by historians and amateurs alike. Yet not one theory has been able to withstand scrutiny. Nor has any evidence gained academic support. The simplest answer is this: because none exists. A mythical figure invented by Brythonic bards in the sixth or seventh centuries, historicised by a ninth-century author to add weight to an invented battle list. But for that battle list or Geoffrey of Monmouth's pseudo-history, none of the subsequent tales would have been written and we might never have heard of Arthur.

The case for the defence of academia's position on this might end the closing argument with a simple statement to all the many theorists and enthusiasts: 'prove it'. The jury, made up of academics and historians, will be forgiven for simply shrugging their shoulders and moving on until new evidence emerges.

The case for a historical Arthur

Despite the above argument, a case can be made for a historical Arthur, mythologised by later bards.

The case against a historical Arthur relies on the author of the HB being either deliberately dishonest, or mistaken about the authenticity of the battle list, with the copyist of the AC blindly accepting it. At the very least it is possible, if not likely, the author expected, or hoped, readers would not find an Arthur defeating Saxons in this period odd. In addition, later hagiographers would not have used a knowingly fictitious figure to bolster their land claims.

Establishing that a ninth- to twelfth-century audience accepted Arthur was historical is not the same as proving he was. However, there is no particular reason to dismiss the figures in the HB's narrative. Ambrosius Aurelianus and the Battle of Badon are both generally accepted by historians, despite relying on late copies of just one contemporary source, *De excidio*. Vortigern is considered to be historical by many historians, even if Hengest and Horsa are doubted. Significantly, there are no known fictitious figures in the HB's narrative between Vortigern and Ida. In placing Arthur fighting twelve battles after Hengest's death, the author demonstrated his audience would accept a historical Arthur in that context.

Many figures noted in Bede and Gregory of Tours have no more support and yet are accepted on balance, as is Riothamus from Jordanes. In addition, the AC may well have derived its information from a separate, likely northern, source.

One criticism frequently heard is that there is no evidence for a historical figure behind the legend. I would argue it would be more accurate to state the evidence that exists is insufficient, rather than non-existent. First we must scrape away all the fan-fiction inspired by Geoffrey of Monmouth's work. We need to be brutal in throwing out every transparent addition acquired as the legend evolved. Some might struggle to accept the concept of a historical Arthur without many of its perceived core components. After all, what is King Arthur without a Round Table, the sword in the stone, the Holy Grail or Camelot? Yet we have seen these were all added by French writers after the legend had become popular. I would go much further and remove Merlin and Avalon, as we cannot trust Geoffrey of Monmouth as a source.

What then are we left with? The twelve battles in the ninth-century HB and two entries in the tenth-century AC. The author of the HB had a political agenda and message, but also wished to be taken seriously. Likewise, the copyist dating Badon and Camlan to 516 and 537 did so with the expectation his tenth-century audience would accept it.

No doubt fifth- to sixth-century Britain had its fair share of heroes, villains, petty kings and warlords. Brythonic kings such as Maelgwn and Urien. Germanic warriors such as Ælle and Cerdic. If historians grudgingly accept these figures, there is no good reason to throw out the baby with the bathwater and dismiss the Arthur of the HB's battle list.

At the very least we can say a historical Arthur is possible. I think we can go further and state that, on the balance of probabilities, it is likely the Arthur of the battle list was a historical figure. How and why he acquired the tales he did is another question.

Some historians do take this position, or at least say it is possible, but caveat it by stating nothing more can be said about him. Any historical figure is completely obscured by centuries of legend and myth before Geoffrey of Monmouth got his hands on it and bent it completely out of shape. Here, too, I would argue we can say a little more.

The when, where and who of Arthur

First, *if* Arthur was historical, the sources are fairly consistent as to when he lived. Almost certainly within a broad range of 450–550. We can be fairly confident in narrowing this down to 480–540. This falls in line with the HB, AC and HRB. Of course they could be wrong, with each relying on the previous source. But we can only repeat what the source says: 'On Hengest's death his son Octha came from the north of Britain to the kingdom of Kentishmen and from him are sprung the kings of the Kentishmen. Then Arthur fought against them ... until the time when Ida reigned.'

Thus our first attested source dates him 488–547 (taking dates for Hengest and Ida from the ASC). Our second attested source dates him fighting battles in 516 and 537. The Saints' Lives associate him with saints in the same period. Lastly, Geoffrey of Monmouth dates his death to 542.

Where Arthur lived and fought is a little more difficult. Welsh tradition places his court at Celliwig in Cornwall (or possibly in northern Wales or Powys). The Saints' Lives have him interacting with events in southern Wales, although not necessarily being from that region. The *life of St Carannog*, places him in or near Devon, ruling with Cadwy. His association with Caerleon appears entirely down to Geoffrey of Monmouth who may have had his own reasons for placing his court there. He also has connections with Dumnonia through his maternal half-brothers, whether they be Gormant (from *Culhwch and Olwen*) or Cador (HRB). There is also the possibility his paternal grandfather was Custenin of Cornwall rather than Constantine of Armorica.

However, while some tales place Arthur in the south-west and South Wales (for example the hunt for Twrch Trwyth in *Culhwch and Olwen*), others associate him with Anglesey and the north (*Pa gur yv y porthaur?*) or Rhyd-y-Groes (on the Shropshire-Welsh border) in the *Dream of Rhonabwy*. Perhaps it is best to take these largely mystical stories with a pinch of salt. Yet the battle list suggests an Arthur fighting a fair distance from the south-west. The battles that can be located with some confidence place Arthur fighting in a wide arc from Wessex to Southern Scotland: Chester, Lindsey and north of Hadrian's Wall. Of the remaining battles, many have northern locations as very likely candidates. An Arthur raised in the south-west but fighting across the former diocese is not a particularly unlikely scenario.

Again we can dismiss the earliest Welsh tales and Saints' Lives as myths. All we can do is state to which areas they point. The genealogies point to the south-west for his familial connections, as does his association with Celliwig in Welsh tradition. The battle list suggests a warlord operating over a wide area, but with more emphasis north of a line between Lincoln and Chester. Figure 31 provides a map of the locations where Arthur may have lived and fought. I have left the former provincial boundaries in place. What is noticeable is that aside from Lindsey, the areas are not within the region that experienced the earliest Germanic settlements.

This would suggest a southern Arthur heading north to lead the Kings of Britons in battles mostly outside the area of earliest settlement. The poem *Y Gododdin* has men from all over Britain, including 'Geraint, before the men of the South'. There is nothing implausible about a renowned warrior fighting far from home. This hints at two things. First, some sort of surviving political or military structure, despite the fragmentation of the former provinces. At the very least, emerging Brythonic kingdoms maintained close political and cultural links.

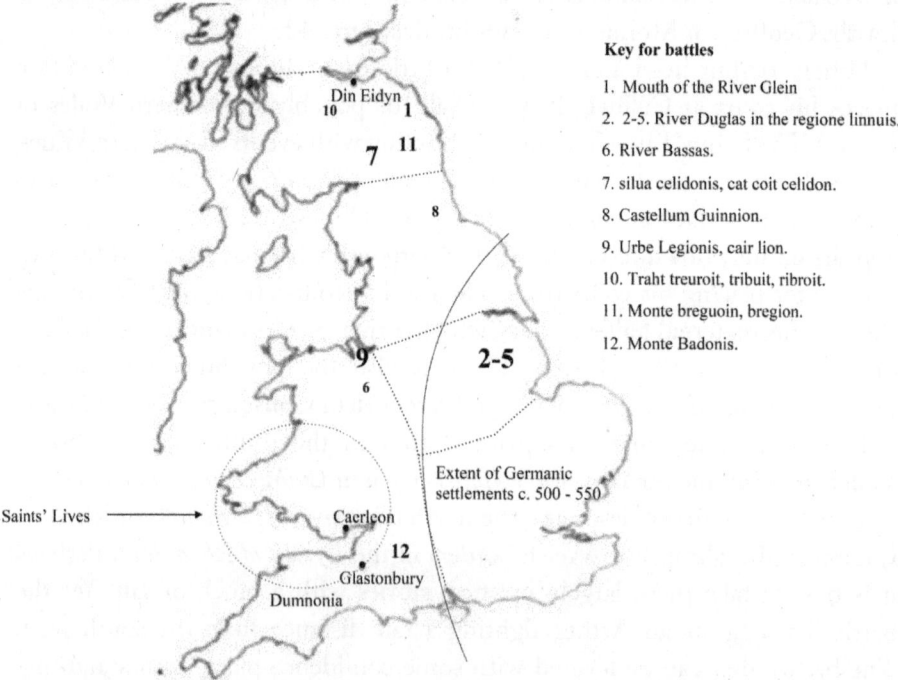

Figure 31: Arthur's Britain.

Second, it points to a far more complex military picture than simply Romano-Britons bravely holding the line against invading Anglo-Saxons pushing the border westwards. Some of these battles could be against raiders, in which case the enemy could be Saxons, Picts or Irish. If they are all against Saxons as the HB claims, then perhaps these are Octha's mercenaries, left behind when he came south to Kent. An Arthur ethnically cleansing small pockets of Germanic troops might be very different from the chivalric king of the middle ages, but possibly far closer to the truth. Especially if he shared the world view of Gildas who saw them as barbarians and dogs, hated by man and God.

If the above is true, then Arthur was a contemporary of Gildas. Living in a world of petty kings such as Maelgwn and an emerging warband culture. That is exactly how the earliest tales portray him. Not a king but, as the HB states, simply *dux erat Bellorum*, 'leader in battle'. None of the king lists for any of the early kingdoms claim Arthur as their own. Who then was he? Certainly not any of the candidates proposed by theories so far.

To answer this we must turn to the genealogies. Again these are late and unreliable. They may well be mistaken. We must also strip away the later confusing contradictions and changes of peripheral figures. All we can do is state what the earliest sources say. First, his name was Arthur. Not some other Arth- or Ath- type name. Not some completely different name with a bear-like nickname. Nor any of the other figures already named in the genealogies, as they have their own pedigrees.

If Arthur was historical then the sources are fairly consistent. He was the son of Eigr, granddaughter of Cunedda, and thus related to a variety of Welsh saints and kings. He was also related to rulers of Dumnonia through his maternal stepbrother or cousin, Cador or Cadwy. In addition, his paternal grandfather was either from Dumnonia or across the channel in Armorica. While we must rely on Geoffrey of Monmouth to make Uther his father, Gwenhwyfar is consistently named as his wife.

A major factor in raising expectation as to his identity is his portrayal as a high-king type figure in some of the tales, especially from the HRB to Malory's *Le Morte D'Arthur*. It is true that some Welsh genealogies do indeed list a series of kings of Britain from Vortigern to Arthur and beyond. Let us accept for a moment this was true. How would this change what the sources say? A warrior elevated to that position might have no association with any of the kings. Alternatively, he could have led the remnants of the council that the 'Proud Tyrant' or Vortigern had sat on. Perhaps some surviving role as *vicarius*, *dux*, *comes* or governor. In these cases we would not have a single reference in any of the genealogies.

The answer to this is far simpler than some have suggested. The issue has been confused by hundreds of years of rewriting, additions, speculations and dozens of modern dodgy theories. The Welsh genealogists tell us who he was: not a king himself, but related to them through his parents. With a fairly consistent immediate family. This is more information than we have for many attested historical figures of the same period.

These genealogies may well be mistaken or deliberately false. They are certainly late and unreliable. Yet they are also reasonably consistent, both with who he was and who he wasn't. Hopefully it has been demonstrated why so many modern theories fall apart on scrutiny.

I will leave the reader with a family tree constructed from the various genealogies. It is my own and thus as suspect as any other from a medieval scribe or later writer. If we trust the tales, then Uther was the second son of a second son, a prince in either Armorica or Dumnonia. The second husband of Eigr, whose first husband ruled in parts of Cornwall. Uther also does not appear as a king in any particular early kingdom. Why should the offspring of such a couple be king of any emerging kingdom? It is no wonder he is not claimed or found in any particular king list of a specific early kingdom. He doesn't belong there.

The HB merely says he led the kings of the Britons. The earliest tales portray a warband leader. Maybe he rose to prominence and acquired a surviving late-Roman civil or military role. Or perhaps he was simply a successful warrior of men and kings, trusted enough to lead them. Later writers could only understand such a figure as a king.

This, then, is the most likely scenario for a historical Arthur. A rather obscure child of a warrior and the widow of a Cornish ruler. No doubt he

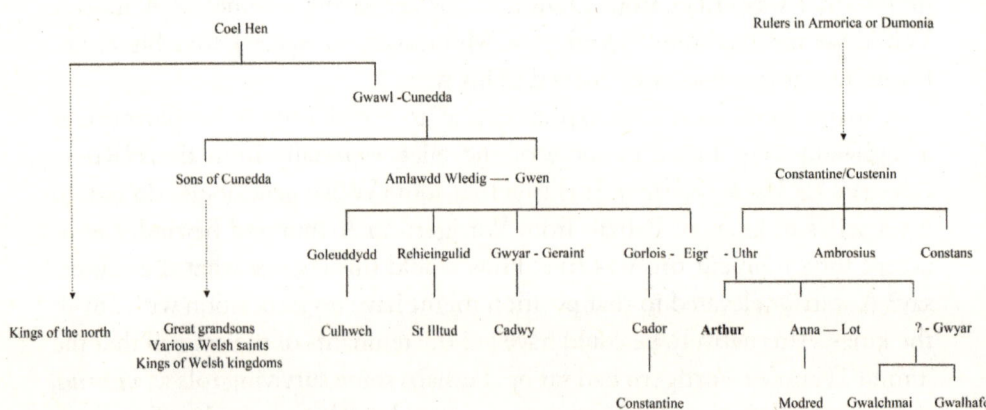

Figure 32: A revised family tree.

grew up close to his half-brother, Cador, and cousins Culhwch and Cadwy (or Geraint). In a world of emerging petty kingdoms that only half-remembered the fragmenting provincial structure. A world of warbands and heroes. Raiding and warfare. With no prospect of inheriting a throne, such a man could gain fame through his own strength of arms and ability to attract men to his own warband. This Arthur might well be called upon by kings and tyrants to lead their men in battle. He might be appointed by a council to wipe out disloyal Germanic mercenaries mostly stationed in the north.

Summary

I began this book with the aim it would save the reader time, effort and money by cutting through the myriad of theories, claims and counter claims. To achieve that it had to do two things; first, to clarify and simplify the history, evolution of the legend and what the original sources and genealogies actually say. Second, to highlight the common flaws in many theories and approaches. If, like me, you are a sucker for anything Arthurian, the next time you spot a book claiming to reveal the 'real King Arthur' you might be better able resist the urge to buy it.

It is possible the more sceptical historians are correct in claiming Arthur is purely the work of Brythonic bards. An invented figure historicised by later writers. If so, all the theories proposing a particular identification for Arthur are wrong and readers can save their money. However, I hope I have shown that it is at least possible, if not probable, a historical figure existed. If this is true, at least most of the theories are still wrong. I would go one step further and say the very evidence they all rely on points to a different Arthur entirely.

It is likely such a figure would have lived and fought c.480–540. Operating across a wide arc from southern Britain, through Wales to southern Scotland. Living on the cusp between a contracting culturally-Roman Diocese and provinces and expanding Germanic kingdoms. However, the King Arthur of Geoffrey of Monmouth, French Romances and Thomas Malory did not exist. Nor does the Arthur of modern films and books. We should not mourn the loss of this version. Swords in stones, round tables, valiant knights, dragons and women lying about in lakes waiting to hand swords to passing warriors are all very entertaining. Yet, I would argue, so is the possibility of a real historical figure leading a warband across early sixth-century Britain. A land full of petty kings and tyrants, shield walls and mead-halls. With its very own ethnic, cultural, political and religions tensions.

In conclusion, the 'Matter of Arthur' is surprisingly simple. Either Arthur is mythical or historical – and there's not enough evidence to decide as yet.

If he was historical, then the evidence points to a specific timeframe and a particular context. The later genealogies place Arthur in a specific position in relation to other figures. If the evidence is there, I suspect it won't be found in manuscripts that have been analysed to death over many centuries. Instead, it is under our feet waiting to be discovered. Perhaps a rich burial or scattering of coins. Or an inscribed stone hidden in the foundations of a medieval church or castle. Waiting to be revealed…

Notes

Chapter 1
1. Morris, 1980: 35
2. Geoffrey of Monmouth, HRB, xi.ii
3. Green, 2009: 20
4. Padel, 2013: 10
5. Loomis, 1959: 60
6. Padel, 2013: 30

Chapter 2
1. Henson, 2006: 49
2. Henson, 2006: 53
3. Salway, 2001: 277
4. Fleming, 2021: 18
5. Crabtree, 2018: 18
6. Zosimus, New History 6.05
7. *Chronica Gallica CCCCLII*, Gallic Chronicle 452 anonymous
8. Goldsworthy, 2010: 337
9. Evans, 2000: 26
10. Henson, 2006: 80–1
11. Henson, 2006: 83
12. Higham and Ryan, 2015: 42
13. Fleming, 2021: 6
14. Charles-Edwards, 2014: 43
15. Fleming, 2021: 5
16. Hills, 2011: 9
17. Gerrard, 2016: 55
18. Wacher, 1995: 150
19. Rippon, 2018: 167
20. Laycock, 2008
21. Eagles, 2018: 2
22. Williams, 2022: 41
23. Lewis in Mitchell and Greatrex, 2000: 77
24. Brown, 2012: 503
25. Salway, 2001: 341
26. Carver, 2019: 192
27. Carver, 2019: 176
28. Bedoyere, 2006: 267
29. Carver, 2019: 189
30. Carver, 2019: 145
31. Carver, 2019: 144

32. Crabtree, 2018: 42
33. Crabtree, 2018: 84
34. Oosthuizen, 2019: 29
35. Charles-Edwards, 2014: 227
36. O Croinin, 2017: 46
37. Morris, 1980: 35
38. O Croinin, 2017: 47
39. Dumville, 1999
40. Procopius, History of the Wars 8.20.6–10
41. Williams, 1999: 4
42. Evans, 2000: 1
43. Evans, 2000: 28
44. Carver, 2019: 637–641
45. Gerrard, 2016: 179
46. Gerrard, 2016: 155–156
47. Goffart, 1980: 3–5
48. Drinkwater in Drinkwater and Elton, 2002: 217
49. Drinkwater in Drinkwater and Elton, 2002: 210–211
50. Drinkwater in Drinkwater and Elton, 2002: 208–217
51. Brown, 2012: 389
52. Brown, 2012: 404
53. Mathisen, 1993: 68–69
54. Brown, 2012: 446
55. Brown, 2012: 448
56. Brown, 2012: 449
57. Brown, 2012: 434
58. Snyder, 1998: 107
59. Snyder, 1998: 107
60. Gregory of Tours, Book II 17–18
61. Morris, 1978: 27
62. Hughes, 2020: 144
63. Charles-Edwards, 2014: 59
64. Charles-Edwards, 2014: 58
65. Charles-Edwards, 2014: 59
66. Stenton, 1989: 12
67. Charles-Edwards, 2014: 70–71
68. Charles-Edwards, 2014: 71
69. Higham, 1992: 8
70. Oosthuizen, 2019: 7
71. Zosimus 1.68.3
72. Cunliffe, 2013: 411
73. Charles-Edwards, 2014: 370
74. Goldsworthy, 2010: 341
75. Haywood, 1991: 37
76. Wallace-Hadrill, 1961: 29
77. Henson, 2006: 108
78. Henson, 2006: 108
79. Dark, 2000: 20

80. Todd, 2004: 208
81. Rippon, 2018: 285
82. Manco, 2018: 119
83. Oppenheimer 2007:382
84. Henson, 2006: 60–1
85. Henson, 2006: 55
86. Rippon, 2018: 241
87. Arnold, 2000: 59
88. Charles-Edwards, 2014: 48
89. Eagles, 2018: 43
90. Henson, 2006: 64–5
91. Henson, 2006: 74
92. Higham and Ryan, 2015: 91
93. Eagles, 2018: xxx
94. Cunliffe, 2013: 424
95. Moffatt, 2013: 182
96. Arnold, 2000: 20 & 21
97. Manco, 2018: 128
98. Henson, 2006: 56
99. Gretzinger, Sayer, Justeau et al, 2022
100. Arnold, 2000: 23
101. Procopius, History of the Wars 8.20.6–10
102. Hills 2011: 10
103. Haywood, 1991: 73
104. Zaluckyj, 2018: 2
105. Bede volume 5 chapter 9
106. Henson, 2006: 62
107. Henson, 2006: 74–5
108. Henson, 2006: 77
109. Henson, 2006: 78
110. Procopius, History of the Wars 8.20.6–10
111. Henson, 2006: 87
112. Henson, 2006: 119
113. Henson, 2006: 70
114. Henson, 2006: 122
115. Henson, 2006: 58
116. Henson, 2006: 120
117. Henson, 2006: 121
118. Henson, 2006: 134–5
119. Henson, 2006: 140–1
120. Haywood, 1991: 51–76
121. Carver, 2019: 3
122. Carver, 2019: 56
123. Haywood, 1991: 55
124. http://www.vortigernstudies.org.uk/artsou/chron452.htm
125. Wood, in Lapidge and Dumville, 1984: 16–20
126. Wood in Lapidge and Dumville, 1984: 19
127. Muhlberger in Drinkwater and Elton, 2002: 34–35

128. Joyce, 2022: 6
129. Joyce, 2022: 31
130. Joyce, 2022: 153
131. Lapidge and Dumville, 1984: 52
132. Joyce, 2022: 158
133. Joyce, 2022: 59
134. Lapidge and Dumville, 1984: 47
135. Lapidge and Dumville, 1984: 50
136. Joyce, 2022: 28
137. Joyce, 2022: 35
138. DEB chapter 3 in Morris, 1980: 16
139. DEB chapter 26.2 in Morris, 1980: 28
140. Hughes, 2020: 130
141. Higham, 1992: 79–80
142. Joyce, 2022: 46
143. Joyce, 2022: 47
144. Joyce, 2022: 136
145. Halsall, 2014: 55
146. Lapidge and Dumville, 1984: 83
147. Joyce, 2022: 158
148. Keys, 2000
149. Woods, 2014
150. Jankulak, 2010: 30
151. Henson, 2006: 24
152. Bede, HE, book 1.22
153. Joyce, 2022: 19–20
154. Gildas, DEB, 23.3
155. Bede, HE, book 5.23
156. Woolf, 2002: 1
157. Joyce, 2013: 59
158. Chadwick in Chadwick et al, 1959: 21
159. Bede, HE, book 1.15
160. http://www.vortigernstudies.org.uk/artsou/bede.htm
161. Bede, HE, book 1.22
162. Swanton, 2000
163. Yorke, 2013: 131
164. Beard, 2005: 263

Chapter 3

1. Jarman, 2005: 64
2. Evans, 2000: 148
3. Koch, 2013: 187–8
4. Charles-Edwards, 2014: 438
5. Halsall, 2014: 63
6. Higham, 2009: 120
7. Green, 2009: 9
8. Charles-Edwards in Bromwich et al, 1995: 21
9. Chadwick in Chadwick et al, 1959: 31

10. Fitzpatrick-Matthews, 2017: 3–7
11. Bartrum, 1993: 565
12. Fitzpatrick-Matthews, 2017: 2
13. Scott, 2017: 15
14. Green, 2009: 101
15. Scott, 2017: 159
16. Morris, 1980: 40
17. Clark, 1996: 4
18. Morris, 1980: 35
19. Morris, 1980
20. Chadwick, 1959: 31
21. Sullivan, 2020: 165
22. Higham, 2009: 146
23. Higham, 2009: 146–147
24. Green, 2009: 54
25. Bromwich et al, 1995: 29
26. Charles-Edwards in Bromwich et al, 1995: 20
27. Charles-Edwards in Bromwich et al, 1995: 28
28. Bartrum, 1993: 26
29. Fitzpatrick-Matthews, http://www.historiabrittonum.net/wp-content/uploads/2018/09/The-Arthurian-battle-list-of-the-Historia-Brittonum.pdf
30. Halsall, 2014: 67
31. Padel, 2013: 3
32. Higham, 2018: 265
33. Halsall, 2014: 67
34. Jackson, 1959: 4
35. Ashley, 2005: 135
36. Higham, 2018: 191
37. Green, 2012: 60
38. Jackson, 1959: 4
39. Milner, 2011: 83
40. Jackson, 1959: 4
41. Jackson, 1959: 4
42. Jackson, 1959: 4
43. Ashley, 2005: 148
44. Higham, 1994: 112–3
45. Jackson, 1959: 4
46. Chambers, 1966: 199–201
47. Scott, 2017: 18
48. Lloyd, 2017: 193
49. Bromwich, 2014: 150, 153, 166, 217
50. Bartrum, 1993: 98
51. Higham, 2009: 194
52. Bromwich, 1991: 26–7
53. Higham, 2009: 209
54. Padel, 2013: 9
55. Padel, 2013: 9

Chapter 4
1. Jones, 2019: 7–8
2. Jones, 2019: 40
3. Jones, 2019: 42
4. Flight, 2021: 52–8
5. Flight, 2021: 84–5
6. Jones, 2019: 13
7. Jones, 2019: 27
8. Bartrum, 1993: 415
9. Bartrum, 1993: 275
10. Scott, 2017: 71
11. Scott, 2017: 72
12. Bartrum, 1993: 275
13. Jones, 2019: 141–66
14. Bromwich, Jarman and Roberts, 1995: 55–7
15. Morris, 1980: 37
16. Bartrum, 1993: 593
17. Bartrum, 1993: 596
18. Scott, 2017: 95
19. Scott, 2017: 29–30
20. Bromwich, 2014: xcix
21. Bromwich, 2014: xvi
22. Bromwich, 2014: lxv
23. Bromwich, 2014: xi
24. Loomis, 1959: 60
25. Loomis, 1959: 61
26. Scott, 2017: 57
27. Scott, 2017: 67
28. Scott, 2017: 78–9
29. Scott, 2017: 89

Chapter 5
1. Padel, 2013: 30
2. Scott, 2017: 21
3. Bartrum, 1993: 104
4. Wade-Evans, 2013: 143
5. Scott, 2017: 22
6. Bartrum, 1993: 86
7. Bartrum, 1993: 385
8. Bartrum, 1993: 575–7
9. Bartrum, 1993: 522
10. Bartrum, 1993: 281
11. Bartrum, 1993: 282
12. Bartrum, 1993
13. Bartrum, 1993: 577
14. Bartrum, 1993: 26
15. Scott, 2017: 19
16. Scott, 2017: 22

17. Thomas, 1981: 198
18. Goldsworthy, 2010: 338, 345
19. Croinin, 2017: 37
20. Dark, 1994: 30 & 32
21. Mathisen, 1993: 93
22. Bede book 1.25
23. Bede, Book 1 Chapter 22
24. Pollington, 2011: 448
25. Dark, 1994: 160–2
26. Arnold, 1997: 31
27. Bartrum, 1993: 440
28. Morris, 1978: 32
29. Morris, 1980: 37
30. Bartrum, 1993: 439
31. Morris, 1980: 45
32. Dumville in Lapidge and Dumville, 1984: 52
33. Bartrum, 1993: 181
34. Morris, 1978: 31
35. Sullivan, 2020: 183

Chapter 6

1. Padel, 2013: 10
2. Jankulak, 2010: 75
3. Burgess and Pratt, 2006: 91
4. Scott, 2017: 25
5. Burgess and Pratt, 2006: 95
6. Burgess and Pratt, 2006: 96
7. Jankulak, 2010: 13
8. Jankulak, 2010: 14
9. Bromwich, 1991: 251
10. Higham, 1992:2
11. Lewis, 1966: 17 & 19
12. Bartrum, 1993: 493
13. Bartrum, 1993: 493
14. Clarkson, 2016: 16
15. Clarkson, 2016: 33
16. Clarkson, 2016: 131
17. Clarkson, 2016: 45–6
18. Tolstoy, 1990: 16–7
19. Tolstoy, 1990: 281
20. Clarkson, 2016: 91
21. Jankulak, 2010: 78
22. Jankulak, 2010: 80
23. Jankulak, 2010: 4

Chapter 7

1. Ashe, 1985: 103
2. Jordanes 65.237

3. Charles-Edwards, 2014: 59
4. Cunliffe, 2021: 232
5. Charles-Edwards, 2014: 70–71
6. Charles-Edwards, 2014: 71
7. Procopius, History of the Wars 8.20.6–10
8. Henson, 2006: 89
9. Wiseman, 2011: 24
10. Procopius, History of the Wars 8.20.6–10
11. Procopius, Gothic Wars book 2.6.28
12. Bromwich, 1995: 262
13. Bromwich, 1991: 251
14. Barber, 2016: 206
15. Scott, 2017: 39
16. Scott, 2017: 40
17. Burgess and Pratt, 2006: 8
18. Burgess and Pratt, 2009: 279
19. Burgess and Pratt, 2009: 281
20. Burgess and Pratt, 2006: 135
21. Rouse and Rushton, 2005: 26
22. Munby, Barber and Brown, 2008: 71
23. Walters, 2006: 721
24. Rouse and Rushton, 2005: 19
25. Rouse and Rushton, 2005: 26
26. Ammianus Marcellinus, fourth-century AD, book 31.23
27. Davidson, 1998: 103
28. Davidson, 1998: 80
29. Davidson, 1998: 104
30. Davidson, 1998: 108
31. Underwood, 1999: 119
32. Marren, 2006: 9
33. Field, 2018: 3

Chapter 8
1. Matthews, 1966: 4
2. Matthews, 1966: 5
3. Field, 1999: 35
4. Field, 1999: 64
5. Field, 1999: 54

Chapter 9
1. Dark, 1994: 30 & 32
2. Brown, 2012: 359
3. Goldsworthy, 2010: 338, 345
4. Higham, 2009: 74
5. Griffin, 1994: 82
6. Griffin, 1994: 83
7. Griffin, 1994: 85
8. Morris, 1978: 31

9. Coe and Young, 1995: 103–5
10. Green, 2009: 30
11. Green, 2009: 27
12. Higham, 2009: 80
13. Scott, 2017: 102
14. Scott, 2017: 4–5
15. Scott, 2017: 159–63
16. Green, 2009: 20
17. Guy, 2020: 344
18. Morris, 1978:32
19. Guy, 2020: 348
20. Guy, 2020: 357
21. Guy, 2020: 375
22. Guy, 2020: 392
23. Guy, 2020: 430
24. Guy, 2020: 434
25. Guy, 202: 341
26. Chadwick, 1959: 52–3
27. Bartrum, 1993: 158
28. Bartrum, 1993: 85–6
29. Morris, 1978: 29
30. Bartrum, 1993: 153
31. Guy, 2020: 428
32. Guy, 2020: 335
33. Clarkson, 2016: 51–71
34. Tolstoy, 1990: 83
35. Morris, 1980: 28
36. Bartrum, 1993: 26
37. Dark, 1994: 79–83
38. Croinin, 2017: 39
39. Dark, 1994: 83–86
40. Bartrum, 1993: 31
41. Bartrum, 1993: 31
42. Bartrum, 1993: 31
43. Bartrum, 1993: 24–9
44. Dumville in Bassett, 1989: 218
45. Dumville, 1993: III.9
46. Marsden, 1992: 27
47. Bartrum, 1993: 28
48. Bartrum, 1993: 589
49. Bartrum, 1993: 636
50. Bartrum, 1993: 636
51. Scott, 2017: 19
52. Bartrum, 1993: 461

Chapter 10
1. Sims-Williams, 2019: 1–2
2. Charles-Edwards, 2014: 250

3. Guy, 2020: 92
4. Thornton, 2003: 30
5. Sims-Williams, 2019: 8
6. Sims-Williams, 2019: 11
7. Bartrum, 1993: 31
8. Sims-Williams, 2019: 55
9. Guy, 2020: 337
10. Guy, 2020: 341
11. Guy, 2020: 347
12. Guy, 2020: 374
13. Higham, 2009: 226
14. Bartrum, 1993: 279
15. Higham, 2009: 230
16. Thorpe, 1988: 281
17. Nitze, 1934: 355–61
18. Alcock, 1989: 74
19. Higham, 2009: 232
20. https://pendragonry.wordpress.com/2018/02/25/cross1/
21. Alcock, 1989: 75
22. Mawrey, 2012: 5
23. https://pendragonry.wordpress.com/2018/02/25/cross1/
24. Alcock, 1989: 77–80
25. Jenkins, 2012: 4
26. Constantine, 2007: 106
27. Constantine, 2007: 109
28. Constantine, 2007: 111
29. Constantine, 2007: 131
30. Bromwich, 2014: 213
31. Constantine, 2007: 201–10
32. Knight and Long, 2004: 121–35
33. Scott, 2017: 132
34. Urbanus, 2019: 34–9
35. Urbanus, 2019: 34–9
36. Tolstoy, 1990: 44

Chapter 11

1. Higham, 2018: 265
2. Higham, 2018: 279
3. Ashley, 2005: 282
4. http://christophergwinn.com/arthuriana/lac-sourcebook/#etymology
5. Birley, 2005: 355
6. Tomlin, 2018: 156
7. Davenport 2019: 493
8. Higham, 2018: 35–38
9. Historia Augusta, Diadumenianus, 8.4–9.3
10. Cassius Dio, book 72.16
11. Tomlin, 208: 160
12. Colarusso and Salbiev, 2016: xv-xvii

13. Colarusso and Salbiev, 2016
14. Higham, 2018: 81
15. Istvanovits and Kulcsar, 2017: 414
16. Halsall, 2013: 149–151
17. Istvanovits and Kulcsar, 2017: 413–4
18. Birley, 2005: 355
19. Tomlin, 2018: 155–7
20. Dark, 2000: 77–96
21. Snyder, 2006, 15–6
22. Skeen, 2020: 61–75
23. Scott, 2017: 130
24. Guy, 2020: 337
25. Guy, 2020: 341
26. Guy, 2020: 347
27. Guy, 2020: 374
28. Bartrum, 1993: 31
29. Davies, 1970: 75
30. Scott, 2017: 142–3
31. Wilson and Blackett, 1986: 7–8
32. Wilson and Blackett, 1986: 171
33. Wilson and Blackett, 1986: 8
34. Wilson and Blackett, 1986: 10
35. Wilson and Blackett, 1986: 11 and 76
36. Wilson and Blackett, 1986: 203
37. Wilson and Blackett, 1986: 159–160
38. Wilson and Blackett, 1986: 7–12
39. Wilson and Blackett, 1986: 18
40. Wilson and Blackett, 1986: 56
41. Wilson and Blackett, 1986: 52
42. Wilson and Blackett, 1986: 71
43. Zosimus, New History 4.47.1
44. Gilbert, Wilson and Blackett, 1998: 38 n.11
45. https://calmgrove.wordpress.com/2020/07/02/unreadable/
46. Gilbert, Wilson and Blackett, 1998: 12
47. Gilbert, Wilson and Blackett, 1998: 178
48. Guy, 2020: 334
49. Bartrum, 1993: 18
50. Morris, 1978: 31
51. Bartrum, 1993: 181
52. Bartrum, 1993: 520
53. Phillips, 2016: 192
54. Phillips, 2016: 205
55. Phillips, 2016: 244
56. Bartrum, 1993: 29
57. Green, 2009: 30
58. Guy, 2020: 395 and 409
59. Guy, 2020: 428
60. Keegan, 2016: 140

61. Keegan, 2016: 143
62. Bartrum, 1993: 242
63. Keegan, 2016: 48
64. Bartrum, 1993: 29
65. Coleman, 2022: 127
66. Ardrey, 2013: 142–3
67. Ardrey, 2013: 139–40
68. Ardrey, 2013: 311
69. Ardrey, 2013: 235
70. Cassius Dio, *Historia Romana*, book 73.8
71. Ardrey, 2013: 144–5
72. Bartrum, 1993: 26
73. Halsall, 2014: 267
74. Fitzpatrick-Matthews 2017
75. Gerald of Wales, The Journey Through Wales, Book 1 chapter 10
76. Dark, 1994: 78
77. Zaluckyj, 2013: 8
78. Crabtree, 2018: 41
79. Crabtree, 2018: 42
80. Scott, 2017: 144
81. Halsall, 2014: 85
82. Halsall, 2014: 307

Chapter 12

1. Field, 2018: 1
2. Scott, 2017: 153–7
3. Scott, 2017: 115
4. Padel, 2013: 47
5. Padel, 2013: 10
6. Padel, 2013: 25
7. Rouse and Rushton, 2005: 10
8. Gerald of Wales, The Journey Through Wales, Book 1 chapter 5
9. Rouse and Rushton, 2005: 79
10. Rouse and Rushton, 2005: 12
11. Scott, 2017: 47
12. Rouse and Rushton, 2005: 19
13. Rouse and Rushton, 2005: 29
14. Rouse and Rushton, 2005: 30–1
15. Rouse and Rushton, 2005: 37

References and Bibliography

Sozomen, *Historia Ecclesiastica*, History of the Church, c.400–450
Chronica Gallica CCCCLII, Gallic Chronicle 452 anonymous
Chronica Gallica DXI, Gallic Chronicle 511 anonymous
Zosimus, *Historia Nova*, New History, c.500
Procopius, *De Bellis*, On the Wars, c.500–565
Prosper of Aquitaine, *Epitoma Chronicon*, Epitome of chronicles, Prosper of Aquitaine c.433–55
Constantius of Lyon, *De Vita sancta Germani*, The Life of Saint Germanus, Constantius of Lyon, c.480
Gildas, *De Excidio et Conquestu Britanniae*, On the Ruin and Conquest of Britain, early sixth century
Bede, *Historia ecclesiastica gentis Anglorum*, An Ecclesiastical History of the English People, c.731
Geoffrey of Monmouth, *Historia Regum Britanniae*, History of the Kings of Britain, c.1138
Nennius, *Historia Brittonum*, History of the Britons, c.830
Annales Cambriae, Welsh Annals, mid-tenth century, anonymous
Anglo-Saxon Chronicle c.900
Jordanes, *De origine actibusque Getarum*, The Origin and Deeds of the Goths, c.550
Gregory of Tours, *Historia Francorum*, History of the Franks, late-sixth century
Adoman of Iona. *Life of St Columba*. (Penguin, London, 1995).
Arnold, C.J, *An Archaeology of the Early Anglo-Saxon Kingdoms*, (Routledge, London, 2000).
Ardrey, A, *Finding Arthur, The True Origins of the Once and Future King*, (Overlook Press, New York, 2013).
Ashe, Geoffrey, *The Discovery of King Arthur*, (The History Press, Stroud, 2010).
Ashe, Geoffrey, *The Landscape of King Arthur*, (Anchor Press Doubleday, London, 1985).
Ashley, Mike, *The Mammoth Book of King Arthur*, (Constable and Robinson Ltd, London 2005).
Barber, Chris, *King Arthur, The Mystery Unravelled*, (Pen and Sword, Barnsley, 2016).
Baring-Gould, Sabine, *The Lives of British Saints Volumes 1–4*, (Forgotten Books, London, 2012).
Barr-Hamilton, Alec, *In Saxon Sussex*, (The Arundel Press, Bognor Regis, 1953).
Bartrum, Peter, *A Welsh Classical Dictionary*, (National Library of Wales, 1993).
Bassett, Stephen, *The Origins of the Anglo-Saxon Kingdoms*, (Leicester University Press, London, 1989).
Beard, D, *Astronomical references in the Anglo-Saxon Chronicles*, (Journal of the British Astronomical Association, Vol. 115, No. 5, p.261, 2005).
Bede, *The Ecclesiastical History of the English People*, (Oxford University Press, Oxford, 1994).
Bennett, A, and Burkitt, T, *Badon as Bath*, (Popular Archaeology, Volume 6(6), 1985)
Bishop, M.C., *The Secret History of the Roman Roads of Britain*, (Pen and Sword, Barnsley, 2020).
Breeze, Andrew, *The Name of King Arthur*, (Mediaevistic, Internationale Zeitschrift für interdisziplinäre Mittelalterforschung, Peter Laing. 2015).
Bromwich, Jarman and Roberts, *The Arthur of the Welsh*, (University of Wales Press, Cardiff 1995).

Bromwich, Rachel, *The Triads of the Island of Britain (4th Edition)*, (University of Wales Press, Cardiff, 2014).
Brookes, S and Harrington, S, *The Kingdom and People of Kent AD 400–1066 Their History and Archaeology*, (The History Press, Stroud, 2010).
Brown, Peter, *Through the Eye of a Needle, Wealth, the fall of Rome, and the Making of Christianity in the West 350–550 AD*, (Princeton University Press, Princeton, 2012).
Brugman, B, *Migration and Endogenuous Change*, in Hamerow, H, Hinton, D, and Crawford, S, *The Oxford Handbook of Anglo-Saxon Archaeology*, (Oxford University Press, Oxford, 2011).
Burgess, Glyn, and Pratt, Karen, *The Arthur of the French, The Arthurian Legend in Medieval French and Occitan Literature*, (University of Wales Press, Cardiff, 2006).
Bury, John, *The Life of St Patrick and His Place in History*, (Dover Publications, London, 1998).
Bury, J.B., *The origin of Pelagius*, (Hermathena, Volume 13, Number 30 (1904): 26–35, Trinity College Dublin).
Carver, Martin, *Formative Britain, An Archaeology of Britain Fifth to Eleventh Century AD*, (Routledge, Abingdon, 2019).
Carver, M., Sanmark, A., and Semple, S., *Signals of Belief in Early England, Anglo-Saxon Paganism Revisited*, (Oxbow Books, Oxford, 2010).
Carver, M, *The Sutton Hoo Story*, (The Boydell Press, Woodbridge, 2017).
Chadwick et al, *Studies in Early British History*, (Cambridge University Press, Cambridge 1959).
Chambers, E, K, *Arthur of Britain*, (Sidgwick and Jackson, London, 1966).
Charles-Edwards, T.M, *Wales and the Britons 350–1064*, (Oxford University Press, Oxford, 2014).
Clarkson, Tim, *Scotland's Merlin, A Medieval Legend and its Dark Age Origins*, (John Donald, Edinburgh, 2016).
Clarkson, Tim, *The Men of the North*, (Berlinn Ltd, Edinburgh, 2016).
Clarkson, Tim, *The Picts: A History*, (Berlinn Ltd, Edinburgh, 2019).
Clearly, S, *The Ending(s) of Roman Britain* in Hamerow, H, Hinton, D, and Crawford, S, *The Oxford Handbook of Anglo-Saxon Archaeology*, (Oxford University Press, Oxford, 2011).
Clemoes, Peter, *Anglo-Saxon England Volume 5*, (Cambridge University Press, Cambridge 1976).
Coe, Jon, and Young, Simon, *The Celtic Sources for the Arthurian Legend*, (Llanerch Publishers, Somerset, 1995).
Coleman, Keith, *Áedán of the Gaels, King of the Scots*, (Pen and Sword, Barnsley, 2022).
Collins, Rob, *Hadrian's Wall and the End of Empire*, (Routledge, New York, 2012).
Constantine, Mary-Ann, *The Truth Against the World: Iolo Morganwg and Romantic Forgery: Iolo Morganwg and the Romantic Tradition in Wales*, (University of Wales, Cardiff, 2007).
Crabtree, Pam, *Early Medieval Britain, The Rebirth of Towns in the Post-Roman West*, (Cambridge University Press, Cambridge, 2018).
Cunliffe, Barry, Bretons and Britons, (Oxford University Press, Oxford, 2021).
Cunliffe, Barry, *Britain Begins*, (Oxford University Press, Oxford, 2013).
Cusack, Mary Francis, *History of Ireland from AD 400 to 1800*, (Senate, London 1995).
Dark, Ken, *A Famous Arthur in the Sixth Century? Reconsidering the Origins of the Arthurian Legend*, Reading Medieval Studies 26 (2000): 77–96.
Dark, K.R., *Civitas to Kingdom; British Political Continuity 300–800*, (Leicester University Press, London, 1994).
Dark, Ken, *Britain and the End of the Roman Empire*, (Tempus Publishing Ltd, Stroud, 2000).
Davidson, Hilda, Ellis, *The Sword in Anglo-Saxon England*, (Boydell Press, Woodbridge, 1998).
Davies, Wendy, *The Llandaff Charters*, (National Library of Wales, Aberystwyth, 1979).
Davies, Wendy, *Wales in the Early Middle Ages*, (Leicester University Press, Leicester, 1982).
Drinkwater, John, and Elton, Hugh, *Fifth Century Gaul: A Crisis of Identity*, (Cambridge Universety Press, Cambridge, 2002).

Dumville, David, *Britons and Anglo-Saxons in the Early Middle Ages*, (Variorum, Aldershot, 1993).
Dumville, David, *Saint Patrick*, (Boydell Press, Woodbridge, 1999).
Dyer, James, *Hillforts of England and Wales*, (Shire Archaeology, Risborough, 1992).
Eagles, Bruce, *From Roman Civitas to Anglo-Saxon Shire: Topographical Studies on the Formation of Wessex*, (Oxbow Books, Oxford, 2018).
Evans, Bryan, *The Life and Times of Hengest*, (Anglo-Saxon Books, Ely, 2014).
Evans, John, *The Tomb of Horsa*, (Archaeologia Catiana Volume 65, pages 101–113, 1952).
Evans, Stephen, *Lords of Battle*, (Boydell Press, Woodbridge, 2000).
Field, P.J.C., *Searching for Camelot*, Medium Ævum 87, no. 1 (2018): 1–22. https://doi.org/10.2307/26871213.
Field, P.J.C., *The Life and Times of Sir Thomas Malory*, (Brewer, Cambridge, 1999).
Fitzpatrick-Matthews, Keith, J, *The textual history of the Historia Brittonum*, (http://www.historiabrittonum.net/wp-content/uploads/2018/09/The-textual-history-of-the-Historia-Brittonum.pdf, 2017).
Fitzpatrick-Matthews, Keith, J, The Arthurian Battle list of the Historia Brittonum, (http://www.historiabrittonum.net/wp-content/uploads/2018/09/The-Arthurian-battle-list-of-the-Historia-Brittonum.pdf)
Fleming, Robin, *The Material Fall of Roman Britain 300–525 CE*, (University of Pennsylvania, Philadelphia, 2021).
Flierman, Robert, *Saxon Identities AD 150–900*, (Bloomsbury Publishing, London, 2017).
Flight, Tim, *Basilisks and Beowulf, Monsters in the Anglo-Saxon World*, (Reaktion Books, London, 2021).
Foster, Sally, *Picts, Gaels and Scots: Early historic Scotland*, (Berlinn Ltd, Edinburgh, 2014).
Gantz, Jeffrey, *The Mabinogion*, (Penguin Books, London, 1976).
Geoffrey of Monmouth, *The Life of Merlin, Vita Merlini*, (Read a classic, USA 2011)
Gerrard, James, *The Ruin of Roman Britain an Archaeological Perspective*, (Cambridge University Press, Cambridge, 2016).
Gidlow, Christopher, *The Reign of Arthur*, (Sutton Publishing, Stroud, 2004).
Gilbert, Wilson and Brackett, *The Holy Kingdom*, (Bantam Press, London, 1998).
Goffart, Walter, Barbarians and Romans, AD 418–584 The Techniques of Accommodation, (Princeton University Press, Princeton, 1980).
Goldsworthy, Adrian, *The Fall of the West*, (Phoenix, London, 2010).
Green, Caitlin, *Britons and the Anglo-Saxons, Lincolnshire 400–650 AD*, (History of Lincolnshire Committee, Lincoln, 2020)
Green, Thomas, Arthuriana, Early Arthurian Tradition and the Origins of the Legend, (Lindes Press, Louth, 2009).
Gretzinger, J., Sayer, D., Justeau, P. et al., *The Anglo-Saxon migration and the formation of the early English gene pool*, (Nature 610, 112–119 (2022). https://doi.org/10.1038/s41586-022-05247-2).
Griffen, T, *Names from the Dawn of British Legend*, (Llanerch, Dyfed, 1994).
Grigg, Eric, *Warfare and Raiding and Defence in Early Medieval Britain*, (Robert Hale, Marlborough 2018).
Gruffydd, Elis, *Tales of Merlin, Arthur, and the Magic Arts*, (University of California Press, Oakland, 2023).
Guy, Ben, (2012). *Did the Harleian Genealogies Draw on Archival Sources? Proceedings of the Harvard Celtic Colloquium*, 32, 119–133. http://www.jstor.org/stable/23630937
Guy, Ben, *Medieval Welsh Genealogy*, (The Boygell Press, Woodbridge, 2020).
Halsall, Guy, *Barbarian Migrations and the Roman West 376–568*, (Cambridge University Press, Cambridge, 2014).
Halsall, Guy, *Warfare and Society in the Barbarian West 450–900*, (Routledge, London, 2003).

Halsall, Guy, *Worlds of Arthur*, (Oxford University Press, Oxford, 2014).
Hamerow, H, Hinton, D, and Crawford, S, *The Oxford Handbook of Anglo-Saxon Archaeology*, (Oxford University Press, Oxford, 2011).
Hamilton, Walter, *Ammianus Marcellinus, The Later Roman Empire AD 354–378* (Penguin Books, London, 1986).
Harding, Dennis, *Iron Age Hillforts in Britain and Beyond*, (Oxford University Press, Oxford, 2012).
Harrington, Sue and Welch, Martin, *Early Anglo-Saxon Kingdoms of Southern Briton AD 450–650: Beyond the Tribal Hidage*, (Oxbow Books, Oxford, 2018).
Haywood, John, *Dark Age Naval Power, A Reassessment of Frankish and Anglo-Saxon Seafaring Activity*, (Routledge, London, 1991).
Henson, Donald, *The Origins of the Anglo-Saxons*, (Anglo-Saxon Books, Norfolk, 2006).
Higham, N.J, *King Arthur Myth-Making and History*, (Routledge, Abingdon, 2009).
Higham, N.J, *King Arthur The Making of the Legend*, (Yale University Press, New Haven, 2018).
Higham, N.J, Rome, *Britain and the Anglo-Saxons*, (Seaby, London, 1992).
Higham, N.J, *The English Conquest, Gildas and Britain in the fifth century*, (Manchester University Press, Manchester, 1994).
Higham, N.J., *The Kingdom of Northumbria AD 350–1100*, (Alan Sutton, Stroud, 1993).
Higham, N. and Ryan, R, *The Anglo-Saxon World*, (Yale University Press, New Haven, 2015).
Hills, C, *Anglo Saxon Identity* in Hamerow, H, Hinton, D, and Crawford, S, *The Oxford Handbook of Anglo-Saxon Archaeology*, (Oxford University Press, Oxford, 2011).
Hooke, Della, *The Anglo-Saxon Landscape, The Kingdom of the Hwicce*, (Manchester University Press, Manchester, 1985).
Hughes, Ian, *Aetius, Attila's Nemesis*, (Pen and Sword Books, Barnsley, 2020).
Istvanovits, Eszter, and Kulcsar, Valeria, *Sarmatians, History and Archaeology of a Forgotten People*, (Romisch-Germanisches Zentralmuseum, Germany, 2017).
Jackson, K.H., 1959 *The Arthur of history*. In: Loomis, R.S. (ed.) Arthurian literature in the Middle Ages: a collaborative history. (Oxford: Clarendon Press, 1–11, 1959
Jankulak, Karen, *Geoffrey of Monmouth*, (University of Wales, Cardiff, 2010).
Jarman, A, *Aneirin, Y Gododdin*, (Gomer Press, Ceredigion, 1990).
Jenkins, Geraint, H, Bard of Liberty: *The Political Radicalism of Iolo Morganwg: Iolo Morganwg and the Romantic Tradition in Wales*, (University of Wales, Cardiff, 2012).
Keegan, Simon, *Pennine Dragon*, (Newhaven Publishing, 2016).
Keys, David, *Catastrophe: An Investigation into the Origins of the Modern World*, (Arrow Books Ltd, London, 2000).
Knight, Peter, and Long, Jonathan, *Fakes and Forgeries*, (Cambridge Scholars Press, Cambridge, 2004).
Koch, John, *Waiting for Gododdin: Thoughts on Taliesin and Iudic-Hael, Catraeth, and Unripe Time in Celtic Studies* in *Beyond the Gododdin : Dark Age Scotland in Medieval Wales : the proceedings of a day conference held on 19 February 2005 [St. John's House papers, no. 13.]*, (The Committee for Dark Age Studies, University of St. Andrews, St. Andrews, Fife, 2013).
Jones, Nerys Ann, *Arthur in Early Welsh Poetry*, (Modern Humanities Research Association, Cambridge, 2019).
Joyce, Stephen, Gildas and his prophecy for Britain, Journal of the Australian Early Medieval Association Volume 9 (2013).
Joyce, J. Stephen, *The Legacy of Gildas*, (The Boydell Press, Woodbridge, 2022).
Keegan, Simon, *Pennine Dragon, The Real King Arthur of the North*, (Newhaven Publishing, 2016).
Lapidge, Michael and Dumville, David: *Gildas, New Approaches*, (Boydell Press, Woodbridge, 1984).

Littleton, C. Scott, Malcor, Linda, *From Scythia to Camelot: A Radical Reassessment of the Legends of King Arthur, the Knights of the Round Table and the Holy Grail*, (Routledge, New York, 2000).
Lloyd, Scott, *The Arthurian Place Names of Wales*, (University of Wales Press, Cardiff, 2017).
Loomis, R.S., *Arthurian Literature in the Middle Ages*, (Oxford University Press, Oxford, 1959).
Loveluck, C. and Laing, L., *Britons and Anglo-Saxons* in Hamerow, H, Hinton, D, and Crawford, S, *The Oxford Handbook of Anglo-Saxon Archaeology*, (Oxford University Press, Oxford, 2011).
Malcor, Linda, *Lucius Artorius Castus, Part 1: An Officer and an Equestrian*, (Heroic Age, 1, 1999).
Malcor, Linda, *Lucius Artorius Castus, Part 2: The Battles in Britain*, (Heroic Age 2, 1999).
Malcor, Linda, A, Antonio Trinchese, and Faggiani, Alessandro, *Missing Pieces: A New Reading of the Main Lucius Artorius Castus Inscription*, (Volume 47 page 415 Journal of Indo-European Studies, 2019).
Manco, Jean, *The Origins of the Anglo-Saxons*, (Thames and Hudson, New York, 2018),
Marren, Peter, *Battles of the Dark Ages*, (Pen and Sword, Barnsley 2006).
Mathisen, Ralph, *Roman Aristocrats in Barbarian Gaul, Strategies for Survival in the Age of Transition*, (University of Texas Press, Texas, 1989).
Matthews, John, and Malcor, Linda, Artorius, *The Real King Arthur*, (Amberley, Stroud, 2022).
Matthews, William, *The Ill-Framed Knight*, (University of California Press, Berkeley, 1966).
Mawrey, Richard, *The Mystery of the Glastonbury Cross*, (History Matters, April 2012: 5)
Mees, Kate, *Burial, Landscape and Identity in Early Medieval Wessex*, (The Boydell Press, Woodbridge, 2019).
Mierow, Charles, *Jordanes The Origin and Deeds of the Goths*, (Dodo Press, Princetown 1908).
Mills, A.D., *A Dictionary or British Place Names*, (Oxford University Press, oxford, 2011).
Milner, N.P., *Vegetius: Epitome of Military Science 2nd Ed* (Liverpool Universety Press, Liverpool, 2011).
Mitchell, Stephen, and Greatrex, Geoffrey, *Ethnicity and Culture in Late Antiquity*, (Duckworth and The Classical Press of Wales, London, 2000).
Moffat, Alistair, *The British: A Genetic Journey*, (Birlinn, Edinburgh, 2013).
Morris, J, *Arthurian Period Sources Volume 3 Persons: Ecclesiastics and Laypeople*, (Phillimore, Chichester, 1995).
Morris, J, *Arthurian Period Sources Volume 7 Gildas*, (Phillimore, Chichester, 1978).
Morris, J, *Arthurian Period Sources Volume 8 Nennius*, (Phillimore, Chichester, 1980).
Morris, Marc, *The Anglo-Saxons, A History of the Beginnings of England*, (Hutchinson, London, 2021).
Mortimer, Paul and Bunker, Matt, *The Sword in Anglo-Saxon England from the 5th to 7th Century*, (Anglo-Saxon Books, Ely, 2019).
Mortimer, Paul, *Woden's Warriors, Warriors and Warfare in 6th–7th Century Northern Europe*, (Anglo-Saxon Books, Ely, 2011).
Munby, Julian, Barber, Richard and Brown, Richard, *Edward III's Round Table at Windsor*, (Boydell Press, Woodbridge, 2008).
Naismith, Rory, *Citadel of the Saxons*, (I.B. Tauris and Co. London, 2019).
Naismith, Rory, *Early Medieval Britain, c.500–1000*, (Cambridge University Press, Cambridge, 2021).
Nitze, W.A., "The Exhumation of King Arthur at Glastonbury." Speculum 9, no. 4 (1934): 355–61. https://doi.org/10.2307/2850219.
O Croinin, Daibhi, *Early Medieval Ireland 400–1200 2nd Edition*, (Routledge, London, 2017).
Oppenheimer, Stephen, *The Origins of the British*, (Robinson, London, 2007).
Oousthuizen, Susan, *The Anglo-Saxon Fenland*, (Oxbow Books, Oxford, 2017).
Oousthuizen, Susan, *The Emergence of the English*, (Arc Humanities Press, Leeds, 2019).
Padel, O.J., *Arthur in Medieval Welsh literature*, (University of Wales Press, Cardiff, 2013).

Pearson, Andrew, *The Roman Shore Forts*, (The History Press, Stroud, 2010).
Phillips, Graham, *Atlantis and the Ten Plagues of Egypt*, (Bear & Company, Rochester, Vermont, 2003).
Phillips, Graham, *Merlin and the Discovery of Avalon in the New World*, (Bear & Company, Rochester, Vermont, 2005).
Phillips, Graham, *The Lost Tomb of King Arthur*, (Bear & Company, Rochester, Vermont, 2016).
Phillips, Graham, *The Search for the Grail*, (Century, 1995).
Phillips, Graham, *The Templars and the Ark of the Covenant*, (Bear & Company, Rochester, Vermont, 2004).
Pollington, Stephen, *The Elder Gods, The Otherworld of Early England*, (Anglo-Saxon Books, Ely, 2011).
Pennar, Merion, *The Black Book of Carmarthen*, (Llanerch Enterprises, 1989).
Phillips, Graham, *The Lost Tomb of King Arthur, Bear and Company*, (Rochester, Vermont, 2016).
Procopius (translated by Williamson, G & Sarris, P.), *The Secret History*, (Penguin Books, London, 2007).
Thomas, Charles, *Christianity in Roman Britain to AD 500*, (Batsford, London 1981).
Rippon, Stephen, *Kingdom, Civitas, and County: The Evolution of Territorial Identity in the English Landscape*, (Oxord University Press, Oxford, 2018).
Rivet, A.L.F and Smith, Colin, *The Place-Names of Roman Britain*, (Batsford, London, 1982).
Rouse, Robert, and Rushton, Cory, *The Medieval Quest for Arthur*, (Tempus, Stroud, 2005).
Salway, Peter, *A History of Roman Britain*, (Oxford University Press, Oxford, 2001).
Senior, Michael, Sir Thomas Malory's Tales of King Arthur, (Book Club Associates, London, 1980).
Sidebottom, Harry, 'Was King Arthur really a Roman centurion?', (*Telegraph* newspaper, 17 Dec 2022).
Sims-Williams, Patrick, *The Book of Llandaff as a Historical Source: 38 (Studies in Celtic History)*, (Boydell Press, Woodbridge, 2019).
Sisam, Kenneth, *Anglo-Saxon Royal Genealogies*, The British Academy, London, 1953.
Skeen, Bradley, L, Artorius Castus and King Arthur, JIES Vol. 48, Iss. 1/2, (Spring/Summer 2020): 61–75
Snyder, Christopher, *An Age of Tyrants, Britain and the Britons A.D. 400–600*, (Sutton Publishing, Stroud, 1998).
Snyder, Christopher, *Arthurian Origins*, in N. Lacy (ed.), *A History of Arthurian Scholarship*, (Arthurian Studies LXV, D. S. Brewer, 2006).
Stenton, Frank, *Anglo Saxon England*, Oxford University Press, Oxford, 1989.
Sullivan, Tony, *King Arthur Man or Myth*, (Pen and Sword, Barnsley, 2020).
Sullivan, Tony, *The Battles of King Arthur*, (Pen and Sword, Barnsley, 2022).
Sullivan, Tony, *The Early Anglo-Saxon Kings*, (Pen and Sword, Barnsley, 2023).
Sullivan, Tony, *The Roman King Arthur? Lucius Artorius Castus*, (Pen and Sword, Barnsley, 2022).
Swanton, Michael, *The Anglo-Saxon Chronicles*, (Phoenix Press, London, 2000).
Thompson, E.A., Procopius on Brittia and Britannia, (Cambridge University Press, The Classical Quarterly Vol. 30, No. 2, 1980: 498–507).
Thompson, E.A., *Saint Germanus of Auxerre and the end of Roman Britain*, (Boydell Press, Woodbridge, 1988).
Thornton, D, Kings, *Chronicles and Genealogies: Studies in the Political History of Early Medieval Ireland and Wales*, (Linacre College, Oxford, 2003).
Thorpe, Lewis (translator), *Gerald of Wales*, (Penguin Books, London, 1988).
Thorpe, Lewis (translator), *Gregory of Tours The History of the Franks*, (Penguin Books, London 1977).
Thorpe, Lewis (translator), *Geoffrey of Monmouth, The History of the Kings of Britain*, (Penguin Books, London, 1966).

Todd, Malcolm, *A Companion to Roman Britain*, (Blackwell Publishing, Malden, USA, 2007)
Todd, Malcolm, *The Early Germans*, 2nd Edition, (Blackwell Publishing, Malden, USA, 2004).
Tolstoy, Nokolai, *The Quest for Merlin*, (Sceptre, London, 1990).
Underwood, Richard, *Anglo-Saxon Weapons and Warfare*, (Tempus Publishing Ltd, Stroud, 1999).
Urbanus, Jason, *A Dark Age Beacon*, Archaeology 72, no. 1 (2019): 34–39. https://www.jstor.org/stable/26822769.
Vermaat, Robert, Nennius, *The Historia Brittonum*, (http://www.vortigernstudies.org.uk/artsou/historia.htm).
Wacher, John, *The Towns of Roman Britain*, (BCA, London, 1995).
Wade-Evans, A.W., *The Lives and Genealogies of the Welsh Saints*, (Ashley Drake Publishers, Cardiff, 1988).
Wallace-Hadrill, J.M., *The Barbarian West 400–1000*, (Blackwell, Oxford, 1999).
Wallace-Hadrill, J.M., *The Long-Haired Kings*, (Methuen & Co, London, 1962).
Walters, Lori., *Re-Examining Wace's Round Table, Courtly Arts and the Art of Courtliness*, in Busby, Keith, and Kleinhenz, Christopher, *Courtly Arts and the Art of Courtliness*, (Brewer, Woodbridge, 2006).
Ward-Perkins, Bryan, *The Fall of Rome and the End of Civilisation*, (Oxford University Press, Oxford, 2005).
Webster, L. & Brown, M., *The Transformation of the Roman World AD 400–900*, (British Museum Press, London, 1997).
White, Roger, *Britannia Prima, Britain's Last Roman Province*, (Tempus, Stroud, 2007)
White, Roger, and Barker, Philip, *Wroxeter, Life and Death of a Roman City*, (Tempus, Stroud, 2002).
Wickham, Chris, *The Inheritance of Rome, A History of Europe from 400 to 1000*, (Penguin Books, London, 2010).
Williams, Ann, *Kingship and Government in Pre-Conquest England, c.500–1066*, (MacMillan Press, New York, 1999).
Williams, Thomas, *Lost Realms, Histories of Britain from the Romans to the Vikings*, (William Collins, London, 2022) .
Wilson, Alan, and Blackett, Baram, *Artorius Rex Discovered*, (King Arthur Research, Cardiff, 1986).
Wilson, Alan, and Blackett, Baram, *The Discovery of the Ark of the Covenant*, (Trafford Publishing, 2007).
Wilson, Alan, and Blackett, Baram, *Moses In The Hieroglyphs*, (Independent Publishing, 2019).
Wilson, Alan, and Blackett, Tony, *Where Jesus is Buried*, Cymroglyphics Ltd, 2021.
Wiseman, Howard, *A British legion stationed near Orléans c. 530 ? Evidence for Brittonic military activity in late antique Gaul in Vita Sancti Dalmatii and other sources*, Journal of the Australian Early Medieval Association, 2011.
Wolfram, Herwig, *The Roman Empire and it's Germanic Peoples*, (University of California Press, Berkeley, 1997).
Wood, Michael, *Domesday, A Search for the Roots of England*, (Book Club Associates, London 1987).
Woods, David, *Gildas and the Mystery Cloud of 536–537*, (The Journal of Theological Studies, NS, 2010, University of Southern California, April 5, 2014).
Woolf, Alex, An Interpolation in the Text of De excidio Britannia 23.3–4, (https://www.academia.edu/313152/An_Interpolation_In_the_Text_of_Gildass_De_Excidio_Britanniae, 2002).
Yorke, Barbara, *Kings and the Kingdoms of Early Anglo-Saxon England*, (Routledge, London, 2013).
Zaluckyj, Sarah, *Mercia: The Anglo-Saxon Kingdom of Central England*, (Logaston Press, Logaston, 2013)

Index

Ælle of Sussex 25, 31, 38, 53–4, 173, 212
Æthelberht, king of Kent 2, 14, 20, 24–5, 38–9, 54, 126, 173
Æthelfrith, king of Northumbria 25, 58–9
Adam of Tewksbury 139
Adventus saxonum 2–3, 20, 23, 27, 32, 34, 40–2, 47, 55–6, 65, 70
Aegidius 39, 45, 145
Aetius, Roman general 28–9, 32, 45, 47–8, 51, 55, 144
Agitius, see Antis
Alt Clud 8, 23, 59, 90, 112, 129, 158, 163, 165
Ambrosius Aurelianus 3, 12, 43, 46–8, 51, 55–6, 61, 66, 71, 80–1, 86, 127, 133, 156, 159, 173, 185, 200, 212
Amhar, Arthur's son 9, 171
Amlawdd Wledig 8, 88–9, 92, 110, 162
Amr, Arthur's son 62
Anglo-Saxon Chronicle 6, 14, 23, 25, 31, 38, 41, 45, 49, 52–6, 67, 69, 80, 88, 169, 185, 213
Anna, Arthur's sister 9, 123, 126, 171–3, 199
Annales Cambriae 4, 8, 78, 158
Annals of Inisfallen 48
Annals of Tigernach 168, 199
Annals of Ulster 23, 48, 168, 199
Antonine Wall 8, 44, 74, 76–7, 147, 204
Arfderydd, battle of 59, 78–9, 99–100, 127–8, 130, 162, 166–7, 198, 204
Armes Prydein 11, 81, 83, 119
Armterid, see Arfderydd
Artur ap Bicuir 4, 157
Arthur ap Pedr 4, 98, 111, 157, 168, 185, 193, 200, 203
Arthur Penuchel 166, 198, 204
Arthwys ap Mar 165–6, 185, 198, 204
Artognou stone 169, 181–2
Artuir mac Áedáin 4, 57, 157, 198–9, 203
Athrwys ap Meurig 168–9, 176, 185, 194, 196
Aurelius Caninus, from Gildas' De excidio 44, 47, 198
Avalon 6, 63, 87, 100, 124, 140, 172, 177–8, 180, 197, 199–200, 212
Avitus, western emperor 29, 45

Badon 3–4, 6, 12–3, 27–8, 38, 43–4, 46–9, 51, 54–5, 58, 64–6, 68, 72–3, 75–81, 97, 105, 106, 119, 123, 125–7, 150, 155, 159, 169, 171, 185, 199–202, 212
Bacaudae 28
Bassas, Battle on the river called 72–4, 202
Bath 54, 64–5, 97, 123, 202
Bede 3, 24, 33, 37–9, 42, 47–53, 55–6, 58–9, 61, 65–6, 70, 74–6, 79–80, 116, 122, 125, 127, 169, 173, 212
Bedivere, see Bedwyr
Bedwyr, Arthur's companion 75, 85, 87, 90–1, 94, 101, 108–9, 173
Beowulf 2, 25, 40, 86
Bernicia 5, 24–5, 41, 57–9, 68–9, 86, 123, 129, 170–1, 204
Black Book of Carmarthen 83–5, 99
Bonedd gwyr y Ogledd 8, 158, 165–6, 198, 204
Book of Aneirin 83–4, 99
Book of Llandaff 117, 168–9, 175–6, 182, 193, 195, 203
Book of Taliesin 81, 83–5, 97–9
Borre, Arthur's son 9
Brewyn, battle of the cells of 75
Britannia prima 7, 15, 20, 44, 75, 129
Britannia secunda 15, 20, 34, 60, 78, 212
Brut y Brenhinedd 84, 161, 206
Buxton 202

Cadbury Castle 21, 106, 147
Cadbury Congresbury 21
Cadell Ddyrnllug 65, 71, 167
Cador, Arthur's half-brother 9, 97, 124, 127, 160, 162–3, 171, 213, 215, 217
Cadwr son of Gorlois, see Cador
Cadwy, son of Geraint 88, 97, 107, 109–10, 127, 163, 172, 213, 215, 217
Caerleon 7, 44, 75, 93–6, 102–3, 109, 120, 124, 147, 189, 213
Cafal, Arthur's dog 62
Cai, Arthur's companion 85–7, 90–1, 94–7, 101, 108–10, 143, 156, 172–3, 203
Caledfwlch 144, 146
Caledonian Forest 73, 76, 81, 188, 202

Caliburn, see also excalibur and caledfwlch 89, 145–6, 210
Calleva Atrebatum 21
Camlan 12, 58–9, 76–82, 87, 90, 97, 99–105, 118–9, 122, 124, 128, 138, 145, 159, 163, 172, 197, 199, 201–2, 212
Camelot 63, 104, 147–8, 153, 186, 210, 212
Canu Heledd 74, 203
Cateryn, son of Vortigern 67
Catterick 57
Cattraeth 57–60, 68, 214
Celestine, Pope 22, 68–9, 75,
Celidonis, battle of cat coit 72–4, 212
Celliwig 7, 64, 86, 89, 92, 101–3, 147, 163, 173, 202, 213–4
Cerdic, first king of West Saxons 25, 53, 124, 169, 171, 185, 212
Cernyw 89, 202–3
Charlemagne 101, 131, 144, 146, 177–8
Chester 6, 73–7, 81, 126, 202–3, 213–4
Chrétien de Troyes 11, 84, 87–8, 105–6, 128, 140–1, 147–8
Cligés, by Chrétien de Troyes 140–2, 147
Climatic event of 536 2, 48, 80
Clovis I 31–2, 38, 55, 123, 133, 136–8
Coel Hen 8–9, 134, 158, 162, 165–6, 173–4, 181, 195, 198
Comes Britanniarum 16–7, 19, 38
Comes Litoris Saxonici per Britanniam 16, 19, 33, 38
Conomerus 112, 138
Constantine of Dumnonia, from Gildas' De excidio 44, 163, 196
Constantine III, western emperor 15, 18–20, 28, 42, 45, 65, 115, 122, 125, 134, 155,
Constantine, father of Uther and Ambrosius 122, 125, 127, 160–3, 213
Constantine, Arthur's nephew 6, 9, 124–5, 160–3, 173
Constantius of Lyon 22, 51, 65
Culhwch and Olwen 7–10, 62, 74, 84–93, 97–9, 103, 105–6, 110, 114, 119, 127, 144, 154–5, 162–3, 169, 172, 191, 209, 211, 213
Cunedda 8–9, 89, 109, 111, 117–8, 158, 162–6, 173–4, 197, 215
Cuneglasus, from Gildas' De excidio 44, 117, 157, 164, 196, 204
Cynlas, king of Rhos 117–8, 164, 185, 196–7, 204

Dalriada 4, 21, 25, 57, 157, 168, 199, 203
Dal Riata, see Dalriada
De Excidio et Conquestu Britanniae 13, 43, 47–51, 55, 70–1, 112–3, 116–7, 157, 212
Deira 25, 57–9, 69, 86, 214

Dinas Powys 21
Din Eidyn, se Edinburgh
Dinas Emrys 66, 101
Droitwich 64
Dubglas, battle on river called 72, 74
Dumnonia 87–8, 110–1, 127, 161, 163, 173, 196–7, 213, 215–6
Dunadd 21, 25
Dux Britanniarum 16, 19, 38, 60, 68, 78, 212

Edinburgh xi, 7, 57, 75, 85–6, 203
Edward Williams, see Iolo Morganwg
Edwin, king of Northumbria 15, 58, 61, 74, 116, 201
Eigr 9, 88, 123, 160, 162–3, 171–3, 203–4, 215–6
Elegy of Geraint son of Erbin 84–5, 87, 119
Elis Gruffydd 100, 196, 206
Eliseg, Pillar of 71, 167
Elmet 8, 21, 58–9, 99, 158, 165
Erec and Enide, by Chrétien de Troyes 87–8, 140–1, 143, 147
Eulogy of Cadwallon 58
Excalibur 139, 141, 143, 145–6, 153, 191

Faustus, son of Vortigern 67, 68, 167
Fisher King 140–1, 143
Flavia Caesariensis 15, 20, 34

Galahad 141, 143, 153
Gallic Chronicle 3, 18, 33, 41–2, 48, 55–6, 65–6
Gawain, see Gwalchmai
Gwallawg, king of Elmet 58–9, 93, 99
Geoffrey of Monmouth 5, 9, 11–2, 32, 48, 55, 61, 64–6, 73, 75, 79, 82–3, 87, 89, 97, 99, 107, 119–21, 123, 125, 127–31, 137–8, 144, 146, 148–150, 154, 160, 162, 166–7, 172, 177, 182, 202, 204, 206–7, 211–3, 215, 217, 219
Geraint and Enid 84–5, 87–8, 93–5, 99, 141, 143, 161
Geraint 84–5, 87–8, 90, 92–5, 97, 99, 105, 110, 119, 127, 141, 143, 148, 161–3, 172–3, 214, 217
Gerald of Wales 113, 127, 177, 203, 210
Gewisse 53, 122
Gildas 3, 6, 12–3, 18, 23–4, 28–9, 33, 37, 41, 43–52, 55–6, 59, 61, 65–7, 69–70, 75–6, 78–80, 90, 93, 97, 99, 100, 104, 107–18, 121, 125, 127, 138, 156–9, 163–4, 168, 174, 196–7, 200–1, 204, 215
Glastonbury 43, 108, 113, 140, 172, 177, 179–80, 183, 210–11

Glein, battle at the mouth of the river of 72–3, 201
Glywysing, kingdom 66, 108, 165, 168
Gorlois of Cornwall 9, 123, 127, 160, 162–3
Gormant, son of Ricca 9, 90, 162, 171, 213
Grail 3, 5, 96, 99, 102, 140–1, 143, 153, 197, 212
Gratian, western emperor 18, 65, 70, 134, 195
Gregory of Tours 3, 24, 29–30, 38, 51, 133, 135, 137–8, 212, 220
Gregory, Pope 33, 43
Guanhumara, see Gwenhwyfar
Guinevere, see Gwenhwyfar
Gwalchmai 9, 104, 123, 127, 142–3, 153, 173
Gwallawg, king of Elmet 58–9, 93, 99
Gwawrddur 57
Gwenddolau 78, 127, 129–30, 166–7, 199
Gwenhwyfach 90, 92, 102–3
Gwenhwyfar 9, 102–4, 113, 124, 141–2, 153, 171, 172, 177–8, 220, 215
Gwen Ystrad, battle of 58
Gwydre, Arthur's son 9, 90–1, 171
Gwynllyw 8, 108–9

Hadrian's Wall 6–7, 16, 45, 48, 60, 66, 73–7, 167, 172, 185, 214
Harleian genealogies 8, 61, 113, 117, 158, 164–5, 167, 176, 193, 234
Hengest 3, 5–6, 12, 23, 25, 42, 51–2, 65–9, 82, 119, 169–71, 212–3
Henry of Huntingdon 72, 126
Hermann of Tournai 87, 119
Historia Brittonum 3–8, 10, 12, 23–4, 42, 46, 52–3, 57–65, 67–71, 75–81, 83, 85–7, 89, 94, 99, 105, 108, 110–11, 113–4, 116–9, 122–4, 127–30, 133, 148, 151, 156–8, 160, 163–7, 169–71, 174–5, 182, 201–2, 204, 206–8, 211–3, 215–6
Historia ecclesiastica gentis Anglorum 47, 50, 61
Historia regum Britanniae 5–7, 9–11, 82–4, 92–3, 97–108, 119–21, 125–34, 142, 144–9, 153–5, 158–63, 169–73, 177, 182, 191, 199–201, 206–11, 213, 215
Honorius 18, 42, 134
Horsa 3, 12, 51–2, 65, 67, 82, 102, 122, 212
Huail 100, 112, 196, 206

Ida, king of Bernicia 5, 24–5, 58, 68–9, 170–1
Igraine, see Eigr
Iolo Morganwg 169, 180–1, 194–5,

Jesus College MS 20 8, 83, 158, 155, 167, 193
Joseph d'Arimathie, Robert de Boron's 154
Justinian, eastern emperor 126, 137
Justinian, plague of 2, 80, 117

Kai, see Cai
Kay, see Cai
Kent xii, 2, 13–4, 16, 20, 24–5, 33, 36–8, 42, 51–2, 54–5, 65–70, 76–7, 122, 124, 129–30, 137, 169–71, 173, 213, 215

Lady in the Lake 5, 141, 143, 145
Lady of the Fountain 84–5, 88, 94, 143, 207, 211, 215
Lancelot 5, 104, 141–2, 153
Lancelot, French Romance 140–3, 147
Layamon 84, 144, 177
Leiden Glossary 49
Le Morte d'Arthur 5, 12, 14, 100, 149–54
Lincoln, also Lincolnshire 6, 34, 73–5, 76–7, 115, 122–3, 184, 214
Lindsey 51, 73, 81, 122, 197, 201, 213–4
Linnuis 72–4, 201
Lindisfarne 58–9, 69, 80
Llacheu, Arthur's son 9, 97, 101, 171
Llandaff Charters, see Book of Llandaff
Llangborth 88
Loholt, Arthur's son 9
Lucius Artorius Castus xiii, 156, 185–8, 191–2

Mabinogion 83, 98–9, 204
Madog, son of Uther 98, 171
Maelgwn, king of Gwynedd 8, 69, 78–9, 97, 99, 108–9, 111, 117–8, 159, 161–2, 166, 196–7, 212, 215
Maglocunnus, from Gildas' De excidio 44, 69, 79, 117, 197
Magnus Maximus 18–9, 28, 44, 65, 69–71, 121, 134, 148, 166–7, 195–6
Malory, Thomas 5, 12, 14, 141, 145, 147, 149, 150–4, 206–7, 210–11, 215, 217
Manaw Gododdin 8, 117, 163–4
Marwnad Cynddylan 203
Maxima Caesariensis 15, 20, 34, 77
Medraut 6, 9, 78, 80–1, 102–3, 123–4, 141, 143, 153, 172–3, 178, 197, 199
Meleaganz 104
Melvas, king of the 'summer country' 104, 108, 113
Merlin 61, 66, 78–9, 99, 115, 120, 122–3, 127–30, 139–41, 144, 153, 166–7, 171–2, 185, 197, 212
Merlin, French Romances 140–4
Mirabilia 3, 15, 61–2, 68, 107, 111, 119, 174, 180, 206, 208, 221
Modena 11, 104, 118–9, 131, 154, 157
Modred, see Medraut
Mons Badonicus, see Badon
Monte Agned, battle at 72, 75
Monte Breguoin, battle at 72–3, 75, 202

Mordred see Medraut
Morgan Le Fay 9, 143, 153, 172–3
Morgana, see Morgan le fey
Morgause, see Morgan le fey
Mynyw, see St Davids
Myrddin, see Merlin
Myrddin Wyllt, see Merlin

Nart Sagas 186, 190–3

Octha 5, 23, 66, 68–9, 76–7, 170, 202, 213, 215
Outigirn 69
Owain, French Romance 84–5, 88, 94–5, 99, 105, 140–3, 146–7
Owain, son of Urien 94, 97, 100, 129
Owain Danwyn 117, 184–5, 196–8, 214

Pa Gur yv y porthaur 75, 84–5, 89, 105, 119, 172, 203, 213
Palladius 22, 68, 79
Pascent, son of Vortigern 67, 123, 167, 185
Pelagian heresy, see Pelagius
Pelagius 22, 46, 115, 156
Pengwern 203
Pen Rhionydd 7, 64, 101–3, 114, 147, 203
Perceval, French Romance 140, 143, 147, 153, 203
Perceval, see Peredur
Peredur son of Efrawg 84–5, 88, 95, 143, 172
Post-Vulgate Cycle 11, 141, 143, 153
Powys 8, 21, 65, 71, 89, 99–100, 158, 167–8, 172, 196–7, 203, 213
Preiddeu Annwfn 49, 98, 105, 172
Proçopius 3, 24, 31, 37–8, 48, 136–8
Prosper 17, 22–3, 42, 115

Red Book of Hergest 83–4, 88–9, 101, 129, 141
Rehieingulid 8
Rheged 8, 57–9, 69, 75, 80, 90, 97, 99, 158, 185
Rhonabwy, Dream of 84, 88, 96–7, 99, 103, 105, 110, 169, 203, 213
Rhun, son of Urien 58–9, 61, 97, 101, 109, 117, 201
Rhydderch Hael 59, 83–4, 88–9, 101, 127, 129–30, 145, 166
Riothamus xi, 31–2, 55, 124, 136, 138, 148, 172, 185, 200, 212
Robert de Boron 128, 140, 143, 145–6
Roman de Brut, by Wace 140, 143, 177
Round Table xii, 5, 62, 64, 140–1, 143–4, 146, 148, 153, 186, 199, 210, 212, 217

St Alban 22, 44
St Albans, see Verulamium
St Aaron 44
St Arthmael 185, 191, 196
St Augustine xii, 2, 13–5, 20, 24, 33, 39, 49, 52, 86, 116, 206, 210
St Cadoc 6, 8, 11, 107–9, 115, 119, 154
St Carannog 6, 8, 88, 117–10, 114, 162–3, 172, 213
St David 8, 78–9, 101, 109–12, 114
St Davids 7, 64, 101, 103, 147
St Dubricius 110–1, 114, 123, 169, 175–6
St Efflam 107, 139, 172
St Galgano 145–6
St Garmon 65, 71
St Germanus 2, 22–3, 27, 42, 45–6, 51, 65–8, 71, 82, 111, 115, 122, 156–7, 167
St Gildas 3, 6, 12–3, 18, 23–4, 28–9, 33, 37, 41, 43–52, 55–6, 59, 61, 65–7, 69–70, 76, 78–80, 90, 93, 97, 99–100, 104, 107–18, 121, 125, 127, 138, 156–9, 163–4, 168, 174, 196–7, 200–1, 204, 215
St Goeznovius 107, 133
St Illtud 6, 8, 89, 107–8, 110–2, 114, 162
St Julius, see St Aaron
St Kentigern 129–30
St Oudoceus 168, 175, 186
St Padarn 6, 8, 107–8, 111–2, 114, 117, 164, 209
St Patrick 5, 22–3, 45, 47, 68–9, 78–9, 109, 115–6
St Paulinus 110, 114
St Samson 86, 108, 110–12, 114
St Teilo 111–2, 114, 117, 175
St Tysilio 84
Salvian of Marseille 28–9, 32
Sarmatians 145, 185–6, 189–93
Sidonius Apollinaris 21, 30, 33, 136, 200
Silchester, see Calleva Atrebatum
South Cadbury 21, 106
Spoils of Annwfn, see Preiddeu Annwfn
Stanzas of the Graves 84–5, 87, 119
Stilicho 18, 42
Sutton Hoo xiv, 2, 24, 40
Sword in the Stone xii, 5, 139–40, 145–6, 148, 153, 186–7, 191, 212, 217
Syagrius, king of Soissons 32, 135–6

Taliesin 25, 69, 81, 83–4, 90, 97–9, 103, 128–30
Tintagel 9, 21, 25, 125, 128, 147, 169, 181–3
Triads of Britain 7, 64, 76, 83–44, 86–9, 98–9, 101, 103–4, 110, 114, 119, 127, 129, 147, 167, 181, 203

Tribuit, battle on the bank of river called 72, 75, 85, 87
Tristan 138, 140–1, 143, 147, 153
Tryfrwyd, see Tribuit
Twrch Trwyth 62, 90–1, 114–5, 213

Urbe legionis, battle at 72–3, 75, 202
Urien, king of Rheged 57–9, 61, 69, 75, 80, 90, 94–5, 97, 99–100, 129–30, 165–6, 185, 201, 212
Uther 9, 55, 84, 97, 122–3, 125, 159, 161, 163, 169, 171, 173, 176, 191, 195, 199, 201, 203–4, 215–6

Valentia 15–6, 34, 60, 78
Verulamium 21–2, 44
Vicarius Britanniae 15, 159, 173, 215
Viroconium 21, 168, 196–7, 203
Vortigern 3, 12, 29, 42, 51–2, 55, 60, 65–71, 82, 101, 122–3, 125, 127–8, 133, 157, 159, 167–8, 173, 201, 212, 215

Vortimer 52, 67, 69, 101, 122, 124, 167
Vortipor, from Gildas' De excidio 44, 113, 125, 168, 185, 196, 200
Vulgate Cycle 11, 141, 143, 153

Wace 11, 140, 143–4, 177
White Book of Rhydderch 83–4, 88–9, 101
William of Malmesbury 43, 87, 119, 125, 209
Wonders of Britain, see Mirabilia
Wroxeter, see Viroconium

Y Gododdin, Welsh poem 2, 4, 8, 57–60, 68, 83–4, 87, 105, 117, 119, 129, 156, 163–4, 201, 214
York 33, 34, 38, 40, 58, 75, 122–3, 134, 147, 150, 152, 156, 186, 188–90, 198, 204
Yvain, see Owain, French Romance

Dear Reader,

We hope you have enjoyed this book, but why not share your views on social media? You can also follow our pages to see more about our other products: facebook.com/penandswordbooks or follow us on Twitter @penswordbooks

You can also view our products at www.pen-and-sword.co.uk (UK and ROW) or www.penandswordbooks.com (North America).

To keep up to date with our latest releases and online catalogues, please sign up to our newsletter at: www.pen-and-sword.co.uk/newsletter

If you would like a printed catalogue with our latest books, then please email: enquiries@pen-and-sword.co.uk or telephone: 01226 734555 (UK and ROW) or email: uspen-and-sword@casematepublishers.com or telephone: (610) 853-9131 (North America).

We respect your privacy and we will only use personal information to send you information about our products.

Thank you!